The Hacker
and
The Hillbilly

The Hacker and The Hillbilly

a novel by

Tilson Klaus

ISBN–979-8-218-52469-2

Edited by MarQuese Liddle of Wild Isle Literature

WILD ISLE LITERATURE

Dedicated to my real-life computer friends
Aaron & Jen, and may they continue to form
like Voltron with their friends and associates
to wax and milk all over the galaxy,
simulation, and beyond.

Author's Note:

No AI tools were used in the creation and editing of this novel. My editor and I believe that using the machine for the creation or editing of the text stifles creativity. We do not sacrifice speed of creation and editing by using even the most basic of suggestive tools. The only computer support used in the making of this novel are the poor spell and grammar check of Microsoft Word and Google Docs' red and blue squigglies. Tilson Klaus encourages all authors, regardless of their popularity and success, not to use AI as it is nothing more than theft which only generates rehashed sentences and phrases of authors that came before us humans. To stay ahead of the machine you must write without its assistance.

Contents

Chapter 1

KNOCK! KNOCK! KNOCK! KNOCK! KNOCK!
From the distinct number, pattern, and force of the knocks, Mukesh knew that the police were at his front door.

"Who is it?" he asked.

"It's the police, Mukesh Patel. We need to talk to you about Tillapah Singh. May we come in?"

Mukesh rolled his eyes, scooted his computer chair back, and opened the door. He stood at the threshold, staring at two policemen.

Mukesh turned away from the two cops to hide another eye roll, beckoned with his hand, and was the first to break the uncomfortable silence. "Come in," he said.

The men shuffled inside. "I assume you know why we want to talk to you."

"It has been on the news for three days straight," said Mukesh.

The two men glanced at each other sideways. The tallest one, a light-skinned half-Indian half-Caucasian, pulled out a small notepad from his rear pants pocket and reached in his shirt for a pen. "I was one of the first ones at the crime scene. I have seen worse, but that was one of the ugliest in years. Singh had two dogs, and by the time we got to the scene, they were both completely covered in blood from where they must have tried to cuddle up to Singh's wife and cousin as they lay in bed." Mukesh hid his cringe, disgusted by the investigator, who related the scene with a slight grin.

The Hacker and The Hillbilly

"Singh only worked for me. I know little about him other than he was one of my best glassblowers." Mukesh spread one arm out behind him at the bins of multi-colored and variously sized glass weed bowls. "I will never be able to replace him." He returned his attention to his laptop and started typing. The policemen looked at each other again.

"Well," said the shorter one, pausing. "Do you know where he might have gone?"

"He was always saying he wanted to become a Buddhist monk one day. I would try Kashmir."

"Seriously, a monk?"

"Seriously," said Mukesh, eyeing the two policemen from over the top of his glasses. The shorter officer half-chuckled. The tall one turned sideways as a sign they were ready to leave. Mukesh stood up from his desk to let the policemen out.

"No one really expects him to show his face around here anymore, but if he does, you let us know."

"I promise," said Mukesh. He watched them walk down the hall, his ears perking as they left. He couldn't make out their whispers, so he went back inside his apartment and locked the door. After checking his laptop again, he brought a box over to the bowl bins and filled it with an assortment.

Medium bright yellows—shipped: 6, backordered: 9. He was going to have to return to blowing glass in a week if he couldn't find a suitable replacement. Singh would toil for pennies and could blow an entire convenience store order in two days. Mukesh filled the order, noting on his whiteboard the back order. Not a single one of the other glassblowers who worked for him knew how to blow the patterns on a bright yellow. Mukesh was going to have to do them all himself. He looked down in his lap and shook his head. He would have to go to the factory and work a few hours of production on Monday, instead of going to the call center. More than anything about the grueling glassblowing work, Mukesh hated the heat.

His iPhone notified him, and a few seconds later, an email notice slid from the side of his Dell. It was from his younger brother, Jeefa.

Dearest brother Mukesh,

I regret to inform you that our father has cancer, and the doctors have given him six to eight months left to live. You are to sell the glassblowing business and production shack, and take the first available flight to Tennessee to take over the business from him as the head of the family. Please let me know when you receive this email.

Thank you,

Jeefa

Mukesh's hands hung above the keyboard, poised to strike. After a few seconds suspended in thought, he typed.

I do not know how long it will take me to sell the business. But as soon as I sell it, I will fly to the States.

Mukesh

That should buy him at least another month. He called up an auctioneer and scheduled the sale in three weeks, then opened up the business logs and started to cook the books. By that evening, he had fudged his sales figures up three hundred

The Hacker and The Hillbilly

percent. He smiled and reasoned that he wouldn't be coming back to India ever again to face the consequences of his illegal action.

He picked up his phone and dialed the factory.

"Hello," the supervisor answered.

"Sunovar, how are things going today?"

"Good, boss. We are behind until you can find a couple more artists to replace Singh. Until then, we will need you to come in for a few hours to run production. Billy Kumar is skilled enough now that you might be able to teach him how to blow bright yellows."

"I just got an email from my father. He has cancer." Mukesh paused to let the news sink in. "Tell everyone they can go home. I will pay them for the rest of the day. After that, the business is closed. I will have your final paychecks ready this Friday."

"Mukesh! That is a very short notice! It might take some of the men and women who work here weeks to find another job."

"I am sorry. These are my father's orders. I can have all the pay that is owed to the workers by this Friday, including the week they are held back. I can pay you all through the rest of this week. That is two days' pay extra for free." The supervisor was silent on the other end. "Is that acceptable? Lock up the door when you leave, and put the key in the mailbox."

"If that is what your father wants, it will be done. Sorry about your father, Mukesh."

"I know," he said. They both hung up. Mukesh climbed onto his futon in the corner of the efficiency and went to sleep.

Since performing office duties was no longer necessary, Mukesh had the whole day to work at the scam call center. He took the bus to an unmarked office building in one of the older parts of the city. The entrance was always locked. He took out his key and opened the door.

Sitting down at his corner cubicle, Mukesh put on his headset and adjusted the twisted dongle from where it had been lying wrongly in the drawer. He opened up the call screen and pretended to look over a few files for the day, eavesdropping on the cacophony around him.

"We need you to pay the prize postage with Steam card... So it will be cheaper postage when we mail you refrigerator... A Steam card is a, uh... ask lady at Kroger, they will show you where to get them... A one hundred dollar Steam card... Ok, I call you back in hour, and you give me numbers on it... No, we don't want you to mail. We just need numbers... Look, I'll explain why once you get Steam card... Thank you, Tracy. You are such a super lady. Talk to you in hour... Yes!" Mukesh heard a hand clap as the newbie caller netted his first Steam card scam and high-fived his cubicle neighbor.

The call center had taken Mukesh off Steam cards months ago. As one of the best in the center and an accomplished hacker, Mukesh was rewarded with a corner cubicle and a nice raise. Because of his language and manipulation skills, Mukesh was tasked with the group's more lucrative and complicated schemes. In five hours of phone calls, most of which were to America, he had hacked into two old ladies' computers and made five hundred dollars in various types of scams. He didn't tell his employers at the scam center he was leaving, as he was

The Hacker and The Hillbilly

going to steal three thousand in Bitcoin from one of the call center computers before he left.

Instead of taking the bus home, Mukesh hailed a taxi. He walked upstairs to his third floor efficiency, opened up his email, and clicked on his brother's thread.

The business is going to be auctioned off in three weeks. I can be home in a little over a month.

Mukesh.

He picked up his phone and called a friend. "Hello. Yadav, I need you to do me a favor. I have to auction off the glassblowing business. My father is sick and is going to die from cancer. I am going to auction off the business in a few weeks. I need you to pretend to be the auctioneer. Father is going to ask for the receipt of the company sale. I am going to tell him I forgot it when I packed and I need you to pretend to be the auctioneer and repeat the sales amount I say."

"What are you going to give me for accomplishing this task, Mukesh?"

"I will give you the rest of the stock from our glassblowing business. You can come by and pick it up tomorrow if you like."

"You know I will have to sell them. I will have to take a loss to sell them quickly."

"Yeah, but there's..." Mukesh looked behind him at his stock. He had ten boxes. "Seven boxes."

"That is not enough."

"Ok. I'll get someone else to do it then. Thank you."

"No, wait. All I have to do is fool your father? I think I can do that for the price of seven boxes."

"Thank you. I will give you the numbers to look out for so you can program them in your phone when father or my brother calls."

"Very well. I am sorry your father is ill."

"Me too," said Mukesh. "Thank you again."

"You are welcome," said Yadav.

A few seconds after he hung up, Mukesh's iPhone notified him about an email. He checked his account and read Jeefa's reply. "That will be acceptable. Father says when you come to America, make sure to bring the receipts."

"Oh, I will be bringing the receipts, asshole," Mukesh said aloud. He turned on the evening news.

"And the latest in the story of last week's brutal murder: Police are looking for the suspect, Tillapah Singh, after the brutal murder of his wife and cousin. They are asking people not to approach the suspect and contact the police immediately, as he is considered to be armed and dangerous. We think he may have skipped town, but be on the lookout."

Mukesh cut off the TV and listened to some soothing Indian music. He opened up another thread in his work email and typed to an associate, "I have some premium vibrant color glass pipes for you. On sale for the low, low cost of one hundred twenty a box." He went over to the bin area and began to pick through the choicest pieces until he had filled up three. He browsed some travel agency sites for the well-deserved vacation he would take in Europe prior to arriving in the United States.

After the auction fees, the Patel glassblowing business sold for one hundred and twenty thousand dollars. Mukesh picked up his phone and texted his friend Yadav. "I need you to say

The Hacker and The Hillbilly

that the business sold for one hundred and five thousand dollars." He sent him three numbers: Jeefa's, his father Bagal's, and the work phone number at Checkers so he would know who was calling.

"K," Yadav texted back.

With his flight booked, Mukesh vacationed all over Europe for a week and made his way from Germany to his new home in the small Appalachian town of Mason, Tennessee.

When Mukesh arrived in the States, he insisted upon getting his own place instead of staying in the Patel family home. With the stipend his father afforded him on arrival, Mukesh settled in a cheap motel rented monthly for fifteen hundred dollars. Any slack in cash, Mukesh was confident his hacker skills could supplement on the side. His main task was to take over store duties while the other members of his family cared for their father.

Mukesh holed up in his motel room and browsed the dark web for long stretches into the night, fueled by the occasional Adderall or Red Bull. Though he seldom took Adderall, an Indian doctor prescribed some scripts for him to sell in the States. The crooked MD prescribed Mukesh one hundred and twenty Adderalls a month and one hundred and twenty oxycodone thirties. Though he wasn't too familiar with Appalachian culture, during his time hanging out with street criminals in India, he learned to spot a drug addict easily. The first person Mukesh met who he suspected of using was a middle aged man who lived in the motel as well, Aaron.

Aaron was a drug dealer and agreed to buy all of Mukesh's prescriptions wholesale. Until his three months of pills ran out,

Mukesh could bank on three thousand extra dollars a month selling to his neighbor.

Aaron met Mukesh in the parking lot of the motel to buy Mukesh's first month's refill.

"How's your pa, Mike?" Aaron asked.

"He's ok," Mukesh said. "The doctors give him about six months."

Aaron shook his head. "Running a convenience store is too much of a headache. I wouldn't want to do it. Hey, let me know if you need anything. I can tell you some names of shady doctors around here to get your scripts refilled when you run out. I see you like Adderall. I got some good meth if you ever want any. I also know quite a few whores if you want some female fun." Aaron grinned at Mike and waved towards his motel room.

"No thank you," Mukesh said, smirking, "I don't take Adderall that often, and I've never had a pain pill, and I don't ever want any meth. Maybe if I get in the mood, I might take you up on a whore."

Aaron was an old GenX head and needle junkie but never took his usage too far. Since he rarely increased his daily dose, he was able to keep his drug habits from interfering with his drug income.

For some small talk and to network his skills, Mukesh tried to tell Aaron about his computer scams.

"I never want to hear any of the details of your online scams," Aaron told Mukesh. "And I don't know anyone that's a hacker like you. I don't understand any computer crap. And about your stories, the less I know, the more people can't say I said something."

The Hacker and The Hillbilly

The next time Mukesh got his meds, they met in Aaron's motel room. Though Aaron had his drug intake under control, his girlfriend was another matter.

Jen was a thin, pale, oblivious-looking girl in her late twenties, with dirty blonde hair and a pleasantly thin but voluptuous build. She leaned over with both elbows on her knees in a chair in the bathroom foyer with her phone by the sink, swiping.

Mukesh was itching to talk to a hacker he'd met on a dark web chat room that night, so he conducted his business with Aaron and quickly left. He hoped to find and join a group of hackers that pooled their resources in their scams. After Mukesh got back to his motel room, he fixed a sandwich, logged into his laptop, and stared at the screen. He thought about how best to prove his worth to a new online contact named Bakertwist81. Mukesh guessed by the handle that Baker was a GenXer, but that could be a ruse.

Mukesh had seen Bakertwist81 in chat enough to guess his habits, so he logged into one of Baker's favorite rooms to chat at ten p.m. Mukesh swapped with Bakertwist a spy software tool, and Bakertwist sent Mike some sample files to prove he possessed genuine hacked data. Mukesh was satisfied with the files, and the hacker tools and software impressed Bakertwist. They progressed in friendship and began bragging and showing off their skills.

After checking with each other to be confident they weren't tracked, they became more candid in chat. Bakertwist81 admitted he was tight with a group of online scammers who could use Mukesh's skills. Mukesh would begin with, of course, Steam card scams, which he'd mastered in India.

10

"I can do so much more than simple Steam card scams," Mukesh typed.

"I don't doubt," Baker replied. "But you're going to have to prove it. And you have to promise to never do any outside scam work on your own or with anyone else if you want to work with the Darknet Collective. If you work with us, we need to know we're all safe from prying eyes. If any authorities try to infiltrate our group, they'll see the trouble they are going to have to go through to uncover our activities and identities.

"Our rules are simple. Make a big enough mistake or break the rules and you're out. Sloppy behavior only means you'll mess up more later. No outside scams or hacking allowed, and everything you do must be sanctioned by the group and go into a shared pool. Based on your hacking skills, we'll also give you some computer tasks on occasion. Your full cooperation will be appreciated during your introduction period, the ending of which you won't know. Our trust doesn't come automatically with your abilities. You are going to have to put the work forward, though of course you'll make more and get bigger scams if you perform well, especially if you gain our trust."

"Alright. When can we start?"

"I'll get you some contacts for Steam card scams tomorrow. Make sure to stay in contact with me."

"Bet," said Mike.

"Lol," said Bakertwist81. "You better be as good with the old folks as you say, because you don't sound convincing with your slang."

"Whatever," Mike typed, chuckling to himself. "Just let me start tomorrow. I will make you proud."

The Hacker and The Hillbilly

"Not tomorrow. It will be a few days. I have to talk to some people." Bakertwist81 knew it was never good for a member starting up to be so overeager, but he hoped there would be no worries and that Mike would make a nice addition to their trusted community.

Three days later, Mukesh got his first block of phone numbers and assignments. By the second week, he found his old groove and made on average fifty percent more money on his marks than some of the Darknet Collective's other top scammers. Most of the people he scammed back in India were American, so not much was new. He proved himself so well in his third week that the Darknet Collective promoted him from simple Steam card scams.

Mike even taught his new online partners a few things. On Mukesh's insistence, he'd received other seemingly unimportant files and information the team had on each victim. Mukesh loved to look up his contacts on social media. He would always find common denominators and subjects to discuss to build his victims' trust. He also learned to steer away from older marks with well-balanced investment portfolios, knowing they would be far harder to con.

"Impressive," Bakertwist replied plainly after Mukesh's fourth week.

Time went on. Mukesh piddled around his father's store during the day and conned from his motel room at night. He became so sure of himself after a couple of months working with Bakertwist and his associates and was confident he could do more one day on his own.

His father's health fell off rapidly on month four of the six month prognosis, and the Patel family assumed he would soon pass. Mukesh's three younger siblings had been running the store well enough on their own for the past few years. He had no doubt Checkers would do fine after his father's passing and that he could do less around the store and have more time for his scams.

When Bagal Patel could sense he was close to death, the dying patriarch summoned his eldest son Mukesh for his final instructions.

"Eldest son," Bagal Patel said in Hindi, "it is your duty now to become the leader and take care of the family and my store. I am counting on you. My good friend Preshanth Pillai will be the executor of the will. The store and all I have will be split evenly among the four."

"Father, I am hoping that I can one day find something else to do in America. I don't like convenience store work."

"It is what you must do as head of the family. I expect you to do this and not to fail, son," the old man sighed.

"I will do my best, father. I will do whatever is right for the family." Mukesh palmed his father's hand and gave it a squeeze. "Everything is going to be ok."

"Good, son. I am glad to hear that."

Mukesh hugged his father and stepped away.

Back at the motel room, there was too much on his mind to try any hacker work, so he watched YouTube videos until he felt like going to bed.

Even though it ate into the family savings, Mukesh suggested that his father stay in a nursing home during hospice so the family could get back to their duties at the store. His three younger siblings would not have it. Asheeda protested about how she wanted to continue to bathe and feed her

The Hacker and The Hillbilly

father, but at her older brother's insistence, they relented and Bagel spent his dying days in a nursing home. The doctor told the family to prepare for Bagal Patel's death in less than a month. The other siblings insisted one of them would stay with the dying man at all times. That was ok for Mukesh, as most of the time it was the youngest teen girl, Asheeda.

The day came when old man Patel passed. The will was read, revealing a caveat. Mukesh had control over Checkers, but if he ever made a big enough mistake, he would lose his stake in the business. As Bagal Patel had specifically stated in his will, Preshanth Pillai, a trusted family friend that lived in Nashville, was entrusted as executor of the estate to make sure Patel's dying wishes were upheld.

Mukesh was solemn at his father's funeral but glad to no longer need to put on so many airs. The Wednesday afternoon after the funeral, he refilled his final oxycodone and Adderall prescription. He took them and the morphine his father had left after he died to sell to Aaron. Mukesh's hacker scam side work was going well enough that he decided against getting an American doctor to prescribe more meds to make him money.

"No," Aaron said bluntly to Mike when he showed Aaron his father's pills. "Morphine only fetches fifty cents a milligram on the street, not a dollar like oxys." Mike looked skeptical. "I give you twenty apiece for your Roxy thirties. Their street value is thirty. I sell them in bulk for twenty-five apiece. That gives you and me both the cushion of not having to mess with too many people. You sell in bulk to me, I sell your pills wholesale to only a few people. Morphine's street value is fifty cents a milligram, so I will give you twenty for these morphine sixties and sell them for twenty-five as well.

"Oh. I didn't know that." Mike said softly.

Aaron thought he might have been too curt to his new friend, so he shrugged it off with a question. "How was your father's funeral?" Mukesh leaned back in his chair and looked down. From the other side of the room, they heard a loud inhale.

Jen was standing in the corner with her phone in the air, filming. She blurted out in a flurry, "In the grocery store there was this woman today that was in the soft drink aisle with her daughter in the push basket. The kid was rocking back and forth and side to side in the cart and the wheels were making scraping noises on the grocery store floor and I got so mad at her..."

Mukesh looked at Jen as she droned on, then back at Aaron and asked, "She has been inside this room all day, right?"

After she finished her rant, Jen lowered her phone and looked. "One minute four seconds. Fuck!" She breathed in and out for a few seconds before lifting the phone to her face for another try.

"Of course she's been in here all day, Mike. I can hardly get her to take out a small bag of trash or get ice. Some of the time, I can get her to buy a soft drink or a snack—if I buy her one, too."

"I still don't get it." Mukesh said in disbelief.

"Get what?" Aaron asked.

"That." Mukesh pointed over at Jen, who had just finished her second take. She mumbled about it taking too long again. Looking sideways in the sink mirror, she prepared herself for a third try.

The Hacker and The Hillbilly

Aaron realized what Mukesh was implying and joked, "All I got to say is, there's a lot more to her than what you think, and she's great in bed. She gets so wild when she's high on meth."

"No meth for me," Mukesh said with a polite laugh. "But since my father has finally passed, I'll take you up on one of those women you know. Can I get something for a hundred dollars?"

Aaron laughed at the price but kept his ethnic jokes to himself. "I can hook you up with a clean country whore for two hundred dollars."

"If she looks good, I'll splurge. Let me see her picture." Aaron grabbed his phone from the nightstand by the bed where he sat and shoved it in Mukesh's face. Mukesh leaned back and looked at a picture of a blonde thirty-year old woman with her head tilted to the side in a mirror reflection. Mike frowned at the picture, which was from her tits up. By the puffiness of her arms, he knew she had to be somewhat overweight, but he was more than fine with hitting it from behind with the lights off. Mike reached in his wallet and took out some money. He had a couple hundreds and a few fifties. He fumbled out two hundred and handed it to his neighbor. Aaron took the money from Mukesh and put one hundred fifty in the top drawer. The other fifty he stuck in his wallet.

"Sure, I'm getting a cut," he told Mike, "but trust me..." Aaron paused and opened up the top drawer on his nightstand. He took out a small baggie of white powder. "She is going to go over to your place...*very inspired.*"

Mike nodded and stood up from his chair. "Text me before you send her over. I'll take a shower and be ready any time after thirty minutes from now." Mike opened up the motel door and walked out. Aaron stood up and flicked the latch.

Jen had finished her first TikTok take in under a minute and said, "Let's see how this one does." She put her phone in her lap and looked down as she started the upload. She shimmied from side to side in excitement until it was complete and the first views started coming in. Aaron prepped a fresh syringe for Mike's whore. He worked up another for himself and shot up. He prepared a needle for Jen as well, laid it down, and began to fumble on Pornhub, sweating.

"I'm ready for you, hon," said Aaron, holding up the syringe in the air in front of Jen.

Jen looked at Aaron and said, "Just a minute, babes, I'm almost done." Aaron set the needle on the nightstand by his porn, phone paused at a point in the video showing a nice closeup. He sat up in bed and looked at Jen, then back at the nightstand. Aaron figured it would take another twenty minutes for Shelly to get to the hotel. He texted her. She texted back she'd be at his door in thirty. Jen put her phone down and scurried over to the bed and crawled in it with Aaron. He reached over with his right hand as she sat on the bed and took up the needle with his left. Jen leaned over the side of the bed by the wall and fastened the loop on the tie belt on her arm. She smacked dramatically at her cupped under-elbow and poised it to her boyfriend. She bit her lip as she watched him inject, and grunted sensually at the needle prick.

"You need to start drinking more water," Aaron said, commenting on the state of Jen's veins. She didn't answer. Jen waited with her head down. She shuddered and started to breathe heavily once she felt the first swells of the speed rush.

The Hacker and The Hillbilly

Aaron grinned at her as she lay beside him and closed her eyes, trembling. Aaron put the moaning girl where he wanted her to be and went at Jen as best as his pickled yet capable GenX body could.

Chapter 2

After sending Shelly away after thirty sweaty minutes, Mukesh washed off, put on an old robe, and sat at his laptop, waiting in a chat room for Bakertwist81 to arrive. Bakertwist gave Mukesh files on three elderly people. Mukesh was worn out from Shelly, so he closed his laptop and went to bed. He had to be at Checkers at ten o'clock the next morning to meet a distributor.

He woke up late and decided to skip his morning shower. Mukesh put on a long-sleeve teal dress shirt and a pair of tan pants with no tie to look like a casual businessman. As his father used to say, appearance is everything to an American. He didn't think that it was much of a change from their home country of India, but he acted as if it was sound advice. Even after skipping his shower, Mukesh's disdain for management led him to arrive at ten-oh-five. The distributor was running late.

"I need to talk to you, Mukesh," Jeefa said. He was taller and stronger than the eldest brother, but meek. Unless distressed, Jeefa never initiated a confrontation. That should have been a sign for Mukesh, his brother's urgency to talk. "There are a lot of papers that need to be taken care of on your desk."

"I have a meeting with the distributor," Mukesh said while looking at his phone. "He is running late."

Jeefa kept his mouth shut, both about how Mukesh was late and also about how Preshanth Pillai came over two days before to talk to him about Mukesh shirking his managerial duties.

19

The Hacker and The Hillbilly

Asheeda had been tracking the store bills and had proved to the Patel family that all of their money matters would be handled well by her. After she showed Jeefa an electric bill that was a month late, he called Preshanth and brought up the issues with Mukesh running the store.

"I will be over later to discuss. This time, don't let Asheeda pay the electric bill. This will be his unacceptable mistake, and we can force him to sell his share of Checkers. I have a meeting in Nashville at three o'clock, so I must be leaving."

"Thank you, Preshanth," said Jeefa.

The distributor arrived for the meeting. Mukesh listened to his pitches for as long as he could stand. He placed the usual order and sent the salesman on his way. Mukesh went into the store office across from the walk-in and sat behind his father's desk. Unopened envelopes lay mixed in with single papers and batches clipped together, some folded over and others lying flat. Mukesh leaned back in the small computer chair and winced at the heap. For two hours, he grabbed sheets at random, taking care of the ones he could settle quickly and without digging deep. Eventually, the monotony of paper shuffling proved too much for Mukesh. He knew he had to take care of all of the papers some time that week, but his nerves got the better of him, and he walked out of the office at one-thirty.

Jeefa watched the live security footage and caught his older brother on his early way out. He pressed him before he left the store, "Mukesh, you need to go pay the bills!" Having given his older brother the respect of enough chances and a fair warning, Jeefa glared at Mukesh as he left Checkers for home.

Once Mukesh was gone, Jeefa walked into the office. Asheeda followed closely behind and reached into the stack of papers.

"This one is past due, Jeefa!" said an excited Asheeda as she handed him an envelope.

"Good girl. But this time, I want you to put it back."

"But I want to write a check again!" Asheeda said, whining. Jeefa bent down in front of his sibling, bracing his outstretched hands across his knees. "I promise you, Asheeda, you are going to very soon be writing *all* of the checks." She grinned at him and went back to finish one of her duties, stocking all but the top two shelves in the walk-in fridge.

Jeefa was glad the electric bill default would be the final straw to get rid of his older brother. The store's electricity being cut off for a few hours would be a serious enough offense. Jeefa logged his brother's work time so Preshanth could see what little attention Mukesh paid the store.

The three younger siblings were doing well on their own, and Mukesh was only in the way. Everything would be like it had been before, except Asheeda would be the one handling the inventory and books instead of their father. Jeefa would take care of management, and Mufa would handle all the errands and tasks. Mufa enjoyed driving around doing company chores. Jeefa eased through the rest of his stressful day, knowing his older brother would soon be out of the Patel family's hair.

Mukesh got back to the motel. He popped open a Sun Drop and sat down at his desk. He sent a coded message to an email address which let Bakertwist know he needed to meet him in a chat room.

The Hacker and The Hillbilly

Instead of Bakertwist81, Hyperthot showed up on the Darknet Collective's behalf and transferred the batch of files to Mukesh.

It was two-thirty in the afternoon. Mukesh studied the files briefly and called a couple of old folks on the phone. One woman paid Mukesh one hundred dollars in Steam cards for shipping a washing machine he made her think she'd won at the mall. Mukesh became bored with his scams and browsed YouTube to tire himself for bed.

The next day, Mukesh researched the files Hyperthot sent him to conjure some potential angles. After spending another five days scamming customers and attempting to hack into some small networks, Mukesh chalked his week up with his first thousand dollar payout from the Darknet Collective. Not bad for any scammer spending five hours on research and twenty-five hours on a phone.

The new contact numbers given to Mukesh by the Darknet Collective were ripe with gullible old women. Mukesh knew he would do well. He had so much fun scamming with his new group. Mukesh began to spend less and less time at his family's store. Feeling guilty, he arrived on time on Friday and went straight to the office to take care of the rest of the paperwork and bills.

He separated everything, placing the administrative ones off to the side and paid all of the bills. Jeefa was polite to his older brother but stayed away from him. Just as Asheeda had seen, the electric bill was already too late by the time Mukesh cut the check. Jeefa patiently waited for the day the store's electricity would be cut off. Mukesh finished sifting through the stack of papers and stocked the top two shelves for Asheeda, putting in a full six hour workday before he left. When he got back into his motel room that evening, he dove back into his scams.

Tonight, he had a special assignment, a remote access hack for the Darknet Collective. Mukesh called a business in California and effortlessly tricked a woman into giving him company information. When Mukesh was done, he hailed Bakertwist81 by coded email. He appeared in the chat room at fifteen past eight, just as planned.

Baker was happy that Mukesh had conned the secretary out of the information they needed and typed, "I knew you were good, but I never would have thought you'd have gotten the answer to that password question so fast. I'd ask you how you did it..." Bakertwist paused to gauge if Mukesh caught on.

"Yeah, yeah..." Mukesh said. "I knew you'd want to erase the recording of my conversation with her after you got into the network and heard my call. I had a lot of fun tricking her into giving me that recovery answer. Have you downloaded any financial records yet?"

"You know I can't tell you that," said Bakertwist. "What I can tell you is that I'm going to transfer you an extra one thousand this week as a bonus for getting the answer to that question. Also, look forward to some nice opportunities to come from this hack in the future. We definitely want to use you for our high level operations. You have that phone charm that makes people lower their guard. AARP is a big fish, and now that we have them hooked, we have an opportunity to make a ton of money. All from your favorite demographic.

"If this works out and we get what we want, Mike," Bakertwist81 typed and sent that sentence before he

The Hacker and The Hillbilly

continued on... "You won't need to go to your family's store anymore." Mukesh wondered if he had ever told Bakertwist81 about his family convenience store, but wasn't sure.

Mukesh thought hard about what kind of plans the Darknet Collective had in store for the AARP. As they had complete control of the AARP's computer network, it could even be a ransomware attack. Mukesh kept his hopes up but stayed reasonable. He might not know the fruits of the remote access exploit for a whole year or more. The excitement of his clever achievement made Mukesh want to get laid. He texted Aaron and asked if he could come over.

"Sure." Aaron texted back. Mukesh walked over to the other side of the building and knocked. A couple seconds later, Aaron flipped the latch. Mukesh walked in, grinning.

Aaron noticed the large smile plastered on his friend's face. "What did you do, and what do you want?" Aaron already considered Mukesh to be a friend. The two shared many traits, namely, taking money from other people and enjoying scams.

"Well, I had a good day at work," Mukesh said to Aaron, wanting badly to brag about how he had tricked a receptionist into telling him the nickname of a janitor's cat. Shaking off his duper's delight, Mukesh asked Aaron, "How about a whore tonight? I'll even take the last one if you can. She was a little chunky, but other than that, not too bad."

Shelly had told Aaron that she never wanted to screw Mike again, so Aaron politely picked up his phone and pretended to text the whore while actually texting his girlfriend. "You look sexy over there, basking in the bathroom foyer glow, staring at your phone. Wanna do a shot later?" Jen perked up when she heard the tone. The personalized notification from her boyfriend annoyed her. She knew the ruse. Aaron was pretending to call someone so she kept her nose in her phone. A half minute later, while her boyfriend and Mike were small-talking, she looked at the nonsense thread.

"Whatever." She texted back to Aaron.

Aaron's phone dinged. He broke off the conversation with Mukesh. He lifted his phone up to his face and stared at Jen's "Whatever" and jiggled his eyes from side to side.

"She's got another date tonight," he told Mukesh. "There is another girl I know, about just as clean, but you are going to want to hit it from behind."

"That's the plan." Mike smiled. "I prefer it like that. How much?"

Aaron grimaced, figuring his cut. "One-sixty," he said loudly. Tammy charged one-twenty, and forty was enough for Aaron to make a phone call.

Aaron was reasonable in his dealings with Mukesh. He wanted his new friend's help. Aaron was trying to plan an insurance scam, having had two lucrative faux-accidents in his life already: one from a fake back injury with a previous employer and one from a car wreck with Jen. He felt certain Mukesh would be able to help him with some good ideas.

Mukesh reached in his wallet and fumbled through his cash. He handed Aaron two fifties and three twenties. Mukesh didn't stay long, eager to get back to his computer while he waited for his whore. He left Aaron's room hastily to shower and prepare for his date.

Forty-five minutes after Mukesh finished his shower, there came a gentle yet not so feminine rap on the door. He opened it with a straight face, in case the woman was ugly enough to

The Hacker and The Hillbilly

scare away a smile. Aaron was absolutely right. Mike was going to have to be very imaginative to keep it up, and definitely was going to have to hit it from behind.

Chapter 3

On Saturday, Mukesh relaxed in his room, reeling with pride at helping his group hack the AARP. He laughed and chatted on a YouTube live-stream. Sunday, he went out on a few errands, including laundry and light grocery shopping for the motel mini-fridge. Mike sat at his laptop, brushed off his pride, and went back to work at hacking, a job that he'd hoped to one day have full-time.

Monday, Mukesh pulled into Checkers at ten. There was a closed sign on the door, and all the lights were off. Confused, Mukesh fumbled out his key, opened the front door, and called inside.

"Mike!" Asheeda said, running to him from the back of the store.

"What is the matter, Asheeda? Why are the lights out?"

"Jeefa went to pay the electricity bill. They cut it off this morning," Asheeda said with her head tilted back.

"I sent it off last week!" Mike exclaimed.

"I don't know," Asheeda said as she broke off the hug, running to the back of the store to stock.

"Where's Mufa?"

"I guess he went with him." Asheeda opened up a small bag of peanuts to snack on.

Embarrassed, Mukesh wanted to get away from the store as fast as he could. He tried to think of something else to do as an excuse to escape and come back once the power was back on. Mukesh was furious at Jeefa for not calling or texting this news to him, as important as it was to the family business.

The Hacker and The Hillbilly

"I'll be back later, Asheeda. Tell Jeefa that I haven't been by. I paid the bill! I am mad he didn't call me!" Asheeda stood, silent. Not wanting to get in trouble by relaying false information, she vowed to keep her mouth shut about everything. Mukesh went to his car and drove around for an hour along a road on an upper ridge so he could see when his brothers got back. At eleven-fifteen, he saw Jeefa's car pull up. A minute later, the blue and red neon open sign cut on. Mukesh drove around town for another fifteen minutes to collect his courage. Once he summoned enough to walk in with his head up, he drove back to his store.

Jeefa ran the register, and Asheeda rearranged the candy aisle. An old white man walked back from the fridge with a Gold Peak iced tea and a frozen Jimmy Dean biscuit. He paid for his food and walked over to the microwave to heat up the biscuit. Mukesh stared at Jeefa, who grinned. Jeefa pointed to the back, and his older brother followed him for their talk. Instead of walking all the way back to the office, Jeefa turned around abruptly and faced his older brother in the center of the hall.

"Mookie, you didn't pay the electricity bill!"

Mukesh stepped back, glaring furiously at his brother for the slight. He raised his hand and feigned a slap. Jeefa flinched. Nobody but Mukesh's mother ever called him Mookie. "I paid the bill. Last week, I paid!" he said, flustered. "Don't you ever call me Mookie. That reminds me of mom!"

"I'm sorry, brother," Jeefa whined. "The bill was very late. We can't have that. That cannot happen. They said they sent you two emails and even tried to call." Mukesh had looked at a few emails that month, but never any from the utility company.

"It will never happen again," Mukesh said plainly.

"I hope not," said Jeefa. He grinned. He caught himself and said, "I love you, brother," and smiled. Mukesh and Jeefa looked off to the sides, both done with their talk.

"Ok," said Mukesh. He walked into the office and fiddled with some inventory logs at his father's desk. A few hours later, he went out front and inventoried half of the stock. Mukesh clocked out at four o'clock, proud he put in a good day of work. He waved at his two brothers and bent over to kiss his young sister before he left. He made eye contact a second time with Jeefa. He nodded at him, letting his younger brother know he had made a mistake. "See you tomorrow, brother."

Jeefa grinned and said, "See you tomorrow." Mukesh looked at Jeefa for a second and turned and walked to his car. Jeefa shook his head and waved at his older brother. Mufa waved as well. Asheeda hummed to herself as she feather-dusted off the bottles of wine on the bottom row.

After Mukesh pulled out of the parking lot, Jeefa looked around the store to make sure there were no customers. "Thank you, Gods!" he exclaimed, loudly. Mufa looked at his older brother, confused.

"What?" Asheeda asked excitedly.

"We had a very profitable month, Mufa," said Jeefa. "Also, Asheeda, you are the one in the family now that will do the orders and pay all the bills!" Jeefa leaned his head down and smiled at his little sister. Asheeda ran over to hug him, squealing.

"I get to write a check again?" Asheeda asked loudly.

"You will get to write all of the checks from here on out."

The Hacker and The Hillbilly

The next morning, when Mukesh pulled into Checkers, old man Pillai's car was parked out front. Instead of pulling in the back, Mukesh pulled up alongside Pillai's. Preshanth Pillai stuck his hand out and waved. Mukesh got out of his car and went to the driver side of Pillai's Tesla.

"Let's go to Bojangles," Preshanth told Mukesh, "we need to talk." Mike took it as a polite order and went back to his vehicle and followed Preshanth to the fast food joint. They parked and entered the restaurant and ordered a sausage and a chicken biscuit. Mukesh got a cup of coffee, and Mr. Pillai got a sweet tea. Bojangles was close to empty that morning. They chose the corner booth to the right side of the restrooms for more privacy. They sat down and faced each other. Mukesh always preferred to sit on the outside of booths but scooted himself to the middle to be directly opposite the elder Pillai. Mukesh sat, silent.

Preshanth looked down as if in prayer, breathed in quickly, and said, "I've got good news and bad news." He paused and looked at Mukesh and searched his eyes for emotion.

Mukesh grinned at the elder, looked around the room, and asked uncomfortably, "Am I supposed to say what I want to hear first?"

"Yes. What do you want to hear first?" Old man Pillai was nice, but his people skills were ancient Indian as hell. Though it was uncomfortable, Mukesh had a hard time not bursting into laughter looking at the old man's face waiting for him to say either "good news" or "bad news."

"I guess the good news," Mukesh said, rolling his eyes.

Preshanth shook his head and spoke straight away: "I am going to have to buy your part of the convenience store and give you one hundred thousand dollars."

"Yeah, so I guess... wait. One hundred thousand dollars? That's the good news, right?" Mike said, confused.

"And the bad news is that you must sell your company stake in Checkers."

Mukesh shifted in his seat and folded his arms in front of him and stared at Preshanth, angered at how it seemed Preshanth always needed a reaction from him to continue on.

"Mukesh, your father warned you to handle the affairs well after his death." Preshanth squirmed a couple times in his chair and sat up straight. He shouted dramatically, "Handle them like a gentleman was what he wanted! And you didn't properly pay the bills! You need electricity to run a convenience store!"

Mukesh wanted to leave. He looked down at his half-gnawed spicy chicken biscuit, folded it up in its paper, and set it to the side of his tray.

"Hold on," Mukesh said. He got out of his seat and took his trash over to the bin and returned the orange tray. Back over at the booth he sat, this time near the outside. Mukesh pulled his half-eaten biscuit in front of him and cupped it with both of his hands.

"One hundred thousand dollars, you say?" Mukesh asked.

"I can have a cashier's check out for you on Friday," Pillai added. Mukesh perked up. It would be a nice sum of money to have all at once. "Tax free?" Mukesh joked, but also as an invitation to bargain.

"Tax free in cash is eighty thousand," Preshanth Pillai said sternly.

The Hacker and The Hillbilly

"Ninety thousand?" Mukesh shot back.

"Eighty-five thousand," Preshanth countered firmly.

"Alright, eighty-five." Mukesh shrugged. Eighty-five was what he figured. After the tax-free inheritance was negotiated, Mukesh sat for a long while in silence while the old man glared at him. Pillai grew impatient with his silence. He opened his mouth, stood up, and spoke: "Your heart was never in the family business, not even the glassblowing one. I know."

"I didn't even want to move here!" Mukesh said to the family friend.

Preshanth Pillai sat back down in the booth. He looked up to the ceiling and sighed. "Your sense of family duty and your father's sense of tradition are what made this complicated. But..." Preshanth added, standing up and shaking a finger, "you should have been a man and talked it out with your family instead of ignoring your duties." Mukesh looked sheepishly up at the old man, who was now being an asshole, giving Mukesh 'I told you so' advice. Preshanth Pillai knew a lot about his past and the strained relationship of the Patel family and some of its causes. Mukesh stood, shaken. The two men briefly chatted about Indian TV shows while they walked back to their cars.

Since the weight of the two men's conversation seemed to linger heavily, old man Pillai reared his head back jovially and said, "One hundred thousand—I mean eighty-five," he corrected, "is fair for a quarter share of your family's convenience store. My conscience would never let me take advantage of you, son."

"I know that," Mukesh said, rolling his eyes as he turned and walked faster to his car.

"We are still family," Pillai said, smiling before he opened the door and sat in his silver Tesla. Mukesh nodded at him and got into his car and drove off as well.

Mukesh arrived at the motel deep in thought. His rage began to focus on his younger brother, Jeefa, and how he had neglected to tell him that the power had been turned off. A flash of clarity cut through Mukesh's angry haze. Jeefa said the electric company had called. If that was the case, it meant he knew, perhaps for days, about the shutoff date. And if that were true… Mukesh began to think that today's confrontation with Pillai was orchestrated.

He stood above the foot of his bed with his phone in his hand. Mukesh glanced around the room, fidgeting, and phoned Jeefa.

"Yes, Mukesh?" Jeefa answered.

"What in God's name, Jeefa..." Mukesh paused.

Jeefa stayed silent. Finally, he replied, "Look, Mukesh..." He paused again. "You messed up."

"You family snake! I know Asheeda goes into my office and looks at the bills. No one told me about the bill being late. You wanted this to happen! This is all on purpose!"

"Brother!" Jeefa yelled. "It would be different if you did anything here other than sit at a desk and put off your paperwork and occasionally stock the top shelves for Asheeda!"

"I never wanted any of this, Jeefa! I didn't want to move to America. It is not any better here for me. In India, I had some real friends! I don't have any here now! This redneck country town is not where I want to be, but now I am here with a place to stay, but other than that, nothing!"

The Hacker and The Hillbilly

"Papa moved to America to take better care of us all!" Jeefa screamed. "Move back to India, I don't care!"

"I shouldn't have been forced to come take care of anyone!"

Mukesh was breathing heavily into his iPhone. Jeefa kept his mouth shut. He didn't care how the conversation would end. "I know dad expected all of us to be together after his death. You were doing well with the glassblowing business. I guess father wanted you and the whole family to be here when he passed. I know we were never that close."

"We were never close," Mukesh inflected back, mocking his younger brother. He was furious. After a pause, he began again. "Whatever, brother. You were always a little, mindless, hateful, obedient dog!" Mukesh wanted to go on, but kept his insults short, hoping to not spend too much time on the phone.

"You have received compensation. This is for the best. That's the way it's going to be," Jeefa ended.

Mukesh was going to mock his younger brother again, but instead said, "Maybe it is for the best."

"Well, you know where the store is, as well as our home." Jeefa said this so callously that Mukesh hung up the phone. He paced around the motel to release his anger. After he calmed down, he sat at his laptop to turn the nervous energy into work. Instead of making scam calls, he probed around networks and tried to pick apart the firewall of a rental car agency.

That Friday, Mukesh met Preshanth Pillai at another convenience store in town and received eighty-five thousand in twenties and fifties in a medium-sized black satchel with two short straps. Mukesh brought the money to his bank, put half of it into a safe-deposit box, and went to Walmart to buy a safe.

He stashed the money in the small concrete and metal box and pushed it under the nightstand by his bed. Since he was keyed up emotionally, Mukesh took two Benadryl and lay down on his motel bed and slept.

Chapter 4

The very next day, Mukesh opened his cheap Walmart safe and went to all of the different grocery and convenience stores in the area that had Western Unions. He had a hacker friend who was profitable with Bitcoin trading in India. He understood his friend's strategy and thought he might be able to make money in trading as well, especially with the lax trading laws they had in the United States. Over the course of three and a half days, Mukesh, through accomplices in India, funneled forty thousand of his inheritance into an online wallet and began trading. He purchased some trading software from a darknet source that would automatically withdraw all of his funds if the market lost more than twenty-five percent in one day. Crypto was risky, but Mukesh was smart and made sure to use one of the more trustworthy online cryptocurrency exchanges. In six days, Mukesh started into crypto trading.

Mukesh explained to the Darknet Collective his emergencies, and was given a pass. "I knew something had to be going on. You seem to really like your work. But yeah, going to a bunch of Western Unions all day for a few days doesn't sound like a lot of fun." Bakertwist paused his typing. "Just keep us informed with what is going on, my friend. We get nervous when people stop working. That goes especially for you after your last access hack. We are watching you, Mukesh."

Mike didn't type a response and pondered what seemed like veiled threats. He could understand Bakertwist81's unease. Mukesh had a foreign background, more difficult to trace. He had just arrived in the U.S. and had gotten far into an accomplished hacker network. Bakertwist81 and his associates had reasons to be wary. Mukesh could be anyone, even an agent.

"Look, I'm alright, man!"

"I'm not trying to be rude. I am just saying that, now moving forward with the nature of our plans with the AARP," Bakertwist81 paused, "everyone is being watched."

That got Mukesh excited. Maybe they were planning a major ransomware attack. If things went well, he might not have to work another day in his life.

The next day, Mukesh bought a 2008 Prius, taking another chunk out of his funds. He was going to have to figure out something. He had no convenience store job to fall back on anymore. He had to make his computer side hustles work or else find another stream of income. Mukesh thought about it for a while and decided that he needed a part-time job. The more time he spent at the computer calling people, the less determined and focused he was on every call. With Mukesh's precise style of personalized swindling, he needed a lot of time to recharge his batteries.

Mukesh collected his thoughts and relaxed for one more day, then continued on with his new scams. He went over to Aaron's later on that evening to chat. After texting, Mukesh knocked, and Aaron let him in.

"What do you want today?" he asked.

"Just coming to say hello," said Mukesh. "You were in a good mood the other day."

"Yep. Yesterday, Jen got that money from the accident we were in two years ago. I was driving, and she sued my insurance company. I'd be driving now, but I haven't been able to get a

The Hacker and The Hillbilly

vehicle since then because of license problems. My disability money pays for this room, and my side hustle everything else. Her settlement will be either emergency money or gravy." Aaron looked over at Jen and joked, "About time she brought something to the relationship." Jen looked over at him like she was pissed, and Aaron grinned to make sure she knew he was only kidding. "We got a few things that we really needed, and we are going to sit on and ride out the rest. If we do well with our money, I figure it can last us years. We can also get a vehicle now if we want."

Mukesh looked around the room but couldn't see anything that they had bought recently, and Aaron and Jen had some pretty raggedy stuff.

Mukesh looked at the TV and asked, "Why don't you get a good flat-screen instead of that hotel generic?"

"We will. We were going to wait it out and find the right one at a pawn shop." Mukesh understood. He was like most Indians who moved from their native country. He tried to save money whenever he could, kept a portion of his savings back, and tried to never dig into it or touch it at all unless it was replenished quickly.

Aaron and Mukesh began to feel more comfortable in their friendship. They talked to each other more freely about their scams. Aaron loved Mukesh's stories of schmoozing and swindling. Mukesh equally loved Aaron's stories of clever and complicated small-time heists.

Aaron told Mukesh his favorite small con story. "This guy I know, let's say his name is Terry. He's about the best con man I've met, so good in fact, that even though everyone knows he's a snitch, he still gets people to sell him drugs. One time, we were driving home from scoring and stopped at a convenience store. Matter of fact, it was your father's, right before he bought it. The other Indian who owned it had a son who just turned fifteen, and his father was teaching him how to run the register. Terry went over to get a fountain beverage. He stood in front of the soft drink station and sipped on it for a while, drinking more than the twelve-ounce container he put it in while standing there, filling up his cup twice. Then he went to the register to pay.

"Terry handed the boy a lottery ticket to pay for his drink, sipping every once in a while at the register. The young boy went to the scanner and checked it. It didn't scan. Terry took the card back and looked. The card was scratched up badly in the bar code section. 'Dang, I must have scratched it too much,' Terry said. 'You can punch in these numbers down here at the bottom and check it that way,' and handed the ticket back to the Indian boy.

"He fumbled at the lottery computer for a while, punching in numbers. A line began to form. I was behind Terry buying a bag of Takis and a Twisted Tea. The boy appeared flustered at the register and said loudly, 'I keep messing up and typing in the wrong numbers!'

"I was impatient, as was everyone in the growing line. 'Let me see that!' I told the boy, who handed the ticket over. BPD were the letters on the ticket, a dud. If it would have been a winner, it would have had FIV or TWO in letters printed at random inside the scratch puzzle box."

Mukesh laughed to let his friend know he was listening.

"It was a beautiful scam. The dollar fountain drink didn't cost the store anything. A lot of clerks, seeing a line like that

The Hacker and The Hillbilly

form, would have let Terry have the cheap dollar fountain drink instead of punching in numbers. If Terry couldn't walk out with his free drink, he'd already had his fill by the time he got up to the register. If anything was said, he could set the cup down and leave refreshed, having not actually stolen anything and a good argument for plausible deniability."

Mike's eyes glowed. "That's a great story, Aaron. I actually believe it's true," said Mukesh, looking down sheepishly to show an ounce of doubt.

"Oh, you can't make up a con like that. Terry could have been a doctor or lawyer, or just about anything he wanted to be. Instead, he became a conman, in and out of jails and prison, using all of his brain power to come up with his next fix. Then he became a snitch, so he could do whatever the hell he wanted to and get away with it."

"How come?" asked Mukesh. "If it comes to making money double-crossing people, being a lawyer seems easier."

"If you knew how fucked up his family was, you'd know how he never much had a chance."

Mike was visibly excited. Hearing about Aaron's exploits made him want to go back to his room to scam. He got up to leave.

"I ain't done with the story yet, Mike." Aaron looked at Mukesh, grinning, sure that his new friend would enjoy listening to more. "The best part about it—that I didn't think of till later—is when Terry pulled that stunt I had such a rush watching him that I paid for his drink. So he conned me, or the way I'd like to think of it, I paid for him to teach me something and also entertainment."

Mukesh smiled, eyes glistening.

"I'll never understand any of your computer talk, but I love to hear how you trick people into giving you information. As a matter of fact, ever since you came around, I've been thinking about a local insurance scam. I have an idea." Aaron stared blankly at Mukesh, who stepped near the door like he was ready to leave. "But I'll tell you all about it next time you come." They both grinned and nodded at each other.

Mukesh was confident on the phone, but not so much in everyday life, so he was hesitant to get involved with any real-life con jobs besides giving advice. Mukesh had a darker complexion, and a lot of uneducated Americans believed he was from the Middle East, so he didn't think he would be that effective in such a small mountain town as Mason, Tennessee.

"I will look forward to hearing your idea, Aaron." Mukesh said politely, smiling at his new friend. He said goodnight and closed the door behind him.

Mukesh went home and called an old woman he had been softening up. He had already dialed her twice a couple of weeks before, when he found out the woman was recently widowed. It was seven-thirty in her time zone, just after dinner. From his past experience working the phones, he recognized a pattern of old women feeling sad and lonely after supper, and since this woman's husband had just passed, he knew that had to be the case. Sure enough, coddling her while she watched Family Feud, he got her to visit a fake website and click a link which infected her computer with several viruses which would give him full access to her laptop.

For bragging rights and a cherry on top, after she clicked on the link, he persuaded the widow to boot up her husband's old computer. He set up another link and told her he would give

The Hacker and The Hillbilly

her another virus scan for only twenty dollars, and she could pay by debit or credit.

"Just a minute, dear," said the old woman. "Is debit ok?"

"Debit is perfect, ma'am," said Mukesh. Mukesh would be going above and beyond in his task by getting the woman's personal credit card information. He wrote down all the numbers, including the CVC number on the back, on a Chinese delivery receipt and set it off to the side.

"Actually, ma'am," he said, schmoozing her more. "You are such a super lady. I will do it for you for free." She clicked on the site on her husband's computer for her free scan. It was a nice Dell, only a year old.

"You are going to want to leave your husband's computer on from now on, ma'am, so we can continue to update it," Mukesh told her. He said how sorry he was about her husband, and that He would call her from time to time to check on and console her, and of course update her software. Her husband's computer was a modern and powerful Dell tower and would be of good use as part of someone's network of zombie computers for denial of service attacks and bots.

As he browsed the Dell, Mukesh noticed a Bitcoin wallet. He transferred it to his laptop. Later, when he cracked into the wallet, Mukesh discovered it contained six thousand in Bitcoin.

The next day, Mukesh reported to Bakertwist81. He gave him the woman's credit card information but never mentioned the cryptocurrency. He was going to spend his six thousand dollars to buy better equipment. He would find an address somewhere a few counties over, an old rural home, and have the packages delivered there where he could collect his new tech unobserved.

After siphoning the dead man's crypto wallet and ordering his new hacker setup, Mukesh logged into the cyber exchange to check on his investments. Bitcoin was down but looked to surge, and Dogecoin and Ethereum had netted him a seven hundred dollar profit, minus trading fees. So far, the system his Indian friend had taught him was working, and Mukesh had already pushed his portfolio value up one thousand dollars. He went to bed happy with the new inroads and achievements of his quiet yet exciting life.

Chapter 5

Mukesh worked another successful week with the Darknet Collective, making fifteen hundred dollars for the first time in seven days. If he could make two thousand dollars or more a week all the time, he would be happy. Mukesh was feeling good. He had such a fun time over at Aaron's the week before that he ended up going over there several times a week.

Aaron sounded happy when Mukesh walked through the door later that evening. Mike pulled over an old, upholstered chair and sat down in front of Aaron. After some "how are you doing" talk, they settled back into bragging about the scams of their pasts.

"The lottery ticket story you told me last week was a good one," said Mukesh. "You always have to think outside the box. That's one reason fraud is so much fun. That lottery con is a very complicated scam for only a dollar soft drink. I like how Terry figured out a way to get exactly what he wanted and more without any chance of getting in trouble. I know what you are saying about people who could have been successful, geniuses born in a different caste or home. Americans might not have a caste system, but sometimes I feel they have something even worse. Americans tend to put people in whatever box they want them to be in based on how someone votes or what they believe. In India, I knew many street thugs and thieves who were smarter than a lot of our leaders. Of course, when you live on the street, you always have to be smarter than the police." Mukesh looked over at Aaron. Aaron nodded at him and listened.

"So..." said Mukesh, pausing to catch his breath, "and I know I don't have to tell you never to tell anyone..." Mukesh began again. "There was this company, and we needed the answer for a security question for a password recovery verification. We had gotten every answer to recover an admin password but one, the office nickname of the CEO's janitor's cat. If we had that one answer, we would have full access and control of their company's network. I had just started working with the people I am working with now, and they knew the more information I could get about an individual, the better. This was such a high-value operation to them that they used a lot of resources to get the contact information of the CEO's secretary, and having already proved my worth with my phone skills in Steam card scams—"

"Hold on now, what are Steam card scams?" Aaron interrupted.

"Well," Mukesh looked up at Aaron, annoyed, "they are not very interesting. They are very simple scams that require too much ass kissing and fake friendship, and for not a lot of money. Steam card scams are ones where you have to be really stupid to fall for twice, and overall, they are not impressive enough to brag about or even explain. They are used a lot by scammers who bully people into sending them money."

"Really? Bullying people to send you money! That's fucking incredible," said Aaron, laughing.

Mukesh continued his story. "We needed to get into a network using password recovery questions, and all I had to do was get the office nickname of the janitor's cat. I was positive

The Hacker and The Hillbilly

I could trick this woman and had already formulated a plan. Because, as you can guess, you just can't ask the secretary of the CEO of a company what the nickname is of a coworker's cat."

"Obviously," said Aaron.

"Also, not to assume the janitor was paid well, but his cat was a beautiful Birman. This woman was a schmooze, and we all thought that she was having an affair with the CEO. We were certain she knew the cat's secret nickname, but I couldn't raise suspicion, so I called her at her apartment pretending I was from a makeup company and that we were going to ship her some free product. I picked up from her photos that she liked expensive makeup. We had her address, and she must have signed up to get free makeup from somewhere, because she remembered signing up to win a gift box. Speaking of, you'd be surprised at the simple fact of telling someone they won a prize can jog a person's memory into thinking they filled out a sweepstakes somewhere when they really didn't.

"Anyway, I pretended that I had a rough day and wanted to talk to her about some things," Mukesh used a mocking feminine tone, "because some of the people I talk to on the phone every day were so awful and she was so sweet." Mukesh chuckled. "I told her about this beautiful cat I had bought, a white one with a brown and black nose, a Birman. She got excited, saying, 'I love those!' I told her my cat's name, Matilda. She laughed, and we joked that Matilda was a good name for a Birman cat, as regal as they look. After I set her up to think about Birman cats, she began to drone on to me about the goofy-looking Birman the janitor of their floor owned. I said, in an affected tone, 'Aww, how sweet. What is the cat's name?'

She told me it was named Carmen, but the office nicknamed it Pootsie because of the cat's dingleberries. It was so fat that it couldn't lick and clean its own ass. I typed 'Pootsy' into the chat window of a partner in our collective. He said that wasn't it. I asked him to check the spelling. He told me that would be one try too many for the password reset for that time but he would try later. I was confident I had gotten what we needed and politely got off the phone. The next day, they tried the iteration 'PootZ' after getting rejected for 'Pootsie,' and we were in."

"Can I ask what it was you guys did once you had the password?" said Aaron, hoping it wasn't too nosy of a question.

"See, I don't even know. That was the big task I pulled off that made them finally trust me. I started to get a lot more complicated scams and freedom after that. I never asked."

"That's fascinating," Aaron said, shaking his head. They both sat, silent for a moment. "Say, I have an idea for a personal injury scam. I know this guy who smashed his foot with a hammer on purpose one time just to get some pain meds. Even though he more or less has a bad limp from that stunt, he wants to fake another injury, though this time not just for pills. This time, he wants to get some real money as well. I bet we can figure out a way where he can injure himself and fake a personal injury lawsuit."

Mukesh lifted his head. "I might be able to think of something. I will look into it. I don't want to be a part of it, but I will gladly help you figure out something, and I am sure if it works you will give me a cut."

"Please be thinking of something," said Aaron, "and of course you will get a cut. Now, I have to meet a guy over here for some of that business of mine that you don't need to know about."

"The less I know, the less things people can say I have talked about," said Mukesh, smiling at Aaron to let him know he had borrowed one of his sayings.

"Indeed," said Aaron pretentiously. "Now, get out of here. But come back now, you hear?" Aaron cocked his head to the side and grinned a goofy grin. Mukesh rolled his eyes playfully as he left Aaron's motel room and closed the door.

Mukesh went straight to his computer when he got back to his room. Soon the computer equipment he had purchased with the old woman's Bitcoin money would arrive at an abandoned farmhouse Mukesh had shipped it to. Mukesh had set the shipping address to a vacant building three hours away. When the package arrived at the home later that week, he would be watching and would pick everything up once the coast was clear. He researched some more identities the Darknet Collective had supplied him with that week and went to bed.

The next morning, he opened his laptop to check on his crypto account and wallet, but when he clicked on the link an FBI seizure page came up instead. He checked the link again. Mukesh was horrified. The exchange had folded, and the FBI was investigating them for fraud. All of Mukesh's Bitcoin money was gone, and there was no chance of him ever getting any of it back again. He emailed Bakertwist81 that he had a big emergency and needed to take the day off.

Mukesh had only thirty-six thousand dollars left in his safe-deposit box, and it would horrify him if his savings dipped below thirty. Mukesh went over to Aaron's to try to drown out his loss. He was visibly pale when he walked in, so much so that Aaron asked him right away what was the matter.

Mukesh sat down. "I lost so much money today," he said plainly, not looking at Aaron but at the wall as he talked. Aaron was afraid to say anything. He put his head down out of respect and listened. Mukesh stayed silent and continued to stare at the wall.

Aaron looked up. "That bad?"

"That bad," Mukesh nodded.

"You'll make it back," Aaron said emphatically. Mike glared at him. Aaron repeated his reply, "You'll make it back. Did you lose everything?" Aaron was too scared to ask Mukesh how much he had lost.

Mukesh lied. "I lost fifteen thousand."

"My God!" said Aaron. "What happened?"

Mukesh was almost too embarrassed to say. "I used the wrong currency exchange to trade my money. They folded yesterday."

"I saw that on the news last night." Aaron didn't say anything else. To try to lighten the mood, Aaron joked, "Sometimes you eat the bear, sometimes Bear Stearns does whatever the hell they want to and gets away with it."

That made Mukesh chuckle. "That is a good way to put it." Mukesh was upset at himself for his stupid decision to try crypto trading. "Thank you Aaron. I am glad I have a person who I can talk about things like this with, someone who doesn't try to make me feel stupid for any of my mistakes."

Aaron put his head down and said, "Well, I don't know if I would call trading crypto stupid, just risky. Also, when a con man gets scammed, it always feels worse."

The Hacker and The Hillbilly

Mukesh tilted his head and looked up. "Now that you put it that way, I guess I can't complain. It always hurts when some banker takes your money, especially when they used it for so many years to make theirs. I lose my money, they go to a country club prison and keep my money when they get out. The head of the company will take the fall for the rest of his family and friends, and after five years he gets out and is set. The accountants and other executives in his firm who, of course, never saw anything suspicious, will have a sweet bank account waiting for him in the Bahamas or Switzerland when he gets done playing golf in jail."

Aaron wanted to change the mood. "Well, instead of switching money back and forth twenty times a day attempting to make more money, why don't you help me figure out some type of personal injury scam? I have seen some people sue and get fifty to a hundred thousand dollars or more for a broken bone from the right kind of fall."

"What are you thinking about, trip hazards or fake car accidents or something like that?" asked Mukesh.

"Trip hazards are difficult to fake. The person is going to have to be really good at faking a fall if there is video footage, and if there is no footage, you'll need a reliable witness. I talked to my friend Todd and he says he is still down. I told him I'll take care of the details and witnesses and we'll split the money. If you come up with a good idea and maybe help by being a witness, I'll cut you in on a quarter of it."

"I'll think about it," said Mukesh, noting that the deal now also included being a witness. At least his involvement would lead to a quarter of the take.

"You'll make a good witness," said Aaron. "Unlike the rest of my friends, you look respectable. You are a foreigner and would appear unconnected to anyone around here, so your story would be believed before the other people I know of I could trust."

Mukesh was intrigued and positive. "I'll come up with something," he said as he got up to walk out the door.

"Good," said Aaron. "Come back whenever. Text me first. If I don't answer, I'm asleep, or if I don't want you to come over, I'll say."

"Bet," said Mukesh.

"Nobody says that anymore," said Aaron. Mukesh smiled and nodded, then closed Aaron's door and went back to his own motel room.

When Mukesh got back, he hailed Bakertwist81 and got a coded email back in spam that told him to be in a dark web chat room at ten-thirty ET. Mukesh nosed around a website to try to find a chink in the firewall while he waited. He stopped at ten after ten and made a fried bologna sandwich out of some naan bread and olive oil seasoned with Indian spices from a glass jar. He folded a couple of large sections of paper towels beside his computer for a plate. He brought the sandwich over along with a half-eaten bag of Chex Party Mix. Mukesh looked at the time, ten-twenty-six. He waited two more minutes and logged into the darknet chat room. It was ten-twenty-nine. Bakertwist81 arrived at the chat room at ten-thirty-one.

Mukesh typed, "Hey Baker."

"Hey. Are you alright? You missed a meeting and said you had an emergency?"

The Hacker and The Hillbilly

"Not good news at all, Baker," Mukesh said. "I lost a lot of money in crypto because the exchange folded."

"I was afraid you had your Bitcoin in that exchange on the news. I know of a lot of people that lost a ton of money there. That's a shame. How much did you lose?"

"Ten thousand dollars," Mukesh told him, lying again.

Bakertwist paused longer than normal, then broke it off. "I won't bother you then. You are doing a good job. If things go well with the new AARP hack, you might be able to afford a better place and even a newer Prius." Mukesh looked off to the side for a second trying to remember if he had told Bakertwist what kind of car he drove. He couldn't. "I will leave you alone for the rest of your evening."

"Thank you for all you have done for me, Bakertwist."

"Before I leave, I forgot to tell you; it was very clever how you got that old woman whose husband just died to do a virus scan. Her husband's computer is now our central location for a large army of zombies and bots. We would like you to call her in an evening or two to remind her she needs to keep it turned on."

Mukesh grew uneasy. He realized that taking the Bitcoin wallet from the woman's desktop was a mistake, but one he hoped would go unnoticed. He shrugged off his doubt. There was little chance anyone would ever look hard enough to find a missing Bitcoin wallet from a dead husband's computer. If they found out, it really wasn't that big of a deal.

"I'll have some more files for you tomorrow evening for next week. Sorry again for your loss. If you are a day late this week, that will be fine. If you want any more files, let me know and we can give you more. You are talented and rising fast. It won't be too long before we have you on the full-time team for our most complicated cons. If you do well, you might make our planning team. The elite strategists with us, based on seniority of course, are some of our highest-paid associates."

"I look forward to joining them one day," said Mukesh.

"I hope you get there. Have a good evening," said Bakertwist81.

"You too," said Mukesh. He logged off and went to bed.

Chapter 6

The next morning, Mukesh woke up early. The equipment he ordered from the stolen Bitcoin would be delivered that day at a vacant home three hours away. He arrived at the location thirty minutes early to survey the area and make sure no one would see him picking up the packages. Mukesh didn't have binoculars but he was close enough to the abandoned building to see a small pile of brown packages left on the flaking gray porch. No one was around, so he backed up to the abandoned home and put the packages in his Prius and drove back to the motel. He piled all the packages in a corner of the motel room and threw a blanket over them to hide them from view. Mukesh was tired after a full day of driving. He spent the rest of his time that evening looking at the Facebook accounts of people he was ready to scam. Bakertwist81 sent him a coded message to meet him in the darknet chat room at nine the next morning.

Mukesh logged into the chat room at one after nine. "Hi," he typed.

"I don't know any other way to tell you this, but we know about the Bitcoin that you stole from that woman's computer and we are severing ties with you." Mukesh was so shocked that he didn't even have time to think. "It was a violation of our rules and ethics, which we had expressed to you when you first started working with us. You used one of our leads and took something for yourself that should have gone into the family pool."

Mukesh was caught and knew it. "But what about the recent hack job that I was such a big help with?"

"Funny you should even mention that. It's like a thinly veiled threat. Let's put it this way, if you say anything to anyone about what you have done with us, there will be extreme consequences. We will be watching you. I won't say anything else." Bakertwist81 left the chat room abruptly. Mukesh's screen on his laptop flashed and went black. The power button stayed lit on his laptop, but the computer was unresponsive. Mukesh stared at his fried laptop with his mouth open.

"How in the hell?..." Mukesh muttered. Then a wave of fear overcame him. The Darknet Collective had hacked into his personal computer, and Mukesh had no idea how. If they could do that, what else could they do? He lay down on his bed and stared at the door, thinking everything through.

He could try to get back into their good graces. How, he had no clue. But as it dawned on him that he'd been part of such a capable group, he couldn't just let his membership slip through his fingers. But how could he do it? Bakertwist had been clear. His firing was final. But there had to be a way.

Mukesh blinked at the door, imagining what it would take. Maybe if he pulled off a high-profile hack that made it into the news, the Collective would give him a second chance. He thought again about what they'd done to his computer, and that gave him a different idea. If he could manage something big enough to impress Bakertwist, would they come after him for a hack that wasn't one under their protection? Images of shadowy fingers clicking keys and summoning SWAT teams to beat down Mukesh's door entered his mind. He snuffed those

The Hacker and The Hillbilly

fantasies before they could get going, and he gave up any notion of trying to rejoin the group.

He checked his phone. Five minutes had gone by, though it felt like more than an hour. Mukesh got up, his body stiff and sore from the shock. He shook it off. There was no need to be afraid, just like there was no need to be overly upset when he lost half of his money. Plus, why would they go through all that trouble to scare him? If they wanted to harm him, they would have done so already without any warnings.

So he was safe from them. But another wave of horror hit Mukesh. If he could not find a way to get the same kind of money that he was getting with the Darknet Collective, he wouldn't be able to make it. Of course, he could purchase some account information off the dark web and call a bunch of random phone numbers, but that would be way too much trouble. There was also little chance of finding any other groups to work with, since his failure with the Collective might also have blacklisted him from all the other hacker groups.

He thought more about what Aaron had proposed, the personal injury scam. Mukesh calmed down and went for a drive to get something to eat. He rode around town to inspire ideas. Since Mukesh was out of work, he would need to save money every way he could. He heard about a food pantry that served hot meals once a day and gave out expired grocery items and leftovers from a local catering company. Mukesh decided to eat there every day to save money. He pulled into the food pantry, and there was a line. He stepped out of his Prius and into the queue. It was five until eleven. Two people up front who seemed to know one another were talking. Mukesh put one earbud in and listened to a classic Indian song while he waited. He tried to keep from looking at people in case they wanted to talk to him. At ten-fifty-eight, a short, pudgy old woman with an apron opened the door.

The people in front hurried in. Mukesh followed behind and looked over to the far left at the two tables where all the rush was headed. He chuckled at the sight of a couple in front scrambling for freebies. They were diving on top of one another, grabbing the best items. Mukesh walked closer to the clamor, amused. After stuffing their allotted pair of plastic grocery bags, the greediest two hurried off and sat down together to wait for the volunteers to bring them their meals.

Mukesh approached the giveaway table, which had been thoroughly pillaged of the choicest items. He eyed two hunks of Manchego cheese and smiled. The people before him were obviously not educated enough to know that they had passed over some really great, expensive cheese. Mukesh sat at a corner table with one other person instead of going to one of the other empty six. They both sat with their backs against the wall. The person sitting next to him got his plate first. It looked like some kind of barbeque sandwich.

"Miss, what is that?" Mukesh asked the woman serving trays.

"RibBQ," said the young woman in a flowery hippie dress.

"I can't eat pork, miss," said Mukesh. Mukesh was lying. He ate sausage biscuits all the time, but he hoped they might have something else, because RibBQs are nasty.

"I'll take care of it, sir," said the radiant woman gently. She walked back into the kitchen and came out with another two trays to pass to a couple of seated people. Others were

The Hacker and The Hillbilly

standing. The woman looked at them and asked, "How many to go? Only two to each person."

"Six," said one woman beside another. The volunteer looked in the back at the person getting food from the table. She gave them the benefit of the doubt that the person at the back table stuffing cakes in a large paper bag was with them.

The young woman called out, "Six to-go meals for these three people here..." She glanced at the two and paused to hint. "And I think..." she fluttered her fingers around in the air while counting those seated, "four more regular trays." She looked over at Mukesh. "And we are fixing your pork-free tray, sir."

Mukesh smiled and nodded at the beautiful, young volunteer woman. She had short hair and was very graceful and feminine in her movements for an American in her early thirties. She returned to Mukesh with his tray and laid it in front of him.

"Thank you, miss," he said.

"When you come, if you don't want the meat option you get the vegetarian option, which is an extra portion of salad, some beans, a portion of fruit and an extra portion of bread." Mukesh looked up at her. She smiled at him.

"Thank you, miss," Mukesh said again. "But it is not a vegetarian thing." Mukesh decided to stick with his lie. "It's a religious thing. I don't eat pork. Do you have Italian dressing? And do you think I could get a real knife instead of this plastic one?"

"What do you want a real knife for?" The woman looked at Mukesh, puzzled.

Mukesh smirked. "I want to cut some of this cheese I just got into my salad."

"Oh," she said and turned to go back to the kitchen. "Yes, I will bring you some Italian dressing and a knife." The shrink-wrap packaging was so thick around the Manchego cheese that Mukesh needed a metal knife to open it anyway. The woman returned again with a bottle of Italian dressing and a stainless paring knife. She handed the knife to Mukesh and squirted some salad dressing on his plate.

"Thank you, ma'am," he said.

"You're welcome," she said softly, and looked around the room. Mukesh stayed silent as he received the knife and cut a long line in the thick plastic packaging. He peeled it back, sliced a section off, and cut the chunk of cheese in small pieces into his salad.

Mukesh looked around the room and pretended to pray. A guy in his twenties walked around and picked up a couple of empty trays. Mukesh slowly ate everything on his plate—except for the slice of bread, a piece of plain white grocery store loaf—and watched the young man. He was pushing a mop bucket back to the kitchen when Mukesh walked over to the bathroom on his way out.

Mukesh walked into the bathroom and slipped, and almost fell. The floor had just been mopped. It was made out of composite tile and was very slick when wet. Nowhere near or in the bathroom was a wet floor sign of any kind, not even the usual bright yellow foldout. In an instant, Mukesh came up with Aaron's insurance scam—a slip in this food pantry's bathroom. The charity organization would be liable for any injuries that occurred if they failed to post a warning about the wet floor.

The Hacker and The Hillbilly

Mukesh broke from his conniving and walked back to the table with the giveaway food. A few pitiful looking bell peppers, a couple medium-sized yellow cakes, and several cans of chickpeas and green beans remained. Mukesh glanced up at the young boy and grinned. He turned to go home.

Mukesh laughed along the drive back to his motel room while imagining more details of his wet floor insurance scam. Home, he sat in his room and spent another half-hour thinking before he hurried over to Aaron's.

"Who is it?" asked Aaron.

"It's me."

"Come on in, neighbor," Aaron said, opening the door for Mukesh.

He entered, excited, and said right off, "The plan with your friend and the injury, I have an idea."

"Ok," said Aaron, skeptical.

"Today, I went to the food pantry. A volunteer down there mops but doesn't put out a wet floor sign after he cleans the bathroom, and I think the boy always mops it before they close every day." Mukesh paused to see what Aaron thought.

"Go on," said Aaron, smiling.

"I can start going to the food pantry every day and be a credible witness. You are definitely right. They will never think I am connected to one of your friends. He can walk in with his pre-injured arm one day and have the fake fall in the bathroom, and I can witness it all."

"That's a pretty good idea," said Aaron. "I'll have to think about it some more and talk to my friend about it. The last time, he smashed a sledgehammer on his foot, and it crippled him up pretty good. He needs money and pills, but he doesn't want to get any more disabled."

"We can do it. I got a good feeling about this," Mukesh told him.

Aaron hung his head, thinking. He lifted it up. "I got it," he said, smiling at Mukesh. "Collar bone. That should fetch some good money, maybe more than a hundred thousand, even. With a collarbone injury, he will be able to walk in, and no one will be able to tell he is injured. Healing from a collarbone injury is tough, but I can convince Todd it won't cripple him up as bad as a broken arm. We can cave his neckbone in with a hammer or something and pretend like he broke it on the toilet in a fall."

Mukesh looked up at the ceiling. "That is a great idea! How are you going to break his collarbone safely without hurting him too much?"

"I'll need to think some more about that," said Aaron, "but so far, this sounds alright. I'm sure a lot of people have broken their collarbone on the toilet. I'll get Jen to nose around on social media and find out who owns the food pantry to get a feel for what kind of insurance they have."

Mukesh bobbed his head up and down in delight as he began to imagine this plan netting him at least what he'd lost in Crypto. His eyes grew wider. "I know it is going to work. I can feel it. We can talk about it more later. I will start going to the food pantry every day from here on and make friends with the crew. They'll see I am educated. Your friend needs to go eat there a few times before we stage the accident. I can make sure in the meantime this young boy always mops before closing and forgets the sign."

The Hacker and The Hillbilly

"Yes, the no sign part is crucial. If not, this will never work. I'll get him to start going in to eat at the food pantry every now and then so he'll look less suspicious."

Mukesh jumped up from his chair. Noticing Aaron's reaction to his sudden movement, he looked over near where Jen sat staring into her phone like always. "May I use the bathroom?"

"Sure, Mike," Aaron said. Mukesh walked back to the bathroom, brushing past Jen.

"Hi, Jen," he said, walking in and closing the door. Mukesh washed his hands, walked out, and stood before Aaron. His eyes were wide, and his lips were grinning. "I'm going to go back to my place to play on the computer and think some more about the food pantry."

"Ok, Mike," Aaron said as Mukesh was halfway through the door.

He paused and looked at Aaron. "When do you think we can do all this, the injury thing?"

"I'd say three weeks or more from now, if Todd is down. I won't bother you with any details until I get my guy on board. I'll have to see him a few times more than I'd like to and throw a few pain pills to him every now and then to keep him interested. I'll even have some grade A heroin not cut with fentanyl for the day of the scam. He'll get half of whatever is left after the lawyer, and you and I split the other half, so you get a quarter. Fair?" Aaron extended his hand at Mike, who shook it. Mukesh closed the door and walked back to his room, exhilarated at the prospect of pulling off his first real-life con.

Chapter 7

Mukesh disassembled the laptop the Darknet Collective had destroyed. He swapped out the parts that were totally fried with working ones from a cheap refurb he got at a local pawn shop and cobbled together a laptop decent enough to sell to a midwit student on Craigslist. Mukesh looked around the room nervously as he proceeded to unpack his new computer equipment. The Darknet Collective must have used some tricks and programs that he didn't know about. From what Mukesh understood, there was no way that his old laptop could have gotten infected with any viruses unless he had made a mistake. He tried to think of what he did that could have allowed their hack, but couldn't. He vowed to be careful moving forward.

Expecting to be blacklisted, Mukesh crafted another identity. He never showed too much personality in dark web chats before, so he didn't think anyone would be able to identify him by a distinctive chat voice.

Mukesh was so frustrated over the opportunity he had lost with his old group that he purchased some random phone numbers for Steam card scams.

Every day, Mukesh ate at the food pantry. He was quiet and polite and gave the impression that he was an educated man going there because he was saving money or down on his luck. After a couple of weeks, Mukesh noticed a pattern when the young volunteer, whose name was Jeffy, mopped the bathroom. Every day, Jeffy mopped ten minutes before the food pantry closed, and Mukesh began to doubt they even had

The Hacker and The Hillbilly

a wet floor sign. Mukesh was nervous and wanted to get the scam over with soon in case that pattern ever changed.

It was fifteen until twelve, and Mukesh had just finished a wholesome meal of baked chicken, peas and carrots, and of course, as always, a salad. A medium-sized, dirty man with a beard came in and eyeballed everyone in the room.

"Do you want a takeout meal or are you eating here?" one of the volunteer servers asked. The man didn't answer. He continued to look around at people and stare. Mukesh put his head down in case this strange man was Aaron's friend.

The server walked up closer to the man and asked again, "Sir, would you like to eat here, or would you like a takeout?"

The man broke from his trance and grunted, "Here." The man nodded at Mukesh and walked to the back and put some tomatoes and cucumbers and a loaf of bread in a bag. As he was leaving the table of food, he scooped up a medium-sized carrot cake and sat down to wait for his tray. He kept eyeing Mukesh in what seemed like short, knowing glances. Mukesh kept his head down the rest of the time while he ate to keep from looking at the man. As his head hung, he fell into a calm state of mind in which his instincts told him that the gruff, dirty-looking man at the table staring at him was the man Aaron was going to use for the con.

When he got back to the motel, he texted Aaron, hoping to find out. As always, Aaron unlocked the door, and Mukesh walked in. The two said their pleasantries, and Mukesh sat down. Both looked at one another like they wanted the other to speak first.

Mukesh broke the silence. "I have been going every day to the food pantry and establishing some trust with the staff." He

64

pitched his tone of voice and said, "I saw someone staring at me today. You said you would send your friend to the food pantry a few times before his accident."

"Yeah, he said he's been there a few times. I think he said once or twice recently. Please don't be upset. I told him that there was a foreign guy that was helping me as a witness and that was why he was only getting half of the settlement. He is a pretty simple guy. The fact that I told him you were foreign might have made him stare."

"Is he short with a beard? This guy today also had a mottled face and stained, dirty-looking clothes."

"That sounds like him, the dirty pockmarked face." Aaron grinned.

"He looks rough. I can see why a witness would be absolutely necessary with a guy like him," said Mukesh. "He doesn't look that smart, that is for sure. When he looked at me, he looked scared, like he knew he shouldn't have been staring."

Aaron started laughing. "That was definitely him today, then." Aaron laughed some more and collected himself. "He is stupid enough to break his collarbone for money and drugs. A broken collarbone hurts something awful, from what I hear, and is a pain in the ass to heal. You basically have to lay around and do nothing for a long time, so that's a plus for him there. I even convinced Todd that a collarbone injury has little chance of crippling him. His foot is lame ever since he caved the middle of it in with that sledgehammer to get some pain pills. He'll really need to take care of himself after we break his collarbone."

"What do you mean by, 'we?'" Mukesh asked, annoyed. "I don't have the stomach for that kind of stuff."

The Hacker and The Hillbilly

"I meant we as in 'our plans,'" clarified Aaron. "I told him he could make one hundred to three hundred thousand or more on this injury, and he's excited. He's nervous about going through with it, especially the part about how we are going to fake the injury." Aaron stared sternly at Mukesh. "A concern that we both have is that something might happen that will keep us from going through with this and we'll break his collarbone for nothing."

Mukesh recoiled in his chair. "I don't even want to know how you are going to break his collarbone," he said. "Let me be clear on that. The boy always mops early every day without fail, and not once has he put out a wet floor sign. I don't even know if the food pantry has a wet floor sign."

"All options," said Aaron, "are not going to be fun for him, but if somebody has to whack his neck with a sledgehammer, he'd rather it be someone with something to gain and not someone that might accidentally miss. I have to learn more about how much force and what steps I can use to break his bone without hurting him too bad. I'll talk to a Pagan I know about that."

"What is a Pagan?" asked Mukesh.

"That's a brutal biker gang with ties to Appalachia. This guy knows a lot about and has broken a lot of bones."

"Oh. It is good that your friend is going to the food pantry now. If he can keep from looking so scared and nervous, everything will be more believable. When are we going to do this?"

"It will be another two weeks. I'm getting some real heroin that's not cut with fentanyl for Todd in a week and a half. If I give him a dose of good diesel a couple days before we do this,

66

he'll be down for anything. I'll string him along until the day comes. That day, he will be so good and high off the good shit he won't be feeling any pain... or not much... maybe."

"I don't want to be there when he gets hurt," said Mukesh. "I don't have the stomach for it."

"I can't wait until that day comes, myself. It has been a long time since I've had some uncut black tar heroin." Jen looked up at Aaron and smiled in anticipation herself. "Don't worry, Jen. You are getting some too." Jen smiled again and buried her face back into her phone.

Aaron looked back over at Mukesh. "Everything is going to work out, I guess, if I can get the bone breaking part right and they believe you as a witness. Oh, I forgot. Jen checked into the food pantry. The guy that owns the property is extremely rich, and people say he donates the majority of the money needed to run the pantry himself. Everyone knows how passionate he is about helping out and feeding the poor. I believe that if the pantry has no insurance, the liability is on the property owner. He definitely has great insurance, and he's so rich, he could take an entire lawsuit hit himself. He is so proud of our local food pantry, he'd pay the settlement money himself before he'd allow the place to close down."

"Sounds like a plan."

"Definitely," said Aaron. "This has a good chance of working."

"I think so too." Mukesh stood up. "Have a good evening, brother."

"You too, Mike." They said goodbye, and Mukesh went back to his room and straight to bed. He lay there thinking about Aaron's insurance scam and came up with a few new

The Hacker and The Hillbilly

ideas while he fell asleep. The next morning, Mukesh got up early and hit the phone lines.

That day, he had to call an embarrassing amount of the random numbers for six solid hours to make only one hundred dollars in Steam cards. Calling random numbers without knowing anything about the individuals was never going to work. Mukesh got sick of his lack of success and quit for the day. He texted Aaron, "May I come over?"

"I have some people coming over tonight. How about tomorrow evening?" Aaron replied.

"That is fine. Let me know what time tomorrow," thumbed Mukesh.

That next day, Mukesh went to the food pantry again. He started showing up at eleven-thirty-five, twenty-five minutes before closing to make sure Jeffy still mopped the bathroom at the same time. Ten minutes before close, the young boy had not mopped. Mukesh went to the front door and pretended to look out at his car while actually investigating the potential threat to their fraud. The mop bucket was in the hall and ready to be used. Mukesh sat back at his table and finished the last few bites of his food. At five till twelve, he could hear the bucket buggy roll down the kitchen hall and stop near the bathroom door. Mukesh walked outside and waved goodbye to the server and kitchen staff members on the way out. The boy was outside of the entrance, scrubbing inside the bathroom with the mop. Mukesh walked back to the giveaway table one more time. The boy finished at eleven-fifty-seven. Way too close.

Mukesh returned to his room and resumed making random calls. He got a text from Aaron.

"Six o'clock I have a friend coming over that I want you to meet. We are going to chat for a while. You can come over at twenty after." Mukesh was sure Aaron was talking about Todd and that they would officially meet.

At twenty after six, Mukesh walked over to Aaron's motel room. Mukesh called out, and Aaron opened the door. The same scraggly-looking redneck that Mukesh had seen a couple of days ago at the pantry was sitting in the chair Mukesh normally sat in, swaying and sagging in his seat with squinted eyes. Mukesh walked over to where Jen sat, said hello, and squatted in a small chair parked beside the mini-fridge.

"Mike, this is Todd. Todd, Mike," said Aaron, watching as Mukesh walked politely over to the man and shook his hand. After shaking hands, Todd leaned off to the side and closed his eyes and mumbled incoherently. Aaron looked at Mukesh and rolled his eyes. "He knows the plan. Hey, what were some details that you wanted to talk to me about?"

Mukesh thought quickly. "What happens again if they don't mop before they close like usual?"

Aaron raised his eyebrows and glanced over at a seemingly sleeping Todd to make sure he wasn't paying attention. Aaron glared at Mukesh and said with soft disgust, "That better not happen." Aaron watched Todd intently. Todd continued to nod off, oblivious. "This guy is going to have to break his collarbone in the food pantry bathroom or else..." He looked back at Mukesh angrily, paused, and shook his head. Aaron corrected himself. "Let's just say that I am going to expect you to make this happen or it won't be pretty." Aaron looked back over at Todd. He was still out. "I don't know how else to tell you. If you aren't certain there won't be a wet bathroom floor with no

The Hacker and The Hillbilly

yellow sign, we need to call this off." Aaron glanced at Todd again, but he was way too high and not paying attention. Aaron leaned toward Mukesh and whispered, serious and intense. "I will have to pay him dearly if this doesn't work out. I will hear about this for the rest of my life. He will wave it in my face for everything. If you don't keep up with your part of the plan, you will pay dearly as well." Aaron paused and looked at Mike with cold, indifferent eyes that seemed to be boring through to the back of his head.

Mukesh shrugged off the glare. "So far, the floor gets mopped early every day. Yesterday, it was three minutes to spare, so it was close, but I have never seen them kick anyone out of the food pantry for staying five minutes late. I will figure something out if not. I want to get this over with. When do you think we can do it?"

"Friday," answered Aaron.

Mukesh got nervous about the possibility of everything screwing up over his part of the plan. "How about Monday? We'll have the whole weekend to think about things and rest."

"Todd!" said Aaron sharply. Todd looked like he was sleeping sitting up. Aaron looked over at Mukesh again. "I want to get this over with. I'm the one who has to break his collarbone, and if we don't do this Friday, that's the whole weekend he will be over here wanting free dope."

"Ok. I see..." said Mukesh.

"The good thing is, my friend showed me the best way to break a guy's collarbone without hurting him too badly." Aaron waved his hand over at Todd playfully. Todd was so high he was beginning to drool.

Mukesh winced. "I don't want to hear anything about it." He looked down to his left and his right a few times as if trying to find something else to say. "Very well. Friday is good. I will come over tomorrow evening, and we can talk more about it then." He looked over at Todd, who now had a line of spittle dripping down the side of his mouth. Mukesh excused himself, intent on escaping his own angst with his laptop, a can of Sun Drop, and some YouTube videos.

The next evening, Mukesh hadn't heard anything from Aaron all day, and it was six-thirty. Mukesh texted him. Aaron texted back, "Things are tense around here, and Jen and I are fighting. We have gone through enough of the details. Tomorrow we are ready. Meet me over here at nine o'clock."

Mukesh smiled and texted back a Xanax reference in code. "I was hoping I could watch the NFL this evening so I could sleep better."

He waited for over two minutes before the response, "Would you please take out the trash for me? I left it by the door. Please don't spill the coffee. Nine a.m. tomorrow."

Mukesh went over to Aaron's door. Outside, there was a white kitchen trash bag halfway filled with trash, pulled loosely by the red plastic strings but not tied. Mukesh carefully picked up the bag. He took it and its contents to the motel's dumpster. At the back side of the dumpster, between the trash bin and the fence, he opened the bag. On the very top was a folded-over coffee cup. When he pulled the paper cup out of the trash bag, he could feel something jiggling and sliding inside. It was a Xanax, a blue football. Mukesh swallowed it down quickly and in an hour was fast asleep.

Chapter 8

Mukesh had set his alarm for seven-fifteen on the Friday morning of their Food Pantry caper. At six-forty-five, he woke up and lay in bed, thinking with his eyes closed until he heard the alarm. He got up and massaged his face with cold water and yawned, still groggy. The benzo morning residual should keep him from being too nervous that big day, and his brain fog was nothing some coffee couldn't fix. He made himself a cup, and at ten til nine, he texted, "Walking over." Mukesh knocked on Aaron's door.

Aaron stepped out of his room and immediately into Mukesh's personal space. Mukesh was not expecting that and stepped back, confused.

"Let's go," Aaron said.

"Go? Let's go where?"

"Let's get in your car and get this shit done." Aaron stared at Mukesh as he buttoned up his flannel.

Mukesh stared back, annoyed, and said, "We can't all go over there together."

Aaron got back in Mukesh's face. "Look, Mike... I know you. You would never understand my part of this plan, and you'd ask too many questions. This is more about me being able to fully trust you. This is half my plan, and I had reasons for not filling you in on everything we're going to do today. You're pretty good with your behavioral science shit and coming up with ideas, but there are some things about mountain folk you wouldn't understand until you see and experience them. And also, like I said, I have to be able to trust you. Now let's go."

Mukesh bowed his head slightly, then he and Aaron got into the Prius. Aaron put on some sunglasses and pulled his worn baseball cap further down his brow. He laid his seat back and rested his arm along the window ledge, sticking his hand outside to catch the cool air.

Mukesh started the car.

"Do you know where Martin's Station is?" Aaron asked. Mukesh looked at him stupidly. Aaron chuckled. "Just drive where I tell you to go. Going out of the motel, take a right." Mukesh took the right, annoyed at Aaron's bark-like commands.

"We're almost there," he said after five minutes of driving. "Take the next right and get ready to turn left at a hundred yards. Turn here." Aaron pointed to the left when they needed to turn in. Mukesh pulled into a lane and slowed down beside a house. "No. Keep going." Aaron swiped his hands forward and pointed at a shed fifty yards behind an old two story house. Mukesh drove slowly along a dirt path. "Stop once you get close to that shed," said Aaron, pointing again.

Mukesh stopped his Prius in front of it and looked over at Aaron. Aaron got out of the car and walked over to the shed. He took a peg out of the latch and opened up the right-side double door and walked inside. A minute later, he came out with a sledgehammer and a two-and-a-half foot long section of a four-by-four chunk of treated lumber. He leaned the sledge and scotch against the shed and re-pegged the latch. Aaron picked up the tools and made his way back to the car. He opened the back door and laid them both in the back seat.

Mukesh was confused and upset, "You need to tell me what is going on! We can't be making any mistakes!"

The Hacker and The Hillbilly

"You have to trust me," Aaron said.

"I trust you, but what are we doing out here? I cannot take Todd to the pantry with me."

"I know that! I got this covered. I hate to break it to you, but you are going to have to help me with Todd. You are going to have to hold the block of wood for me and be a witness in case something happens." Aaron looked at Mukesh, whose mouth hung open. Aaron chuckled. "It is going to be ok, Mike. It's one of those things that's like this... I'm not going to be in on something like this with someone unless they take the culpability for some of the nastier things. You hold the block of wood, I'll do the hammer swinging. If you hold it right, I won't kill him, and there should be very little blood. I hope not, at least. There is a chance this could give him a heart attack, and then of course I'd need some help getting rid of the body."

Mukesh looked pale and started hyperventilating. "You are going to give me a heart attack!"

Aaron smirked. "Mike, you look like you are having another one of your panic attacks. I got something for you." He reached in his watch fob pocket and retrieved a blue Xanax. Breaking it in half, Aaron ate one and handed the other half to Mukesh. Mukesh swallowed it. Just the thought of the pill kicking in made him feel more at ease. Mukesh looked over at Aaron.

"Let's go get a biscuit at Bojangles. I could also use a beer," Aaron said to Mukesh. It was nine-forty-five. Mukesh started backing out of the property and turned around in a large gravel parking section.

Mukesh glared at Aaron in disgust.

"What's your deal?" Aaron asked him.

"I did not want to be driving you around, nor do I want a biscuit, and I told you I did not want to be there when Todd gets hurt. I don't even want to know his last name."

"Todd Carlin," said Aaron.

"Now why would you…"

Aaron cut him off. "It's about trust. Maybe his first name isn't even Todd, maybe I want to make sure you don't ever repeat that name and I'll find out if you do." Mukesh stared, blank-faced. "And," Aaron continued, "the only way I am going to do this is with you." Aaron pointed at the back seat where the sledgehammer and block lay. "The block will keep me from hurting him too badly with the hammer if I use the right amount of force…" Aaron paused, "but if something does go wrong, I'm going to need you to help clean up the mess. Because of that, you have to be there with me on this and hold the block for me. If that's not ok with you, I can still call this off."

Mukesh didn't like how Aaron said "I." It was both of their plans.

"Listen, Mike…" Aaron said sternly, "if you can't deal with crazy shit like this, you'll never be a good con artist." Aaron leaned all the way back in his seat again. "You need to learn how to be level-headed and cool under pressure, especially in real-life scams." Mukesh kept his eyes on the road and listened. "That Xanax kicking in? God, I hope so. You're acting like a little bitch." Aaron looked over at Mukesh with his stupid, raggedy hat and shades and grinned.

The Xanax was indeed kicking in. Mukesh began to relax and flashed Aaron back a smile. He returned his attention to the mountain road. Aaron had made several good points.

The Hacker and The Hillbilly

Mukesh would definitely need to be calm while playing his part at the food pantry.

They both were quiet the rest of the way to Bojangles.

"Buy me a biscuit for doing this for you," Mukesh said with a slight pout.

Aaron shook his head and smiled. "I'll buy you a biscuit." They walked inside the restaurant and got a two-for-five dollar steak biscuit deal to split. Mukesh started to walk out the door with their bag of food. "Where are you going? Let's have a seat and relax." Mukesh followed him to a booth in the corner of the store. "Remember, relax is the key word. You should know better than to get frustrated. You're going to have to get in character. This is real-life stuff, with more mistakes to make than over the phone. Do you get upset over stuff you can't control when you are tele-scamming an old woman?"

Mukesh felt the urge to explain how complicated it could be, how sometimes it was beneficial getting folks fired up, but instead he said, "No."

"That's right!" Aaron said.

Mukesh smiled, feeling childish that he allowed his unfamiliarity with Aaron's plan to affect his disposition.

Aaron chewed on his finger. "So, I hope I won't make you nervous if I ask you again... Are you sure this volunteer dude always mops without fail, every day with no sign, right before they close?"

"You already asked, and yes," said Mukesh quickly, not wanting to be chided and second-guessed about so much for so long. "I will figure something out if not."

"I have to stress it, though." Aaron cut his eyes at Mike to let him know how serious he was. "Todd is not going to want to go through what I am about to do to him unless he's gonna get some good money for this. This is a good scam, and I have no doubt it'll work and that, in about a year after the second or third offer from the insurance agency, we all will get a nice chunk of money. You get a quarter of the take for details of the plan and to be a witness, and I get a quarter for picking out the local idiot and breaking his collarbone with a sledgehammer." Aaron chuckled and smiled at Mukesh. "Then the local idiot spends half of what he gets with me on dope." He grinned again and started laughing. "So I guess you can say in the long run I get most of the money anyhow."

Aaron checked his watch. "Speaking of Todd's dope—I left it at home. It's ten fifteen. We have time to ride back to the motel. He's going to want a shot. I'm not the biggest of fans of pain meds, but there really is nothing quite like good heroin that's not cut with fentanyl. I had to pay double the street value to get some wholesale uncut shit."

They rode back to the motel. Aaron walked inside his room and returned a moment later.

"Ok," he said after he got in Mukesh's Prius, "we are meeting him in a field by Carrey's Bridge at eleven o'clock." Mukesh opened his mouth to say something, but Aaron interrupted. "But I know you don't know where Carrey's Bridge is, so just follow my instructions." Mukesh frowned nervously as he drove, head and eyes fixed on the road. Aaron had Mukesh pull into a logging trail. After a quarter of a mile, they came to a clearing in the back. Todd sat in the corner of the field on a stump.

"Don't say anything more to him about the plan. I'll do all the talking about that. He gets confused easily." Aaron got out

The Hacker and The Hillbilly

of Mukesh's car. Mukesh stayed in his Prius and watched Aaron walk over to Todd. He returned shortly after and poked his head inside. "It would be better if I could prepare this guy's pain medicine in your vehicle." Mukesh nodded and got out. He stood in front of his car and stared off into the distance, having no desire to speak to the sketchy dude on the stump. Aaron stepped out after five minutes of fumbling. He looked at his phone. It was ten after eleven. He walked over to Todd, handed him the needle and walked back to Mukesh's car. Before he got to the Prius, he called out to Todd, "And turn around! The driver slash witness doesn't want to see any needles or blood." Mukesh already had his head down to keep from looking.

Aaron walked over and whispered to Mukesh, "There really shouldn't be much blood if we do this right. I have to hit the hammer dead in the center of the wood block directly over the point I want to break. All you have to do is hold the block of wood still on top of his collarbone. Whatever you do, keep it flat. If it gets twisted or a corner of the wood is poking into Todd when I strike, we might hurt him more than we want."

Aaron opened up the back door and fetched the sledgehammer and wood block out of the back. Aaron handed Mukesh the block of wood, and they both approached the stump where Todd sat. The black tar heroin was coursing through Todd, who showed little reaction to two criminals encroaching and brandishing a sledgehammer with malicious intent.

Mukesh had to focus to keep his hands from shaking.

They stood in front of their short, goofy-looking victim, half-nodded out on a stump. Aaron glanced at Mukesh, reached out, and felt around the right side of Todd's neck. He dropped the sledgehammer by his side and pulled at Todd's shirt collar with both hands to get a good look at the bone. Aaron took the block from Mukesh and positioned it to the right of Todd's head, flat on the clavicle to show Mike how he wanted him to hold it. "Just like this." Aaron handed the block back to Mukesh.

Mukesh looked at the block in his hand, then back at his friend.

Aaron took his finger and prodded the part of the collarbone that stuck out the most from Todd's neck. He began to wake up. "Let the block rest gently on this spot." Aaron shook Todd's left shoulder. "And you are going to want to tilt your head off to the other side real good, Todd, to keep it from getting hit with the hammer." Aaron hefted the ten-pound sledge into the air, letting the head slam ominously onto the palm of his free hand. He smiled.

"Let's get it over with," said Todd in a drowsy voice. Todd was so high, he had to strain to keep his eyes half-open. Mukesh rested the block gently on the side of Todd's neck. He winced and looked away.

"You can't look away, Mike! You have to watch to make sure the block of wood stays flat against the bone. You also have to make sure you keep it still." Aaron stepped back and lowered the sledgehammer. "Hold up. What time is it?"

Mukesh removed the block from Todd's neck and looked at his phone: "Fifteen after eleven."

"We have a few minutes. We want the wound to be as fresh as possible. Let's talk about this."

The Hacker and The Hillbilly

Mukesh was annoyed at Aaron for assuming a strong leadership position, but there was nothing he could do about it. Aaron shuffled around for another couple of minutes, thinking. He looked at his phone and back again at Mike and Todd. "All right. The bone that is going to be broken is on the right side of your neck. How are you going to lie in the bathroom after the fall?'" Aaron asked Todd. Todd's eyes lulled across the ground.

"Todd!" Aaron poked him in his chest with the hammer handle. The junkie gawked at him, confused. "Get up and pretend that stump is the toilet. How are you going to lay on the floor around the commode to fake this wound?"

"I don't know. I'll lay on the floor with my head near the bowl, I guess."

"So you walk into the bathroom and slip, your feet go backward, you fall forward and hit the bowl. Just make sure you lay on your stomach and not your side so it looks more natural. Also, take a little blood from your collarbone wound and smear it on top of the side of the toilet bowl."

"Blood?" Todd asked.

"Trust me, both of you. I have talked enough about this bone-breaking thing with my Pagan friend. You'll be alright, and I'll always have something better for you than the pain meds they are going to give you at the hospital. You can even trade the pills they give you to me for heroin. That's some good diesel, ain't it? Of course, if you want the good-good like what you've had the past couple of days, you are going to have to pay a whole lot more."

Todd looked up at Aaron and said, "When you get done, if I'm in pain, I want another shot."

Aaron smirked and said, "You've had plenty. You have to appear like you are halfway sober at the pantry. You can't be so high that you are nodding out like you are now. I'll give you a real good one once we're done with the hospital and get back to the motel room. I'll give you such a good shot, I'll have some Naloxone spray ready in case you die." Todd shrugged and yawned, then rolled both his shoulders around to loosen and brace his body for what was about to come. "What time is it now, Mike?" Aaron asked.

"Eleven-twenty-two."

"Time enough." Aaron looked at Mukesh. Mukesh, eyes bulging, stared at the block of wood in his hands. Somehow without shaking, he rested the four-by-four flush with Todd's collar, just the way he had been shown. Aaron hoisted the sledgehammer above his head and test-touched the iron end on the block face. Todd winced. "Close your eyes, Todd, and tilt your head further to the other side." Aaron raised the hammer again and dropped the head with moderate intention. It was a clean, even stroke. The shock hardly shot past Mukesh's palms. The same wasn't true for Todd. He grabbed at his neck and jerked away, screaming.

"Fuck! It ain't broke, you bitch!" he spat at Aaron's feet with his head hanging, breathing heavy through gritted teeth.

"Todd, I'm sorry, but you know I'm trying not to hurt you too bad. I'll make sure to get it done the next time."

"You better get it right, you piece of shit!" Todd screamed. Aaron swung the sledge-end up and snatched the iron head dramatically again with his fist choking the handle's shaft. Inspired by Todd's insult, he nodded at Mukesh, who repositioned the block on Todd's shoulder. He screamed out loudly.

"What?" Aaron asked.

"Just touching that block on my neck hurts like hell now!"

"It'll break it this time, I promise. The block has to touch the bone, or there might be too much blood. Lean your head over and close your eyes, dammit!"

Reluctantly, Todd obeyed.

This time, Aaron floated the hammer above the block to keep from touching it so Todd wouldn't flinch. He lifted it high into the air and brought it down harder. The smack sounded so loud, for a second, Mukesh thought Aaron had smashed the four-by-four. Todd gasped and hopped off the stump. He rolled his eyes and tumbled backwards onto the ground, limp. Mukesh and Aaron dropped the wood and hammer and stared at each other, mouths open. Aaron rushed over to check on Todd. He was still breathing but otherwise knocked out cold.

Aaron stood and calmly said, "That ain't good."

"What!" Mukesh yelled.

"He must have passed out from the pain. I didn't hit him all that hard. Go get something to put some mud puddle water in, and let's try to wake him up."

Mukesh raced to his car to find a container while Aaron bent over and slapped the sides of Todd's face. Mukesh found an old to-go box and scooped some puddle water in it. He handed the water to Aaron. Aaron took the container from Mukesh, dipped his fingers in it, and flicked some flecks into Todd's face. He didn't move. Aaron splashed the rest of the water hard into Todd's face, but he still didn't budge. Aaron checked Todd's vitals again. He was breathing and had a pulse.

"Looks like we'll have to try something else to wake him up." Aaron went to the Prius and sat in the front seat. A couple of minutes later he got out with a needle full of clear liquid in his hand.

Mukesh felt beyond nervous. Things were not going according to plan. He shouted at Aaron. "How the hell is another shot of heroin going to help?"

"This ain't heroin dumbass!" Aaron squatted down and pulled one of Todd's limp arms up on his lap, jabbed him, drew back, then slowly pushed the syringe in. Aaron stood up, stepped back, and stared. Five seconds later, Todd's eyes began to flutter. His body jerked upright and slumped against the stump, hunched up, face wincing. He gasped and lightly palmed the side of his neck.

"What the hell, Aaron! You know I don't like meth! What the hell happened anyhow?"

Aaron leaned in closer to Todd. "You were knocked the fuck out, dumbass! We had to wake you up. We tried everything else." Todd dried his face with his sleeve. Aaron leaned in closer. "Move your hand and let me see your neck." Todd moved his hand. It was a good, clean break. One side of the bone caved into his neckline; the other side stretched his skin where the half-clavicle protruded. The injury was so fresh, it still looked pale. They were going to have to hurry before Todd swelled up too much.

"Aaron, you asshole!" Todd yelled. "Go get me another shot of dope!"

"You aren't going to feel it on top of that meth," Aaron said.

"That's your fault, motherfucker!" Todd cradled his right arm to his body to keep the weight from agonizing his neck.

The Hacker and The Hillbilly

Mukesh looked at his phone. "It's eleven-thirty. We have to go. What are we going to do now, boss?"

Aaron grinned and rolled his eyes at Mukesh. "Let's get in the car. You drop me and Todd off up the street a few blocks and go on to the food pantry. I'll catch a ride back to the motel, and Todd will walk in right behind you." Todd got up and pussyfooted to the car holding his right arm to keep it from swinging. "You know that you are going to have to walk normal and not hold your arm like that, right?"

"Fuck you," said Todd.

Aaron was pissed now, thinking Todd was using the situation to berate him openly and potentially get more free dope. "Look now asshole..."

"I don't want to hear any of this!" screamed Mukesh. "Let's go get this done!" Aaron and Todd stopped arguing, and the three marched silently to the car. Todd let his arm swing naturally for two or three steps to see how it felt before pulling it back, wincing and mumbling. Aaron fetched the hammer and block of wood and returned them to the back seat of the car. Mukesh started the engine, and they took off.

"I want another shot!" Todd told Aaron a minute down the road.

Aaron spun in his seat and scowled. "I'll give you a real good one after the hospital. It's on you if you die and I have to wake you up sick as a dog. You are, for the first time in your life perhaps..." Aaron paused dramatically, "now worth a whole lot more alive than dead."

Even through the pain, Todd couldn't hold back a grin. "Yeah, well... this better work and I get some real good money in eight or twelve months, like you said."

Aaron glared sideways at Mukesh. As they neared the food pantry he sighed and said, "It's all on you now, Mike. Make it work."

Mukesh thought about his recent luck and considered, just maybe, this new career of in-person cons was meant to be. "I am sure it will. I have faith."

Chapter 9

Mukesh drove to the block behind the pantry at eleven-thirty-three. "Where am I dropping you two off at?"

"Somewhere close. This is beginning to hurt something awful," Todd said from the back seat, cradling his arm.

"Pull up here. I will walk with Todd to the front of the pantry and be on my way." He turned toward the back and smirked. "I'll even hold your hand if you want."

Mukesh pulled over on the street behind the pantry. Aaron got out to open Todd's door. He stuck his head back into the open passenger-side window and asked, "What's that Cardi B WAP song say again? Something about you're going to need a bucket and a mop?" Mukesh looked at him blankly, unfamiliar with the song. Aaron didn't explain. He smiled as he pulled his body out of the car window and refocused his attention on Todd. Todd had managed to get his legs out of the back and planted on the street, but Aaron had to help him the rest of the way out of the car. Mukesh looked at his phone. It was eleven-thirty-five. He gave Aaron a thumbs-up and rode around the block to park at the front.

Todd stared at Aaron. Aaron stared at Todd. They collected their thoughts. "Let's go through this one more time. May I pull back your shirt and look?"

"Hell, no," Todd folded the collar back himself to show his wound. Aaron saw blood on the shirt and reached to touch Todd's collar and investigate. Todd flinched.

Aaron stopped. "Slight problem. You got too much blood on your shirt earlier from this wound, and it's beginning to dry.

That's going to look suspicious. Here..." Aaron unbuttoned his shirt, a light fall flannel with a large checkered pattern and earth tones.

Todd twitched and yelled, "You mean I gotta take this shirt off?"

What a bitch, Aaron thought, but he said, "Don't talk so loud, and stop freaking out. It's just a t-shirt. Getting it off shouldn't be too hard." Unlike Todd, Aaron liked to wear long sleeves to cover up his daily track marks. He shrugged his flannel off and balled it in his right hand, looking at Todd.

Todd squirmed at the thought of getting the long-sleeve on, then he remembered he still had his own t-shirt to take off. "Can't we just cut it off?"

"No, we can't cut it off. That would look suspicious, and we don't want people watching us. I'm sure there are cameras somewhere. We've been bullshitting back here way too long anyways. We need to get you to the food pantry soon, so you can get situated. Mike might get nervous if you don't show up on time. I'll get you another gram of black tar on top of the one I got you. I can have it next week. For as long as you heal, I can keep you in some real heroin. Getting on full-time pain meds with the hospital and your doctor is all on you. I'm sure you can get it done, so... suck it up, and let's get that shirt off you." Aaron grabbed the sides of the bottom of Todd's shirt.

"I need you to help me lift my right arm in the air more than anything."

"Oh. Ok," Aaron responded.

"I can't lift it up without it hurting real bad."

"I think I got this figured out. Come on, we got to roll man! It has to be almost eleven-forty. It will take us two or three

The Hacker and The Hillbilly

minutes to walk down there!" Aaron yanked the left side of Todd's t-shirt, and they got the side with his good arm out of the armhole. Aaron rested the bunched-up shirt on Todd's left shoulder and focused his attention on the other side. He held Todd's arm high as Todd pulled the right side up with his left arm. Slowly, Aaron peeled Todd's shirt over his head and off his hurt arm. He dropped it on the sidewalk behind him and picked up his flannel. Aaron held it in front of him, looking Todd up and down.

"I'm trying to think of the best way to do this... Here," he said and picked up Todd's old shirt again and handed it to him. "I really think you should ball the end of your shirt up and bite down on it. There ain't no way we can do this without it being excruciating. Don't call out, and don't struggle with me, please. You know this is going to hurt." Aaron stood in front of Todd, holding the left armhole open for his good arm. After he slid the sleeve on, Aaron circled behind Todd and positioned his right arm. The flannel stopped short, stretched taut across the broader man's shoulders.

Todd looked sideways at Aaron.

Aaron spoke. "Seriously, put that shirt in your mouth and bite down hard. You know how it is, putting on a stiff long-sleeve. We are going to have to reach your right arm around a lot to get it into the hole, so bite down hard, and try not to scream real loud." Aaron took hold of Todd's right arm and slowly bent it at the elbow. "Think about the motions you have to make to put on a button-up. This is not going to be fun." Todd winced and bit down hard on his shirt. "Just think of the motion you make, and let me help you move this arm the best

88

I can to get it in the sleeve. Ready?" Todd groaned with his eyes closed and strained.

Aaron lowered Todd's arm and twisted it backward where it would slip into the right armhole. Todd couldn't help but cry out a little through the cloth, and sweat beaded like tears on his forehead. Aaron paused with Todd's right arm poked inside the shirt sleeve to give the injured man a break.

"Ready?" he asked again.

Todd didn't nod or speak, but bit down harder on the shirt and strained to let Aaron know he was. After a few muffled cries and a couple more beads of sweat, Aaron had Todd's arm pulled halfway through his shirtsleeve.

Todd relaxed some.

"We're almost done," Aaron said, sliding the sleeve onto Todd the best he could before the next step.

"Ok, Todd, we're going to have to rotate this shoulder and get your arm out in front of you to get this shirt on. You can do it. Let's get this over with." Aaron stared at Todd intensely. "Last step. Close your eyes, and make sure you bite down hard."

Todd closed his eyes, which welled with tears. He bit down hard on the rag. Aaron pulled Todd's arm around in front of him, watching the muscles around Todd's collarbone tense and spasm. The caved-in section of the bone break heaved in and out with the exertion, and Todd's face and neck burned rouge red. The wound was beginning to swell. Beads of sweat became flows of perspiration, mixing with tears, stinging his eyes, doubling the saltwater flood pouring out of Todd's head. They had to hurry.

The Hacker and The Hillbilly

"You're ok now," Aaron said, patting him on the chest. "That's the worst of it." He racked his brain for something to say to lift Todd's spirit. "Just remember, whatever pain you have to feel to keep from looking like a cripple when you walk in and get a tray will be made up for by the massive shot I'll have ready for you when you get back to my motel room." Todd closed his eyes and grimaced.

Aaron and Todd had spent too much time putting on the flannel, so they decided not to tuck it and tossed Todd's bloody shirt in a trash bin on their way to the food pantry. Aaron hoped they didn't stand out too much, with Todd now in long-sleeves fit for the fall and him stripped down to the yellowed tank top that he always wore underneath his flannels.

"Quit holding your arm, Todd. You have to. I mean it!"

Todd winced as his arm dropped to his side, groaning. "Oh, man that hurts." They were almost at the corner of the road of the food pantry. Aaron stopped Todd. He looked at his phone. It read: eleven forty-five.

"I'm going to turn and walk away here. This is almost over. All you have to do is go in and fake the fall. You got this. I promise when you get to my place later, I'll have one of the best shots of your life ready, and the rest of this half-gram of heroin you can take home with you." Todd said nothing. He turned to the left, gritted his teeth, and walked to the food pantry entrance.

Aaron glanced back at Todd twice while he walked up the street toward the Patel family convenience store. "He'll be alright, the piece of shit," he muttered to himself. He took his time walking, texting someone to pick him up. "I've done my part. Now Mike better do his."

90

Chapter 10

Mukesh pulled in front of the food pantry and looked at his phone as he stepped out of his car. It was eleven-thirty-seven. He walked up the ramp and paused before he went in, looking through the glass. The nice young lady was there in a short yellow dress. He skipped going to the back to look at the table of expired food for an excuse to nose around it later. It was the perfect position for someone to witness Todd's fall.

"Hi, Mike," said the young woman. Her name was Debra.

"Hi," Mukesh said. He went to his normal table in the corner with the rows of stacked chairs at his back and sat down.

Debra brought Mukesh his tray, a double portion of salad, a piece of plain white bread, some navy beans, and two baby cupcakes. There was no meat. He looked over at another table and saw they were serving fake RibBQs again and that was the reason for his vegetarian plate. He smiled at the attentive young server and began to compose himself and relax. Debra smiled back. Mukesh nibbled on his salad and stirred his spoon around in his navy beans. He put some salt and pepper on the navy beans and stirred some more.

Mukesh fished his phone out of his pocket. It was eleven forty-one. He set his phone to the left of the green plastic tray and tried to pace his eating. Mukesh had not seen nor heard the mop bucket yet and was getting anxious. He stood up, and went over to the front door hurriedly and acted like he was going out to his car. He eyed the kitchen corridor, but there was no sign of the boy. That was especially worrisome. The boy had always bustled about before, staying busy, whether it was filling salt and pepper shakers, wiping off tables, or sweeping the floor. Horror filled Mukesh when he realized Jeffy might not be there at all. He began to tremble and dart his eyes around as he walked outside to get some fresh air and think.

Mukesh had to figure out how to fix this big mess. He relaxed and composed himself and slowly walked back in through the door. It was eleven-forty-two, and no one had even prepped any mop water yet.

Mukesh meandered back to his seat in the corner. He sat down and rubbed his face and ran his hands through his hair. He picked up the phone and looked at it, eleven forty-five, and set it back down on the table. He glanced around the room, trying to think of what to do. He heard the front door open and knew it had to be Todd.

Todd shambled into the room, wincing and gritting his teeth. He walked with a half-zombie stride but showed little evidence he was injured. He eyeballed Mukesh all the way to his seat and sat at the table directly across from him. He looked around the room before making a suspicious gesture, picking up his right arm with his left hand and placing it gently on the table. Every movement of Todd's arm caused him visible discomfort and pain. He glared alternately at Mukesh in front of him and to the right for his food. Debra brought Todd a tray. Mukesh put the phone in his pocket and watched the clock on the wall, which showed two minutes behind the time on his phone display. It was eleven forty-eight.

Mukesh started sweating. He began to shake. Suddenly, a strange yet familiar peace came over him. He closed his eyes and saw a scene as if in a dream: he stood in the bathroom with his penis out, pissing on the floor. In the vision, as Mukesh cut short the stream and put his prick away, a line of backpressure piss hit his slacks right above his shoes, leaving a thick, wet line. Following that, he saw a short scene of a chubby woman in an apron mopping the bathroom floor.

Mukesh opened his eyes and broke out of the vision with a sudden jerk. Todd stared at him, mouth-breathing. Mukesh calmly ate another bite of his salad and two more spoonfuls of navy beans. He put the utensils down on the top of the tray, transferred his glass of iced tea to its rounded tray hole, leaned back, and stretched his arms. Todd stared at him, his mouth still open.

Mukesh pointed at his food and gestured to Todd to eat. Todd shook his head and pointed at his shoulder. One more time Mukesh gestured and pointed at the RibBQ on Todd's tray, then at his shirt pocket. Todd perked his head up, confused. Mukesh glanced to see if people were watching and motioned again at Todd. This time he moved his lips and mouthed a silent, "pocket." It was eleven-fifty. Todd still sat there looking stupid. Mukesh stood up, swiped the RibBQ off of Todd's tray, walked over and threw it in the trash to make it look like Todd had eaten something.

Mukesh walked inside the bathroom and shut the door. He pulled down his pants and pissed a medium-sized swipe on the toilet seat and floor. As in the daydream, he cut his pee stream short and began to put his penis back into his boxers. The scene played out in life exactly as it had unfolded in his mind, down to the precise patterns of pee splotches on the toilet seat — except this time, Mukesh pulled back his leg at the last second to keep from getting urine on his pants and shoe. It splashed in

The Hacker and The Hillbilly

the middle of the bathroom floor instead. Smiling, he walked out of the restroom. Debra turned and looked at him in the hall. Mukesh raised his finger up and motioned her towards him.

The woman met Mukesh at the bathroom door, and Mukesh whispered, "I need to use the bathroom, ma'am. I hate to trouble you, but someone has peed all over the toilet seat and floor in there."

"Oh, I'm sorry, Mike," Debra said to him, frowning. She walked over and poked her head into the kitchen. "Glenda, do you mind mopping the floor right now? I'll take care of the rest of those dishes for you if you do. I have to plate and serve the last two trays." There was a pause, and Mukesh heard a woman's muffled voice coming from the back of the kitchen. Debra stuck her head further inside and said, "I know you don't like mopping, but Gary must have pissed on the toilet seat and floor again, and Mike needs to use it." Mukesh waited for half a minute in front of the bathroom. The same chubby woman with the apron from his vision, Glenda, appeared in the corridor. She walked out of the kitchen and headed over to the sink area with a mop.

Glenda wore curly brown hair, the type older women get with a perm and a hairdresser visit every week. It was obviously dyed, hair curled and sprayed into a helmet shape, contained in a white plastic hairnet. Glenda mumbled to herself and squirted some dish soap on the mop head. She turned both the hot and cold spigots on and blocked the drain with the mop strings, soaking the mop in dish soap water. She turned the faucet off and wrung the mop head out in the sink with both her hands. Bubbles from the dish soap squished out of the mop head and into the sink. She brushed the bubbles off the mop and walked towards Mukesh. He moved out of her way, relieved to have found a quick solution.

Glenda cussed lightly under her breath as she mopped all over the perimeter of the bathroom, saving the middle portion with the piss for last. After she finished the floor, she walked out and said to Mukesh, "I'll be right back with a rag to get that toilet seat." Mukesh beamed and thanked her, grateful that the plan was back on track. He thought the floor was probably slicker since Glenda used Dawn instead of bleach. There were bubbles, large ones even, on the floor, and the soap painted an oil-slick-looking sheen on the tile when she was done. After she finished wiping off the toilet seat, she dried it with brown paper hand towels.

"Thank you, ma'am," Mukesh said to Glenda. He went inside the bathroom and emptied his bladder, flushed the commode, washed his hands, and walked back to his seat. He glared at Todd until Todd looked up at him. Mukesh nodded.

Todd stared at him, looking stupid. Mukesh, annoyed Todd didn't understand his nod, perked up and put his fist forward, poking his thumb up while grinning, both an American thumbs-up and a Middle Eastern "fuck you." Todd rolled his eyes around and readied himself to stand. He stood up slowly, bracing the arm that rested on the table as he picked himself up to walk away. The volunteers were in the kitchen. A fat woman sat at a table adjacent to Todd's, and she was almost done with her tray. She stared into her half-eaten food, spooning beans into her mouth. Barbecue sauce from the processed pork sandwich slathered her face and lips.

The Hacker and The Hillbilly

Todd glanced at Mukesh sideways and began to make his way to the bathroom to fake his fall. Mukesh followed behind him, walking to the back table to position himself to be a witness. Mukesh watched Todd closely. With the first step as Todd broke the threshold of the bathroom, he slipped and fell for real. Todd's foot shot out from under him, and down he went, hard. He hit his head on the toilet seat and tumbled off onto his left arm, which he had stretched out behind him to catch his fall. It twisted and folded behind Todd's back as his body collapsed. Todd let out a sharp squeal, which abruptly stopped at the wet smack of his head hitting the hard tile. Todd was knocked the fuck out. Again.

Mukesh raced over to him to survey the situation. Everything looked according to plan except for the blood missing from the toilet lid. Mukesh pressed his finger on the focal point of Todd's injury, which luckily was still oozing. Todd woke up at the touch on his collarbone wound and screamed out again, louder. Mukesh dabbed his bloody finger on the toilet bowl, then rubbed the rest of Todd's blood onto the inside of his left pant leg. Debra looked into the bathroom and gasped.

Mukesh stood up calmly and slowly and said, "I saw it all, miss. He slipped and hit his neck on the toilet, then his head hit the floor, and he twisted his arm under him when he fell." Mukesh stood back. Todd tried to lift his torso, hollering some more. He pulled his mangled arm from behind him as he struggled upright. It was twisted near the wrist, and the index finger on that hand was bent backwards, dislocated at the lower knuckle. Mukesh fought back a grin.

"Glenda!" Debra shrieked out. "Call the ambulance!"

Glenda took out her Cricket flip phone and thumbed 9-1-1. She ran over to take in the scene, shook her head, pursed her lips, and put the phone up to her head.

"9-1-1, what's your emergency?" the dispatcher asked.

"A man has fallen and can't get up. His forearm is broke, and it looks like he might have hit his head real bad."

Todd couldn't resist and shouted dramatically for the phone recording, "Ow! My neck!"

Glenda bent over to look closer at his neck. "My God! Looks like he bashed his collarbone in real bad as well." Since the two women were busy attending to the broken body sprawled on the soapy tile, Mukesh slipped away, back to the seating area. He couldn't help but crack a smile. Things were going perfectly. The old woman speculated to the police the exact same fake fall Mukesh was supposed to have seen. He allowed himself a couple inaudible chuckles and then forced himself to keep a straight face. Todd's real fall and extra injuries, paired with the two women's hysteria, wrapped this whole insurance fraud up with a bow. Mukesh was sure they were all on their way to a nice payday. No one should question the collar bone injury, because Todd obviously didn't come in with a twisted wrist and dislocated finger.

"I guess I have to stay for a while to talk to the ambulance. I saw it all when I was getting food at the rear table," Mukesh told the two volunteers.

Todd, who had been whining and grunting up to this point, groaned at Glenda, talking on her flip phone with the dispatcher. "My neck... my back... and also my arm!" Glenda paced lightly in the hallway in front of the bathroom and gnawed on her hand between words.

The Hacker and The Hillbilly

Debra stood up from trying to comfort Todd and faced Mukesh. "What happened?" she asked him.

"I'd rather wait until the cops get here, ma'am, so I only have to tell the story once. It was almost exactly how your cook said." Mukesh pulled one of the café chairs from under the tables and sat. He relaxed and stared at the scene, grinning a sly grin. Todd lay back down on the bathroom floor and moaned.

Chapter 11

The policeman and paramedics arrived shortly after twelve-fifteen. Mukesh stayed as far away as he could from Todd while the two paramedics strapped him to a black-padded gurney and wheeled him away. Mukesh waited patiently in the chair. He cleaned his glasses when he heard the policemen wrap up their talk with the two volunteers. Once they were finished, an officer approached Mukesh.

"So, you are the gentleman who witnessed the fall?" the policeman asked.

"Yes," said Mukesh plainly.

"What is your name?"

"Mukesh Patel."

"What do you do for a living?" This was an irrelevant question and irritated Mukesh, who was hoping that the policemen would be quick with their questions so he could leave. Mukesh figured, however, that the officer might be sizing him up, so he put on his best show.

"I run the convenience store up the street with my brothers and sister."

"The one across from the Bojangles on Main?"

"Yes," Mukesh answered, lowering his eyes in disgust. He shook it off and lifted them back up and continued the act. He knew it was best to swallow his pride and coddle the cops rather than raise any unwanted attention.

"Start from the beginning. What did you see?"

Trying to be as brief as possible after thinking everything through, Mukesh paused and inhaled deeply. "I was on my way out and went over to the table to grab a few things before I left, and that guy tried to walk into the bathroom." The other policeman was at the bathroom door on one knee, taking pictures with his phone. "As soon as he stepped inside, he slipped and fell. His neck hit the toilet, and he tried to catch himself with his left arm as he fell. His arm slipped and bent underneath him. When he woke up and pulled his arm out from behind him, it looked like he crushed it with his upper body when he tried to catch his fall. I went over to help, but didn't. You can get yourself into too much trouble nowadays if you try to help someone and something goes wrong."

"Ain't that the truth," said the officer by the bathroom, taking photos. He snapped a close-up of the floor and stood up and joined the pair in the dining room. The officer showed his phone to the other policeman and swiped through some photos. "Look at that floor." The officer scrunched up his face, scrutinizing the pictures.

The officer paused and looked away from Mukesh towards the kitchen. "Excuse me for a minute." He marched into the corridor and hollered for the two women. "Ma'am, who mopped the floor?" The officer who had questioned Mukesh bent down and examined the tile, which still bore bubbles from the excess soap. He swiped his finger on the floor and rubbed the suds between his finger and thumb.

Glenda came over. "Yes, officer?"

"What kind of soap did you use?"

"Dawn," Glenda said, immediately realizing her mistake. She became frantic. "But I only used it this one time!" Instead of chiding her, the officer tilted his head toward the kitchen.

Glenda fled into the rear kitchen area, sobbing. The policeman returned to Mukesh and his partner.

"My name is Officer Morton." He eyeballed Mukesh. "Mukesh, right?"

"That is my given birth name, yes. If you want, you can call me Mike."

"Mike, if you don't mind," said Officer Morton. "It's shorter."

Mukesh didn't like the cocky cop, but he endured by turning his thoughts to the insurance fraud unfolding flawlessly.

"Do you know the guy?" Officer Morton asked.

Mukesh liked that question because he could answer it honestly. "Yes, he comes in here and eats every so often. I have never really talked to him much. It is a shame he hurt himself so badly."

"Well, what I am having problems figuring out is... What I mean is that we are trained as investigators to be able to visualize all the movements of projectiles and body positions of crimes or accidents. I am having a hard time figuring..." The officer paused and squinted at Mukesh. "How did this guy hit the right side of his neck, snap his left wrist with his body, and, at the same time, smack the back of his head?"

Mukesh looked down for a second. He flinched as a vivid daydream hit. No, not a daydream. It seemed too real, a strong hallucinogen overpowering his senses. He saw Todd fall, hit the toilet, and then the floor. He lifted his head quickly and met the officer's stare. "As soon as he walked in, it was like he sidestepped to position his body to take a piss and reached his left hand out to close the door. He slipped with his side facing the toilet and cracked his neck on the side of the rim. He hit

The Hacker and The Hillbilly

the toilet so hard that his body seemed to bounce. He spun halfway around and twisted his arm behind him trying to catch himself. He hit his head as he fell."

Officer Morton searched his eyeballs around in his head and brought them back down and looked at Mukesh. "That sounds right. Well," Morton looked over at his partner, Milton, then back at Mukesh. In a rehearsed speech, Officer Morton broke everything down for Mukesh. "Normally, how this goes is, we send this police report off to the insurance company. On the report, you are noted as a witness who corroborates the evidence. It's only if they need to speak with you or if you need to be a witness in court you'll be called. But I don't think they are going to trouble you over this. This injury case is pretty cut-and-dried." Mukesh fought back a smile. "Sorry you had to spend so much time with us today answering our questions, but it's important you spoke to us so this man can get the fair compensation that he needs and deserves. You are free to go about your day." Mukesh released a pent-up smile at the policeman's dismissal. He walked over to the doorway, turned to the left, and yelled softly at Debra and Glenda.

"Sorry about today, ladies!"

Debra poked her head around the corner and smiled, "You didn't do anything, Mike. This was all a horrible accident. Thanks for helping!"

"Yes, it was a terrible accident, indeed, ladies. See you later!" Mukesh turned and smiled broadly at the food pantry as he walked back to his car. He started it up and stared alternately at the police cars parked on either side of him and laughed. He slapped the top of his steering wheel and hissed, "Yes!" in a loud, raspy whisper then pulled out and drove around the mountains for a while to revel in the success of his well-thought out and executed scam. After Mukesh had driven around enough to clear his head, he pulled in front of his motel room. He sat in his car and propped his phone on the steering wheel.

He texted Aaron, "Are you at home?" Aaron hardly ever texted right back but rarely failed to answer, so Mukesh stuck his phone in his pocket and went inside his room. He opened the shades and booted his computer, bringing up a blank spreadsheet and typing in some numbers, trying to figure out how long he could last on the money he currently had if he couldn't make what he needed on scams. He could hold out for over 6 months on his savings if inflation didn't rob him. It looked like their scam was going to pay off. Still, if he couldn't figure out a way to make money with online side hustles, he was going to have to get a part-time job.

It took over thirty minutes for Aaron to text back, "I am not at home. I will text you when I am." To kill some time, Mukesh tried to network with some hackers in a dark web chat room. There was a lot of buzz about Bling cameras and how easy it was for those accounts to be hacked. Mukesh thought there must be all kinds of ways to con someone if you have access to all their surveillance footage. After the excitement of the day's events at the food pantry, a cooped up life of sitting at a computer in a dark motel all day long no longer seemed satisfying to Mukesh. He felt antsy and wanted to go over to talk to Aaron. He closed his laptop in a nervous fit and left the motel room for another drive.

The Hacker and The Hillbilly

When he got in the vehicle, he texted Aaron again, "I am going for a ride. When do you think you will get back? Is everything ok?"

He was pulling out when Aaron texted back, "Be an hour or two, I think. I will let you know when you can come over." Mukesh drove past his father's old convenience store then aimlessly through the mountain roads. Even in a Prius, the beautiful view and the breeze seemed to mix well with the excitement of his real-life scam.

The rush of a real-life con was a lot better and more satisfying than defrauding people over the phone. Plus, Todd's extra injuries had the potential to net a lot more than what Aaron and Mukesh had first thought. It wasn't the money that Mukesh was excited about. It was the excitement of watching plans unfold in person and in real time.

While rounding a bend on a mountain road, Mukesh reveled in the strange trances he had at the food pantry earlier. It was an entirely different experience than having a eureka moment when he scammed on the phone. They were genuine premonitions, except for the one where he saw Todd's fake fall. That vision provided the kind of foresight to be able to convincingly lie to the police.

He slowed around a pass at the crest of a small hill and gazed out of his car window. The sun shone, hidden behind a single large cloud, and there were some low-lying thin ones that crept above the mountaintops.

Mukesh turned around and drove back the same way he came. The sun had broken through the side of the large cloud and cut a bright line on the valley floor: half sunlight and half shade. The border between the light and shadow seemed to ripple with the outline of the large, puffy cloud.

Mukesh drove slowly all the way back to the motel room. Someone was standing at Aaron's door. The door opened, and Aaron let the man in. From the light of the motel room, Mukesh made out Todd's silhouette. Mukesh went into his own room and turned the lights on, shut the shades, and powered up his laptop. He logged into a darknet website to chat.

Bling cam hacks were still trending. Mukesh lurked and listened to hackers bragging about their exploits. He was given shared access to a few Bling cam systems from random locations and Mukesh accepted them to get some experience with the software. He didn't like to lurk around a single darknet chat room for too long, so he logged out of chat and investigated the Bling cam accounts.

It was obvious that most of the supposed Bling cam "hacks" to which he'd been given access were actually exhibitionist accounts. The dialogue between one couple, who had cameras in every room, sounded as rehearsed as reality TV. Some of the other couples consistently posed in the best spots for the cameras when they performed their "real-life dramas." Mukesh became bored with the contrived nonsense, but at least he familiarized himself with the Bling system well enough to navigate a hacked account.

A text notification sounded from his phone. He got out of bed and looked. It was Aaron saying he could come over to his place in thirty minutes. Mukesh smiled. He watched three ten-minute videos on YouTube to wait out the half-hour before closing his laptop and heading over.

The Hacker and The Hillbilly

Mukesh knocked. Like always, Aaron called out, "Who is it?"

"It's me," said Mukesh.

"Come on in, Mike."

Mukesh tried the knob, but it was locked.

"Sorry about that," said Aaron. He stood up, unlocked the door and cracked it open. He lay back down on his bed. Mukesh sat in his usual spot, the motel chair with upholstered arms, which was always positioned in front of Aaron, facing him on the bed. The chair cushions were still warm from Todd.

Aaron hopped up from his supine position in bed and clapped his hands. "So, how was your day? I hear it went well."

Mukesh shook his head and smiled. "The finest scam I have ever pulled, and so much fun. Things went about as well as they could. How is Todd, by the way?"

"He got out of the hospital and came over here to get high about an hour ago. He was nodded out here in the chair until right before you came. Unfortunately, since he has no use of either of his arms until he heals up some, I am going to have to give him his fix when he needs it. I told him I'd do it twice a day for him and that's all. Two shots of good heroin is all you need a day anyway. One, actually, but that's too uncomfortable for most junkies."

"What about the lawyer?" Mukesh asked.

"Todd meets with her tomorrow. Everything should be fine, and we all should get more than what we expected."

"We still split it like we said?" asked Mukesh.

"Of course," Aaron said sharply. "I already heard Todd whine about that earlier, how he hurt himself extra fucked-up and deserved more. I told his dumb ass he should have done like we originally planned and pretend to fall instead of actually doing it. The lawyer says she thinks Todd could get two hundred fifty thousand after her fee. That's not bad. Fifty or sixty thousand apiece for you and me. I can do something with that for a while. As long as I can keep her happy." Aaron pointed over at Jen, who was hunched over like always, staring into her phone.

"You got exactly what I need to keep me happy, hon," Jen said to her boyfriend. Her quick response surprised Mukesh. He began to see she could always be counted on to eavesdrop on every single conversation.

"Is it the heroin, or is it the meth, or is it me?" Aaron asked her.

Jen looked up at her boyfriend. "Both," she said, grinning, before returning her attention to her phone. Aaron chuckled, and Mukesh grinned as well.

"So, tell me what happened. I wish Todd hadn't messed up his left arm like he did so he could shoot his own self up."

Mukesh shifted upright in his chair. "It was too perfect. Because the other woman in the back mopped the floor and not that young boy, she used Dawn dish detergent instead of normal bleach water. It looked like your friend didn't expect the floor to be that slippery, so he fell for real and tried to brace the fall with his good arm and twisted his wrist and bent his finger out of socket. The police were confused over the details of the fall because Todd had so many injuries."

Mukesh glanced toward the floor for a second, amused. "I brushed it off and remained calm. I came up with a good description of how Todd hit his neck on the toilet like we talked about, then I said he rolled off the toilet afterwards, and that

The Hacker and The Hillbilly

caused the arm injury. I also remembered to smear some blood on the toilet when Todd was knocked out. He woke up and screamed when I touched his wound to get some blood on my finger." Mukesh laughed.

Aaron smiled the whole time Mukesh was talking and started laughing after he was done. "That's pretty funny, how he fucked himself up extra on accident. I already told him today he could expect to get a lot more than what we had first talked about, so he could forget any extra percentage share. The injury to his left arm isn't even that bad. When he came over tonight to get his shot, I set him straight. The deal is he gets half, you and I split the other. So tell me how it was with the cops. They had no trouble with your story?"

"No," Mukesh laughed. "They were the first ones to notice the floor was extra slippery." The memory of the visions flashed through his mind. "Every bit of it was thrilling. It was the best feeling of my life." Mukesh stared at the wall past Aaron. "The ideas just popped into my mind automatically."

Mukesh went suddenly reticent, so much so that Aaron began to press him. "Mike, why are you looking strange like that all of a sudden?"

Mukesh shrugged and looked at Aaron. "It was almost like I had a premonition at the food pantry today. A couple of them, actually."

Mukesh's look and tone gave Aaron genuine cause for concern. He tried shaking it off with a laugh and a light joke. "I ain't ever been in your room, Mike, but I hope you don't have an altar with some incense and a brass idol." He piped up to his girlfriend Jen, "Honey, you better not ever let Mukesh get near our hairbrush!" Jen had already stopped paying attention to

108

the two men once Mukesh started talking strangely. She stared into her phone by the bathroom mirror and put in her second earbud to avoid the conversation. Aaron waited for him to continue and hoped the mood in the room would change.

"I am sorry," Mukesh said, breaking out of his trance.

"No need to apologize," Aaron said to him, amused. "I have seen some strange things in my life. But when it comes to things like that, I don't talk about them so as not to draw the wrong types of attention. Of course, you're a close friend. I think you would know it if I didn't like you. Jen and I don't have too many people who come and small-talk without them always having to hand me money."

"That reminds me," Mukesh grinned. "Can you get me a whore tonight?"

"You and your conquest fucks. Every time there is some excitement in your life, you want to get laid." Aaron started chuckling.

Mukesh grinned, "So?"

Aaron had already had a full day with Todd and didn't really want to fool with it, but he grabbed his phone on the end table and made a call. "Sandy, you want to do some work tonight? It's here at the motel... Yeah... You can stop over before, of course... I guess... in two hours or so... eight-thirty?" He looked up at Mukesh and winked. "Ok, see you then."

Mukesh glared at Aaron.

"What?" asked Aaron.

"We did not talk about how she is or what she looks like!" Mukesh said.

The Hacker and The Hillbilly

"I know what you like," Aaron shot back, slightly disgusted. "Sandy has black hair. I know that's not your favorite, but other than that, she's pretty clean for a hundred-dollar whore."

"Only a hundred dollars!" Mukesh protested.

"She sells herself short," Aaron said, smiling. "She will be of the same quality as one of the last ones you had, but of course you will pay me one hundred fifty. If you need to feel like you'll get a better quality, you can always pay me more if you want!" Mukesh rolled his eyes away from Aaron for trying to sound so clever. "I know what you like, basically not too disgusting of a face is a must for when you meet her at the door, but other than that, from what you say, you'd rather be looking at the back of her head anyhow!"

Mukesh smiled at his friend.

"Don't worry about Sandy. I think I got you pretty well figured out and you'll like her," said Aaron.

Jen came over between Mukesh and Aaron and rummaged in the end table drawer for a needle and spoon. She returned to her seat by the mirror and put them both on the bathroom counter. She reached into her purse and retrieved a little baggie.

"Make sure you do that in the bathroom to be thoughtful of Mike," Aaron told her sternly.

Jen rolled her eyes at Aaron and went into the bathroom to fix.

Mukesh relaxed in his chair. "It was an exciting day." The premonition flashed through his mind again.

Aaron sensed Mukesh was thinking of something unpleasant, so he steered the conversation clear of the discomfort. "Tell me again about the cops!" His eyes went wide like a kid's.

Mukesh began to grin. "That was what reminded me of the strange stuff. The police officer asked me how Todd got all of his injuries, and at first, I was stumped."

Aaron hung his head pensively and said, "Oh." He popped it back up and asked, "What did you tell him?"

"A scene sort of flashed and unfolded in my mind."

"Sometimes being under pressure is inspirational."

"Yes, but I closed my eyes and saw it in my head just like looking at a picture."

"Like I said, let's not talk anymore about that stuff. People's minds are funny when they are stressed. I've come up with some good ones like that under pressure; excuses for cops, lies to my..." he paused, glancing over, thinking of Jen. She was still in the bathroom. "Employers, if you know what I mean." He winked to let Mukesh know he meant Jen.

Mukesh thought about the whore he'd be seeing soon and wanted to wrap up the conversation and go back to his room to prepare. He thought of some final things to say about his great day. "The best thing was... well, nothing was better than Todd hurting himself unexpectedly for more money..." He carefully framed his words to hide the near mishap with the mopping. "... was how Glenda used Dawn dish detergent, and the floor was too soapy after she mopped. The police even took pictures of the residue. That's why Todd slipped for real in the first place. It's in the police report, and that shows even more fault with the food pantry employees."

"I don't know how it will work or how the food pantry is run, but the man who owns that property loans the space to them and is also one of their biggest donors. Mr. Jenkins owns a lot of property and he has to have good insurance. The guy might drive around town in a beat-up, rusty Honda and dress in dingy sweaters like a slob, but he is one of the richest men in town. I'm optimistic about this payday. Give it eight months, maybe a year. The longer Todd holds out, the better for him and us both."

"I can't wait," said Mukesh, thinking of how good it would be to replace what he lost in the Bitcoin fiasco. Maybe he'd even get a little more. He was tired of talking and stood up. "I'll talk to you more about it later." He turned and walked over to the door, unlocking it. "Oh..." Mukesh said, turning around, "Let me get a Xanax for after the whore."

Aaron fumbled in his drawer. "Put five dollars on the top of this end table." Mukesh took an old five out of his wallet and put it on top of the table. Aaron opened up a small tube, palmed a pill out, and handed a blue football over to Mukesh, who put it in the front chest pocket of his shirt.

"And please, Mike, don't talk about any of this stuff with anyone, especially that supernatural shit. Remember, you don't want to draw attention to yourself."

"Alright," Mukesh said and walked out the door.

Chapter 12

Mukesh woke up the next morning at eleven, invigorated. He dressed and opened the curtains to let in the sun. The weather was so welcoming; he drove around the hilly roads just for the sight of the valleys and the crisp mountain air. After an hour's ride and a short stroll, Mukesh returned home. He opened his laptop and dove into some dark web chat rooms. Few were chatting. It was ten a.m., an unpopular time for chatter. Mukesh looked on Craigslist for jobs. A deli position was open in a grocery store in the nearby city. He emailed them. It was almost ten-thirty. Mukesh had not been to the food pantry since the incident, so he decided to head over and eat.

He pulled up to the pantry early, and there was a line. So as not to deal with the scramble for the rear table, he sat in the car until five after eleven. When he walked in, Debra was in the kitchen hall, prepping trays.

"Hello Mike!" she chirped. Mukesh smiled at her and walked to his usual seat in the corner.

"Hello, Debra," he said when she brought him his food. It was the first time he had called her by her first name.

She stood over him and cupped her hands in front of her breasts, one palm over the other, and spoke. "It's a shame what happened to that man the other day. Jeffy had been mopping the floors too early anyway, and we should have been using a wet floor sign." Jeffy, the boy who was absent the day of the fraud, walked around with a pitcher of water. "I am really glad Jeffy wasn't here, though. He would have been devastated if someone would have gotten hurt from something he did."

Mukesh ate his food and kept his mouth shut about the accident. Once he was finished, he got a loaf of wheat bread from the rear table and left.

After a drive and short walk, Mukesh went home and took a nap. He needed to stay awake and chat later at what he considered to be prime time for hackers, two or three a.m. He walked to the drink machine and bought a root beer. When he got back, he logged into a dark web chat room. Again, few were talking. In that particular room, the number of people logged in was not shown, so no one knew how many were lurking. Mukesh went into lurk mode himself and waited for more verbose folk to trickle in. He watched a few YouTube videos while he waited, popping back in and out to check the chat.

No luck. The room remained mostly silent, so Mukesh popped back in and asked, "Anyone got any good info on Bling cams?" He waited. No immediate response. He flipped back over and watched the latest Darknet Diaries on YouTube. Still no one in the chat room talked. He popped in and out of a couple of other rooms he had heard good things about, but there was little activity anywhere. Eventually, he found himself back in the first room he'd visited. About halfway through a rewatch of a classic Why Files video, "Mel's Hole," a few people came in and started chatting. Mukesh was glad that he had spoken to the room earlier so he wouldn't look too much like a lurker. That way, he might have a better chance to get involved in their conversation about a large packet of Bling cam hacks.

"Two Bitcoins," said the chatter with the hacks, KMan23.

"For how many hacked profiles?" asked Zippytoes.

"546, from all over the United States, mainly on the two coasts."

"That's way too much money."

"Well, I am going to get it, or I'm going to sit on it. I don't think I'm asking too much, and two Bitcoin is a nice round number."

Mukesh decided he would chance speaking up. To emphasize his seriousness, he acted like he had the money for the entire packet of hacks. "I'd think about it. But I would have to know if there were any hacks that were at a certain location, preferably in a certain county or town."

Chat went silent. After a long pause, KMan spoke up. "Who are you, and why are you here now?"

"You know I can't tell you that, and of course I was told to be here tonight."

Chat went silent again. KMan23 typed: "If you want hacks that are from a certain city or county, I probably can find something for you, but of course you are going to have to pay extra."

"Shoot me an email, and I will mail you the coordinates for the locations of the hacked accounts I need," Mukesh keyed.

Kman typed back, "fredturner1968b2@yahoo.com"

Mukesh went to his own trash email account and logged in. He sent the mail requesting a hundred-mile radius of a zip code thirty miles away from his motel. Kman checked it lightning-fast, which added to his legitimacy.

"Come back here to this room at this time tomorrow night, and I'll see what I have. We might be able to work something out." That small success was a good enough stopping point.

The Hacker and The Hillbilly

Mukesh logged off for the evening and went to bed, listening to some storytellers on YouTube until he fell asleep.

The next morning, Mukesh's alarm woke him at nine-thirty. He had an interview over at Food City in the nearby town. He dressed in his usual tan slacks with a pullover polo. He chose a long-sleeve navy blue one, a good neutral look for an informal interview at a grocery store deli.

He arrived at the interview twenty minutes early and walked around the store. He took note of the gourmet cheese and decent wine and beer selections. Ten minutes until the interview, Mukesh went to the deli and asked to speak with Kim. The guy at the bakery counter pointed over to the sushi section, where a man thinly sliced a nice slab of tuna.

"I have an interview with Kim," Mukesh told the man making sushi.

"She should be here soon," the Japanese man said with a heavy accent.

"Thank you, sir." Mukesh roamed around the deli while he waited. When he saw a forty-year-old Oriental woman come in, he approached the sushi station and stood at attention. The old man looked up from his hunk of fish, speaking to the woman in Japanese and pointing at Mukesh with a butcher knife. She smiled at Mukesh and stuck out her hand.

"Hi. I'm Kim," she said. Mukesh shook her hand. She scanned the few booths in the deli for a place to sit but found them all occupied. "Do you mind if we stand over there and talk?" She pointed to a hallway in the back of the deli. They walked over and stood beside some shelves where employees stored their belongings during their shifts.

Kim started her questions. "So, you have some experience?"

"A lot of kitchen experience, yes ma'am. None with sushi, but plenty of restaurant and deli experience in India." Mukesh had never worked in any restaurant but was handy enough around a kitchen to know he could fake it.

"So you know your way around a commercial kitchen. Good." She asked him several other questions, and he answered them all to the best of his ability, spiced with clever lies. "Are you looking to make this permanent?"

"Yes," said Mukesh, another lie.

"What we really need is for someone to roll sushi. Do you think you can do that?"

"Absolutely," said Mukesh.

"Do you mind rolling some up now? I will be able to tell how well you will do on your first try."

"Sure," said Mukesh.

"Alright. Come here, and let's see what you can do." Mukesh made sure to walk over to the sink beside the Japanese man's workstation and wash his hands first. Kim nodded in approval. The Japanese man glanced over his shoulder at Mukesh when he walked by. Kim handed Mukesh a pair of thin serving gloves and stood beside him at the rolling station. "Watch me," she said. She picked up a small avocado, quartered it, peeled off the skins of each section, then pitched them in the trash. She sliced the naked sections into thirds for a total of twelve long slivers. Mukesh mimicked her movements, slicing his avocado in what he thought was a fair amount of time. Kim nodded at him.

The Hacker and The Hillbilly

Kim took out a rectangular piece of seaweed and placed it under a small stainless steel appliance and pushed a button. A section of the machine dropped down and squished some sushi rice on top of the dried seaweed patch. She flopped that one down on the workstation across from the rice-squishing device to prep three more sushi rolling papers. One she flopped next to the one in front of her. The other two, she set down in front of Mukesh.

"Now we do California roll." Kim lined a row of avocado slivers on her seaweed and added what looked like cucumber strips and spread them on the roll. Mukesh mirrored Kim as best as he could as her fingers fondled the fake crab, deftly and delicately dropping it onto her sushi. Lastly, Kim rolled the seaweed and rice wrap tightly, starting in the middle and patting the avocado and cucumber strips back into the roll where they squished out of both ends. "Now you try," she said.

She stared at Mukesh as he attempted his first roll. "A little tighter," Kim said. Mukesh unrolled the seaweed and started again. He rolled it tighter and looked sideways to his teacher. Kim nodded. He completed his second roll, and she nodded at him again. The Japanese man watched and smiled. "Good," Kim told Mukesh. "Now let's see how you use knife." She placed a knife in his hand, one of those that wasn't serrated but had a wavy blade instead.

"Watch this," she said. "Cut in half. Then take a finger-width off of each half, then cut other section in half and then in half again." She cut the sections up quickly on both of her rolls, then turned and looked at Mukesh. "Now you try." Mukesh did his best to replicate her slices. "No. Bigger for finger size you first slice off." Mukesh tried again and made the next first slice bigger. Once he finished cutting his first sushi roll, Kim nodded again in approval. The second one he cut quicker, again looking up at Kim when he was done. "Good job!" she said.

"Thank you," Mukesh replied.

Kim took off her gloves, so Mukesh did the same. Again, they shook hands.

"Thank you," said Kim. "For helping, here is a pack of California rolls for you to take home." She went around to the front of the display and got an older package rolled a day or two before and handed it to Mukesh.

"Thanks again," said Mukesh, and smiled at the Japanese woman, taking home his pay for the impromptu training session.

"I will let you know by email tomorrow if we want you to work. I have all the other interviews this evening, so I let you know. You did well. Most men don't know how to use knife as good as you."

Mukesh smiled and looked down. "Have a nice day, and I hope to hear from you." She smiled at him. They both lightly bowed to each other, and Mukesh walked off.

An employee at the front door stopped Mukesh on his way out. "You have to pay for that, sir," he told him.

"Kim gave me this sushi after my job interview," he told the clerk.

"Wait here while I go check on that," the young man said to Mukesh.

"Ok," said Mukesh. He stood there until the employee turned the corner out of sight, then walked out to his car and drove home.

Chapter 13

Mukesh woke up late the next morning. He rubbed his face and dressed, then pulled back the thick, brown curtains and sneezed at the bright sunlight that shone on the motes of dust that floated like golden snowflakes around his room.

Instead of making his own breakfast, Mukesh went to Bojangles for a biscuit but bought his coffee from Mickey D's. When he pulled out from the McDonald's drive-thru with his java, a text notification came through.

"Come over later this evening. Text me after seven," the message read. Mukesh hoped Aaron might have heard something about Todd and his lawyer.

Swiping through his apps, he noticed a Gmail notification. He checked his inbox. The Food City sushi place had emailed him back. "We would like to hire you to roll sushi for us! Come in this Wednesday at 10:30 to go over the paperwork. Please acknowledge that you have received this email to accept this career position." Mukesh thumbed on his iPhone that he would be there and stopped at the Salvation Army Thrift Store to get some black pants and more short-sleeve blue polos to match the color and style of everyone else at Food City.

After buying his work clothes, Mukesh decided to drive the mountain roads and walk in the park for a while. When he got home, he took another short nap and woke up at five o'clock that evening. He watched a few YouTube videos until seven-fifteen and texted Aaron. He texted back to come over after eight.

"I'll be there then," replied Mukesh. A few videos later, he turned the corner to walk over to Aaron's and saw someone who looked like Todd leave and get into a large Ford.

Mukesh knocked on Aaron's door.

"Who is it?"

"It's me," he said, like always.

Aaron unlocked the door and Mukesh sat down in the chair pulled out in front of Aaron's bed. It was still warm. Mukesh glanced at the bedside end table. There was a baggie full of a black goo, a syringe, and a spoon. Aaron saw Mukesh staring at the drug paraphernalia and put them back in the drawer.

"Todd just left. Good news from the lawyer. They are hoping that, after a few rounds of rejections, we could be looking at half a million dollars, maybe more. Todd says his lawyer says it's a sure thing. Hopefully in a year we'll have a large sum of money."

Mukesh grinned. "Good."

"If I think of any more insurance scams that would need your help, I'll let you know," Aaron said. "For instance, if we want some more car accident money, we could all pile into your Prius and Jen could drive." Jen looked up at her boyfriend and rolled her eyes. Mukesh smiled at Jen and looked down, shaking his head at Aaron.

They chatted jovially for another thirty minutes. Mukesh looked at his phone. It was twenty til nine. "I'd love to stay and talk to you more, but I have to be back in my room by nine o'clock for a meeting. I almost forgot," said Mukesh, who turned to face Aaron sitting on the bed. "Do you have another Xanax?"

The Hacker and The Hillbilly

"Not a Xanax, but I have a Klonopin. They're similar but not quite as good."

"Sure. How much?"

"These are one milligram for four dollars," Aaron told him. Mukesh pulled out a five-dollar bill and passed it to Aaron, who gave Mukesh a small green pill and a one. Mukesh swallowed the pill and went back to his room and opened his laptop. He watched a ten-minute YouTube video until the time came for him to meet Kman23 in the darknet chat room. He went into the room five minutes early. Kman came in at three after nine. Mukesh had already posted a "Hello," in the chat room to let Kman know he was present.

"Hello," said Kman23. "I got six of them inside of that location."

"What locations are they?"

"I am not telling you the exact locations."

Mukesh changed the subject. "How much?"

"Five thousand in Bitcoin."

"That is a lot!" Mukesh typed. "Can you tell me anything about the locations? What kind of places are they?" There was a pause. Mukesh was hopeful.

"Two are residences, one is a church, one is a convenience store, one is a warehouse, and one I can't figure out. It stares at a shed that no one ever goes to. That's all I can say," Kman answered.

Mukesh paused before typing, "I'll tell you what. You let me know if any are in or near zip code 38964, and I will consider getting them."

"You'll consider getting them if any are near that zip code?"

"I have to talk to a partner. If one or more is in that area, I think we might get them."

"Well," Kman typed in, "you'll be happy to know that there are two in that zip code."

A wave of relaxation overcame Mukesh. He stared at his computer screen and felt a supernatural nudge to buy the hacks. He lifted his head and said, "If you have two in that town, I will take the batch. I can get the Bitcoin tomorrow. Let's meet in this chat room at seven." He was confident he would be able to get his money back from one of the Bling cam account holders, though he couldn't say how—that must've been the Klonopin kicking in.

"I will be here at seven tomorrow evening, then," said Kman23.

"I will get a site moderator over here to monitor the transaction."

"K. I will see you then."

Mukesh shut his laptop and lay down. The next morning, he went to fill out his paperwork at Food City. They copied his visa and green card and gave him the schedule for next week: three six-hour days and two seven-hour days. Starting pay would be thirteen-fifty an hour. Kim offered Mukesh a couple hours that day if he wanted to work, but he declined. He had to retrieve five thousand from his safety deposit box for the Bitcoin transfer later.

When Mukesh arrived at the bank, he took out six thousand dollars to have some extra cash on hand, and stuffed it all into his coat pockets. He used the same contact from India to siphon the crypto into an anonymous wallet through Western Union. Like before, Mukesh had to go to a few different

The Hacker and The Hillbilly

locations, a pain in the ass, but worth the extra anonymity. When he got back to his motel after all the transfers, he texted Aaron, "May I come over?"

Aaron texted back immediately, "Todd is coming over. As soon as he leaves, I will let you know." Mukesh got everything settled and ready for the Bitcoin transfer. Hopefully Kman would show up to the chat room later with the goods.

Seven o'clock arrived, but this time he stayed silent to see if Kman would speak first. He waited until five after seven. Since no one was speaking, he announced himself, "Hello."

The lurking Kman23 answered. "Good evening."

A site moderator, Moonflower, mediated the swap for a small fee. The mod scanned Kman's files and told Mukesh the Bling hacks were legit. Mukesh sent the mod the Bitcoin and the transfer was initiated. After it was complete, Moonflower said goodbye and left the room. Mukesh thanked Kman and likewise departed.

He promptly closed the darknet chat window and watched some YouTube while he waited for Aaron's text. At around eight o'clock, a text said, "Come on."

Mukesh went over and knocked. Aaron flicked the lock, and Mukesh opened the door and walked in. Again, the seat was warm from Todd.

Aaron spoke as soon as Mukesh sat down. "Sounds like you wanted to talk about something."

"I have an idea for a new scam. Plus, it seems that the gods are with me again, because I had another one of those premonitions over this packet of files I bought."

"I don't understand anything about what you are talking about. What packet of files?" said Aaron, sounding snippy.

"I am sorry," Mukesh said, looking over to Jen and back at Aaron, who had to fight rolling his eyes.

"It's ok. Jen knows and sees everything that goes on in this room. It's always good to have a witness. Trust me..." Aaron paused, and stared at Jen. "This is my girl, and she's not going to tell anyone anything." Jen shifted in her chair, then stared back at her phone. "She knows everything that goes on with my life. She's capable of a lot more than what you think." Jen looked over at her boyfriend and smiled. Aaron laid it on some more. "She's actually one hell of a thief and conman, whenever I can get her agoraphobic ass out of the house." Mukesh grinned slyly, thinking about how it was rare Aaron got out as well.

Aaron continued flattering his woman with his clever tricks. "You can trust her, Mukesh. She's a real good girl." He waved his hand as if clearing the air and said, "Continue on with your scam idea. I'm intrigued."

"I just purchased six Bling cam hacks. Two are in this town. I don't know much more than that. I wanted to come over to tell you. Don't ask me how I know this will work. It's almost like the last time when I had those visions at the food pantry."

Aaron's expression soured, now annoyed. "What about these Bling cam files is good for us in a scam?"

"I paid five thousand dollars for six Bling cam hacks. We are going to use them and whatever information we can obtain from them to figure out something. I know that everything is going to work out. I can feel it."

"Facts don't care about your feelings," said Aaron. "Sounds risky. Why would you go about spending that much money on surveillance when you don't already have a foolproof plan?"

The Hacker and The Hillbilly

"As I said, I know everything is going to work out. I can feel it." Mukesh smiled at Aaron again.

Aaron switched his expression from sour to serious. "I would never spend any money on some Bling cam bullshit based on some woogedy-boogedy whims. All of this seems so risky. I saw something about Bling cams on the news, how you can remotely view the footage from any device and how easy they are to hack."

"I am going on my hunch. I have already bought the files."

"How much did you say you paid?"

"Five thousand dollars," answered Mukesh.

"If this works, I will pay my part." Aaron started laughing. "But truthfully, you never asked me what I thought about any of this before you purchased it, so I don't really owe you a damn thing."

"I never asked you for anything, Aaron," Mukesh said firmly. "I am sure I will get my money back somehow from something I see in these feeds. Even if I have to blackmail a cheating husband, I'll get my money back."

Aaron grinned at that. "If you get some juicy footage, you better show it to me and Jen. And it would be best if you shared these hacks with us anyway, because we can tell you the dirt on all the locals."

Jen spoke up, "You'd better share with us, Mike!"

Aaron rolled his eyes and shook his head and pointed at his girl. "She's more about drama and stuff like that than I am!" Jen stared at Mukesh with a look of longing.

Mukesh rolled his eyes and shook his head, as amused as his friend. "I don't even know anything about these places, so if anyone can be of help, of course I will let them." He looked over at Jen.

She stared at Mukesh and said, "I would love to help you watch the surveillance system, Mike. Let me know. I promise you I'll be a good help."

"That would be great. Just let me see what I have with these files first, and I will let you know." Mukesh turned to Aaron, who said nothing. "I will come over in a couple of days after I look at the hacks."

"Suits me fine," said Aaron.

Jen stared at Mukesh longingly.

Mukesh went back to his room. It was too late to sort through his hacks, so he went to bed and dreamed of another successful con.

Chapter 14

The next day was the first day of Mukesh's formal sushi roll training. He learned fast from Kim, who personally supervised him and provided laminated pictures of all the various rolls. She made no major objections to his work, except for a style complaint about sauce drizzle, which he quickly corrected. While he was rolling sushi, he thought about the six Bling cam accounts that needed looking into that evening.

Mukesh got back to his motel room and looked at his laptop. It was going to be a long night. He texted Aaron, "May I come over real quick?"

Five minutes later, Aaron texted back, "Come now. Real quick." Mukesh walked out the door and went over to Aaron's room. This time he didn't sit down.

"Hello, Jen," Mukesh said. He had begun to see some signs of depth in Aaron's TikTok-addicted girlfriend. There had to be something to her other than sex, as cool as Aaron was.

Jen smiled and lifted up the hand she used to tap her phone and trinkled her fingers at Mukesh a cute 'hello.'

"Hi, Jen!" Mukesh smiled.

Seeing his friend still standing, Aaron asked him, "What did you need?"

"An Adderall if you have one." Aaron squinted at him, knowing from Mukesh's habits he was more into sleep than staying awake. Aaron stayed silent as Mukesh continued on. "I'm going to go over those Bling cam hacks tonight, and I need to pull an all-nighter studying them. I don't normally like

Adderalls, but they have their time and place." Jen perked up from her phone and ogled Mukesh.

Aaron groped around in the top drawer of his nightstand and pulled out a bottle from the back. "You're in luck," he said, as he scooped an orange tablet from a pile of assorted pills he poured onto his palm. He dropped it on the table and returned the bottle of pills to the end station drawer. Aaron paused. "You also wanted a Xanax yesterday. I got one today. Twenty dollars for both that and the Adderall."

"Yes, thank you. I will take both." Mukesh fished his wallet out of his front pocket and found two fives and a ten. He handed them to Aaron, who nodded at the end table at the two pills lying there. Mukesh pocketed the pills, nodded, then turned toward the door to leave.

"Have fun tonight!" Aaron said. "Let us know if you see anything good on those tapes."

"Please do," Jen added, smiling. Mukesh grinned as he went out the door.

When he got back to his room, he made ramen noodles and a salami sandwich and swallowed the Adderall with a Mountain Dew.

Opening his laptop to check out the hacks, he chuckled to himself, struck by the strange confidence that overcame him when he first heard about Bling cam hacks. He now possessed six local ones, two within the town of Mason.

Mukesh hovered his mouse over the hacked file folder and clicked. Six subfolders appeared in standard configuration, with gibberish letter and number combinations with corresponding GPS locations. He recognized the two that were

The Hacker and The Hillbilly

in his town right off and began to copy and paste the other GPS locations into Google maps, saving the Mason hacks for last.

The first one was just a doorbell. Mukesh was upset and hoped that they all weren't like that. The next one was a convenience store, a four camera system that was also the furthest location from Mason. He logged in and checked a saved file of that day's feed. An older man and woman were working in the first camera stream. The old man sat with some paperwork, and the woman bustled at the cash register, swiftly serving the line of customers. Mukesh shuffled back and forth between the four camera feeds and noticed that the two near the front register had icons for sound. He plugged in some headphones and listened.

The woman chatted in broken English with the customers. After the line died down and they closed up for the evening, it was five minutes before the married couple spoke. Mukesh thought their accents sounded North Indian, and by the Indian decorations and icons around the store, Mukesh pegged them as a boring traditional couple that never broke the law. Another dud, but better than a doorbell cam.

He looked at another file, a suburban home with four cameras, one watching each side of the standard, square house. He shook his head and clicked off this location and onto another. The next one was a decent-sized warehouse and office. It had six cameras, two for the office, one for the loading area, and the other three surveyed storerooms. Mukesh cycled through the live feed of the three storeroom cameras. It was very late, so of course no one was working. He zoomed in on the boxes to see what the warehouse sold: it was a bunch of bedroom furniture and bedding. Tall stacks of futon racks lined either side of the middle row. And that was it, so far as he could see. The storerooms were dimly lit, and the office showed pitch black on his screen. He looked down, disgusted, when he remembered that Kman23 had told him one of the Bling cam feeds was a camera pointed at a rarely used shed. Mukesh hoped that the church feed would be his saving grace.

He joggled his cursor over the two remaining folders. He opened one of them at random. It was the church feed.

The church had eleven cameras with audio available on ten. He got excited but clicked off the folder and opened the last hacked feed, which indeed showed a shed with a single light shining from somewhere off-camera. He clicked back on the church feed. In the same instant, the Adderall kicked in, honing his focus into a knife-sharp edge. He toggled through the various feeds. The parking lot and the front foyer each had a camera. As Mukesh gazed at the array, he felt that strange sensation come over him. He closed his eyes, and a heavyset, short man appeared, standing in the church, arms folded. A familiar comfort blanketed Mukesh. He smiled and shifted in his chair, glancing back and forth at the logs. He made a mental note to buy a large monitor from the pawn shop the next day so he could more easily see the feeds. For the rest of the night, he pored over older saved footage, starting with the earliest: the Sunday morning from thirty days before.

Mukesh opened all camera angles in thumbnails and observed the general patterns of movement to get a better feel for what he had. Besides the parking lot and foyer, one camera eyed a segmented room with many tables and computers, which Mukesh supposed must be the church office. The larger, shared part of the communal office had a camera, and so did

The Hacker and The Hillbilly

two children's rooms and a nursery. There were two cameras in the sanctuary, which ensured the entire room was in view. Then there was a fellowship room, a kitchen area, and one camera that monitored the hallway in between the sanctuary and other rooms. Every camera system, except for the parking lot, had a microphone.

Mukesh chuckled as he watched and listened to the congregation filing in. He was happy with this church hack but didn't want to look through any more of the footage that evening. Now he felt annoyed that he had taken Adderall. He thought about taking the Xanax to make himself sleep but saved it. He had to roll sushi the next morning, so Mukesh powered through and looked through more footage.

During the second service, Mukesh saw the same man from his vision standing in the foyer with his arms crossed. Churchgoers entered the building while a different man and a woman shook people's hands. The man from his vision came into view, stoic-looking, eyes forward and arms crossed. Mukesh zoomed in on the man's gruff demeanor. Whatever was going to become of this scam, Mukesh knew it revolved around the stout manlet maximized on his laptop screen.

By six in the morning, Mukesh had painfully skimmed through two of the oldest saved Sundays and one Wednesday church meeting. He gathered that the manlet acted as some sort of church bouncer. Every Sunday service, he or one of the other potbellies posted up in front of the entrance, eyeing everyone they didn't know.

The Bling cam system was set to either archive or erase old footage every thirty days. Sunday was just around the corner. Mukesh had been hoping the whole night that Jen could look through the majority of the footage in his stead. She and Aaron might even know a few of the churchgoers. Of course, Mukesh would need to see how observant Jen was before he could trust her judgment. After all, the best thing going for her was what made him think less of her at first: the time and attention she spent on her phone.

Mukesh took a shower and felt refreshed even though he had been up all night. After his bath, he closed his laptop and reminded himself to be more cautious, that he could be caught while hacking a Bling cam system if he forgot to log out when he showered or left the room.

Mukesh looked at his phone. It was seven-thirty. He had two hours to kill before work. He watched a few YouTube videos and left early to ride around and clear his head.

Arriving at Food City, Mukesh parked his Prius on the opposite side of the farthest shopping cart rack. He was twenty minutes early, just like he'd planned. He got out of the car and yawned and stretched. By the time he walked into the deli, it was fifteen till. No sign of Kim.

The old man nodded at Mukesh and reached out his hand. "My name is Sugami."

"Hi, Sugami, my name is Mukesh."

"Moo-keshi," repeated the old Japanese man.

"You can call me Mike if you like," Mukesh said with a grin.

"Hai. Mike," said the old man. "Wash up and we start your day." Mukesh took off his coat and put it in a bottom cubby on the shelf in the back hallway. At his workstation, he put on a pair of large vinyl gloves. The old man brought a ring binder with laminated sushi roll pictures and set it on the right side of the cutting board. He put up his finger for Mukesh to wait, then

The Hacker and The Hillbilly

walked away and came back with a printout of what needed to be rolled that day. Mukesh took the sheet from the old man and laid it on the left of his work space.

California rolls were first. He pulled out the seaweed sheets and placed them beside the sushi rice-squisher directly behind the roll station. He made four seaweed-rice rectangles and placed two of them at his prep station. He fixed the bare spots where the rice squisher machine missed with finger pinches of pressed rice, just as Kim had shown him days before. The other two unrolled squares he placed caddy-corner in the far section of his workspace. After completing two rolls while the old man watched him, he turned the page on the laminated instructions and arranged the sushi trays as they were shown in the picture, with the wasabi dabs, ginger slices, packets of soy sauce, and all. He closed the containers and sealed them with a sticker.

"Very good," the Japanese man said. "I think you do well. I go watch from there." Sugami pointed with his butcher knife at his station, where he cut and formed the gourmet sliced sushi that wasn't formed in rolls. Not intimidated in the slightest, Mukesh kept on working and, in fewer than forty-five minutes, had rolled, cut, and decorated all ten trays of California rolls. Sugami came over to make sure Mukesh knew what type of tuna he needed to put in the spicy tuna rolls and left him to continue working unsupervised with his picture instructions. By the time Kim arrived at three that afternoon, Mukesh had almost finished the whole list. She smiled at him when she saw his progress and the quality of his neatly arranged and garnished trays.

"You are doing well," Kim said. "Every day after you finish sushi, we need you to do dishes in sink. The lists of things that need to be done every day and things that need to be done once a week are posted on the wall as well." She went into the back area to her office. Mukesh washed all of the pots and pans in the sink and performed three of the fourteen weekly chores before the end of his shift. He walked back to the office to check in with Kim. She walked out and checked all of the tasks he had performed and praised him for a good day's work. Before Mukesh left for home, he bought some groceries and a small container of self-serve salad bar items and rode back to the motel.

When Mukesh got back to his room, he looked at his laptop folded on the table. He texted Aaron. "May I come by for a while tonight?" Most of all, Mukesh wanted to see Jen.

"I'll let you know when you can come."

Mukesh knew that Todd must be stopping by for his nightly fix. It would be more than a few minutes, so he scrubbed through a week of Bling cam thumbnails to kill the time and get a feel for the church's schedule. Two nights a week, the church held Bible studies, and a small administrative staff worked from ten until two, Tuesdays and Thursdays. On Wednesday evenings, the church held leadership meetings. It was all quite boring, and Mukesh was getting restless when Aaron texted him to come over. He logged off immediately, remembering his warning to himself, and went over to his good friend's.

"Who is it?"

"It's me again," said Mukesh. He had his hand on the doorknob, waiting to hear the lock unlatch. Aaron unlocked it, and Mukesh walked in. This time, the upholstered chair in front of Aaron's bed was cold. "How is Todd doing?" Mukesh asked, smiling.

The Hacker and The Hillbilly

"Still coming at least once a day. Most of the time he gets his brother to give him his fix in the morning."

"Yes, but I mean how is he doing? Is he healing well?"

"Oh. His collarbone is going to take a long time to heal. He still has a full cast on his left arm and limited mobility with his right." Aaron grinned, knowing Mukesh didn't come over to talk about Todd, but kept silent and let Mike lead the conversation.

Mukesh stared at Jen, who swiped on her phone. "Hey," he said to her, beaming.

She peeked up from her phone, smirked, and said, "Hey," back. Aaron gazed at Mukesh..

"You told me to tell you if I found anything interesting. I have a local church's entire camera system under my control," he said, still smiling at Jen.

Aaron and Jen started laughing. "No way," Jen said. "That's too cool." Mukesh looked back over at Aaron, who was smiling.

"What church is it, Mike?"

"To be honest, I don't know. I could have gone to Google Maps or zoomed into the front sign, but it wasn't important to me at the time."

"Have you seen anything good so far?" Jen asked.

"I am glad you asked. I scanned through a lot of the footage last night. There is far too much for me to watch by myself, and I need some help. Also, I don't know any of these people, but you two might."

Aaron spoke up, cutting off his girlfriend's gushing, "I think we can help you. Jen likes to look at security footage. Sometimes I do too. Being able to watch and listen to people in a church has got to be one of the best ways to hear town gossip. I'm sure I know a few of the people that go there as well, or know of them." Aaron nodded. "I see now how this might be a good way to come up with a con, but even if nothing ever comes of it, we'll have a laugh at the locals and hear all their gossip. This is going to be great."

"I just wanted to see what you two thought about it. As far as everything working out, I had another one of those strange visions. I will show you which guy I saw. It was clear as day in my mind, even the same pair of dark slacks and striped shirt."

"Look, Mike. I am glad you are so confident, but I told you, I really don't want to hear about the strange visions crap. I need to see things work out for myself."

Mukesh turned and faced Jen. "Of course, I would love to get your help watching footage. You are familiar with how to work a laptop, right?"

"Yes," Jen said. "I learn fast with stuff like that."

"Good. I'll get you a computer tomorrow. I will talk to you then about what you should look for and things like that."

"She is going to be a natural." Aaron smiled at his girlfriend. She rolled her eyes at him and returned to swiping.

"I saw enough last night and I am glad that the Adderall finally wore off. I am done with that mess. I was up all night looking at the six accounts and hated every second of it. I would love for you to help me, Jen." Mukesh grinned.

Jen beamed back. "Of course I would love to, Mike!"

Mukesh turned to face Aaron. "And about the strange stuff going on, I am your friend and am just as confused about things. I am only trying to process them with you."

Aaron nodded. "That's fine. But there is a time and place, and never in front of a phone. I had a friend who once..." Aaron paused and looked at Mukesh, who looked tired from his all-nighter. "It's a long story. I'll tell you later. Around these parts, we all have seen some strange shit, and sometimes it hasn't worked out well for folks who talked about them."

Mukesh was intrigued but exhausted, so he stood up, intent on heading home.

"Wait! What other hacked accounts did you get?" interjected Jen, excited.

"Do you mind if I tell you about them tomorrow when I bring over your new computer? I just want to go home and take that Xanax and go to bed." Jen smiled at the thought of her new computer and chore.

Mukesh smiled again to validate Jen, and the three said goodnight. Mukesh walked back to his motel room and swallowed the Xanax he bought the night before. He forgot to set his alarm but woke up right on time with an hour to kill before his second full day at work.

Chapter 15

Mukesh took an hour off for lunch the next day. He rode around looking in pawn shops for a computer for Jen. At the second place he checked, he found a used, mid-grade Dell Latitude. It cost him three hundred and fifty dollars and had decent speed and a medium-sized monitor. It was a small expense if Jen could save him from looking through the footage. He went by Walmart and picked up a seven dollar wireless mouse and went back to work.

Mukesh's sushi rolling improved rapidly. That day, he performed two extra chores and washed all the dishes with ten minutes left to piddle around and spot-wipe counters and door faces with a rag. As soon as he got home, he set up Jen's pawn shop laptop. He downloaded the Bling cam software as well as some other programs like the TikTok Studio app. Finished preparing his "present," he closed the software, hid the Bling cam icon in an obscure folder under GAMES, and stashed the laptop in a backpack.

Mukesh took his phone out and texted Aaron: "May I come over again sometime tonight?"

"You can come over right now," was the reply.

"Be right over." Mukesh took up the backpack with the laptop and a spare mouse and walked over to Aaron's. Once inside, he occupied his usual chair across from Aaron's bed and angled it slightly to point at Jen. Aaron noticed this and chuckled.

Mukesh yawned. "You know what I could use tonight. A Xanax."

The Hacker and The Hillbilly

"You have been taking too many of them lately, Mike. You don't want to go down the road of benzo addiction. The withdrawals are the worst. They can cause seizures and even kill. You should take one only every now and then. Please lay off of them for a while. I say this as a warning from a friend. I'll get you any drug you want, but I always like people to know what they are getting into, especially my friends. Plus, do you have five dollars a day to spend? Five dollars a day is what it will cost if you take only one, but take them too many days in a row and they stop working like they used to. Next thing you will want two a day, and that's ten dollars.

"You have a good point," Mukesh admitted, eyebrows high and head low. He turned the conversation toward Jen, reaching into his bookbag. "I got you something!"

Jen put her phone on the counter in the bathroom foyer. "Is it what I think it is?"

"Maybe," Mukesh said. He took out the laptop and mouse. Jen's face brightened, elated, as he stood up from the cheap upholstered motel chair and handed them over. She opened up the laptop and laid it on the bathroom counter and scooted up her chair.

"Awesome. It's a Dell, too," Jen said to him.

"Of course. The pawn shop had five Acers, and ten Hewlett-Packards and a piece of shit Microsoft. This was the only Dell. I know enough about computers to buy anything Hewlett-Packard."

"I know, right?" Jen agreed.

"Now you'll be able to have a computer to edit your TikTok videos to make them look more professional."

"I don't know," said Jen. "Swinging the phone around doing different poses is very popular right now."

"I am talking about filming it on your phone and then editing your videos on the computer."

"Oh," said Jen. "That would be sweet!" Mukesh was worried for a second that she might not know enough about computers. He hoped that her meth determination and focus would overcome any technological handicaps. He might even enjoy spending the time to train her on how to use the software and any other hacker tricks that would help better weaponize her with the important chore. Mukesh picked up the mouse from where Jen had let it fall to the hard motel carpet. He tried handing it to her, only to meet rejection. "Oh no. I'll use the pad on the laptop for the mouse. I prefer that." Mukesh had to fight rolling his eyes as his doubts about Jen's computer skills crested again. Their scam hadn't even started, and already he'd experienced more ups and downs than a pinball.

Mukesh set the mouse on the counter. "I'll leave it with you. I think you will find out it is going to be easier than using the trackpad after a while." He studied Jen some more and chuckled. "Check this out." He leaned in and reached over her left hand. "The monitor doubles as a touchscreen like an iPad or phone screen." He extended his finger and thumb and swiped and pinched and pulled on the screen. He grinned at Jen's computer greenness on how she hesitated figuring out if she should use the mouse or touchscreen in different applications.

"You'll get it." Mukesh hoped. Aaron leaned back against the headboard with a couple of large pillows and turned on the TV.

The Hacker and The Hillbilly

"That stuff's bad for you," Mukesh told him.

"What?"

"TV."

"But it's only the network news!" They both laughed, and Jen giggled politely as she played with her new laptop.

"Do you mind if I sit in your chair for a second and show you some things?" Mukesh asked Jen. "I want to show you about the Bling cam system so we can be on the same page. Again, I want to tell you all," Mukesh's voice grew louder and stretched with an ethnic drawl, "I am positive that this is going to work out, and I appreciate your enthusiasm and help."

While Aaron watched the local news Mukesh gave Jen a short Bling cam tutorial. When the national news came on, Mukesh sat back and observed Jen perform some basic tasks, correcting her when she needed it. When the hour was done, Mukesh felt confident Jen could work the Bling system adequately and would only get better.

"Aaron," said Mukesh.

"Yes, Mike?" said Aaron.

"Please come over here, I want to show you something." Mukesh stood up and watched Aaron walk over. "I'll say it plainly. This guy is the mark." He pulled up a screenshot of the over-eager church bouncer in the foyer.

Aaron nodded. "That's Jerry Dirk. He's Judge Robert Dirk's brother and a real douche-canoe. I know a lot of the people that go to this church. It's called Community Compassion Presbyterian. It's a pretty stuck up institution which contains most of the town's uneducated's old money."

Mukesh smiled and continued on. "What I need for you to do," he looked and nodded at Jen, "is to find out all scandalous information or town gossip, any information that you think we could use for our scam."

"Like blackmail?" Jen asked.

"Yes, but better than blackmail if we can. Look at patterns and behaviors and focus on this one guy. We have the potential now to know everything that this church is doing and thinking and to use that information against them."

Aaron, who stood behind Mukesh and Jen, said, "I'm sure we'll figure out something. Jen and I are going to recognize a lot of people there, and Jen can find out the scoop on just about anyone in town from Facebook. I am going to go lie down again. As far as someone with a keen eye for drama," Aaron waved his finger up and down at his girlfriend while walking backwards to his bed, "you are dealing with a pro."

"I am beginning to see that," said Mukesh with a smile. "I believe I underestimated her. But dear," he said, turning and facing Jen, "it really doesn't look like much when someone stares at their phone all day."

Jen lifted her eyebrows and smirked. Mukesh watched Jen for a while longer from behind while she fumbled with the software before he finally took his seat to discuss things further.

Aaron asked Mukesh, "Tell me, what are some things you are thinking about when you say, 'better than blackmail?'"

"I mean, maybe we can manufacture some type of accident or injury with someone at this church like we did at the food pantry. Anything that can net us a large, winnable lawsuit. Any information we can use against someone is good, too, as it might lead us to other local scams. The best thing about this church is that it looks like they have plenty of money."

The Hacker and The Hillbilly

"Community Compassion Presbyterian has lots of money," Aaron said, smiling, "and the folks in their congregation have plenty of stuff that can be used against them." Aaron put his hands behind his head and leaned back some more. He kept the television on but turned the volume down. He alternated between staring at the TV and back and forth at Mukesh and Jen.

Mukesh stood up to leave but then remembered something. "Before I forget, this is important." He looked once more at Jen. "You have to make sure you log off from the Bling cam church network when people come in." He paused, trying to remember whether there was anything else. "I think that's it. I'll show you some more things tomorrow. Have fun. I am sure you will do well. Watching the church will be time better spent than mining for TikTok views and likes."

"But I am almost monetized!" Jen shot back.

Mukesh rolled his eyes. "I promise this will pay off better than any TikTok money you might ever get, if you ever get any."

Aaron laughed. Mukesh went over to him and pulled out a five-dollar bill and stood in front of Aaron's bed. Aaron fumbled for the bottle in the back of the end table drawer and passed Mukesh a single oval-shaped blue pill. Mukesh swallowed it down and walked out of Aaron's.

Chapter 16

The next morning, Mukesh woke up to an alarm at eight o'clock, two hours before he had to roll sushi. It was Thursday. People splurged on payday and weekends, so Thursdays and Fridays were always big for production. Even with the extra workload, Mukesh rolled the Thursday quota quickly and tackled more weekly chores. After work, he bought some chicken and vegetables from Food City and a jar of Indian spice rub at the World Market across the street. That night, he planned to prepare one of his favorite Indian dishes.

When Mukesh got back to his room, he opened the curtains, washed his hands, and prepped his meal, chopping the vegetables and marinating the chicken in spices, placing them in bowls in the mini-fridge to cook later. He sat down in front of his laptop and opened the Bling cam app. After fiddling with the church footage for a while, he thought about any instructions or tips that he forgot to mention to Jen the night before.

He texted Aaron, "I was going to come over tonight and hang out with you if that is ok."

Aaron texted Mukesh back, "I'll let you know when you-know-who is gone. Speaking of, I'll have some news for you when you come."

Mukesh was overjoyed. He prepped a file that compiled all of the church bouncer's footage and put it on a thumb drive. He put the drive on the table beside his laptop to take to Jen. He opened a batch of Wednesday's meeting footage. He watched a gaggle of women cackling, gesturing wildly in the

The Hacker and The Hillbilly

office frame. Mukesh opened up the audio, isolated the frame, and listened in on the conversation. The women were talking about how someone in town had recently died and left the church four million dollars.

In the few hours he spent studying the behaviors and vocabulary of the congregants in Community Compassion Presbyterian, Mukesh agreed with Aaron about their intelligence. It was clear from their shallow conversations that the church was comprised of either the stuck-up working middle class or the simple-minded children of upper-class old money.

Aaron texted back. "Come over whenever."

Mukesh texted. "20 or 30 minutes." He set the phone down beside his laptop and thought more about what he needed to school Jen on and the things at the CCP she should pay special attention to. He skimmed over some of the Wednesday meeting footage again and yawned, logged off, and walked over to Aaron's. After the usual knock, call-out, answer, and entrance, Mukesh went straight to the back and stood behind a seated Jen, who was in the middle of the two sinks of the bathroom foyer, glued to her laptop with six church panels open.

"How's it going, Jen?" Mukesh said louder than normal since she had her headphones on.

She turned around and smiled. "Hi, Mike! I'm going over one of the sermons now."

"That's why she's wearing earphones," Aaron added. "Normally, I'll listen to the conversations, and I can even see what's going on from my bed if it's full screen, but I'm not trying to listen to one of their sermons." Jen grinned at her boyfriend.

"Would you please take your earphones off, Jen? I wanted to go over some things."

"Sure." She took the headphones off and paused the sermon, handwriting the timestamp on a notebook next to her computer. Proudly, she showed it off to Mukesh. "I got a notepad here, so if there's anything important I need to remember or a time stamp for an event I'll have it written down."

"That's good," Mukesh said, nodding. He put his hand up to his chin. "Let me know any important information you have discovered."

"I've only been over one full week, but I went over it completely. In two or three more days, I think I'll have everything watched, even the first and second duplicate sermons. If you want to watch their music, you're going to have to do that yourself. After hearing how bad the worship team was the first Sunday, I skip all their songs. I've been keeping a close eye on Jerry Dirk as well. He does seem to be a little too excited about being a church bouncer."

"Just like his brother, the judge, he's a real jerk," Aaron interjected.

"That's good." Mukesh was impressed with Jen's progress for only one day on the Bling system, which, knowing Jen, had been a twenty-four hour stint. Mukesh was going to point out to Jen some of the things he had noticed, like the four million dollars, but he kept his mouth shut so he could see if she could uncover that for herself.

"She's doing good," Mukesh said to Aaron. "You say you have listened in on some of their conversations. What have you seen or heard? Do you know anyone else who is of interest?"

The Hacker and The Hillbilly

"I know a couple of them," Aaron said. "As far as it goes with Jerry, he's a hothead and it looks like he is being self-righteous with his church bouncer position. What are your thoughts so far for a scam?"

Mukesh relaxed, hoping for another clairvoyant revelation, but no visions came. "I don't know yet, Aaron. Brainstorm some things yourself if you want."

"Maybe we can get him to assault someone who doesn't have it coming as they try to walk into church when he is on security detail."

"That's a good idea," Mukesh said. He took off his glasses, wiped them and grinned. "Let's continue to see how he interacts with other people as they come into the church. I will keep that in mind. What we need to do is see how he treats a stranger who appears to be threatening."

Mukesh closed his eyes, this time for just a long and weary blink. A vision came to help him. It was of him walking into the church wearing a long coat. As Mukesh tried to bypass Jerry in the foyer and into the sanctuary, the bouncer reached out and grabbed Mukesh's shoulder.

Aaron noticed the strange change in Mukesh's countenance and spoke. "Hey... Mike..." Mukesh didn't move a muscle. Aaron leaned off the bed and touched his friend's leg. Mukesh shuddered and rolled his eyes.

"What was that, Mike?" Aaron asked.

"I told you about the visions! That was a heavy one. It was so powerful, it was almost like watching a video." Mukesh put his head down in his lap and shook. He brought it back up again and looked at Aaron. "But something about it, through all the apprehension... felt...exhilarating."

"I see that you are serious about the visions you say you have been having. That almost looked like a possession, and believe me, I have seen possession. But I want to emphasize to you again, Mike..." Aaron rolled his head in disgust and put his head down and spoke in a louder, sharper tone. "You have to be careful about what shit you say and who you say it to around here." The change in Aaron's tone and facial expression made Mukesh uncomfortable.

Aaron calmed down and leaned back and stared at the ceiling. "It was a few years back, about five, and I'll tell this story even though I shouldn't, because I don't want to see you get hemmed up in a bunch of shit." Mukesh looked at him blankly. Jen put her headphones back on to avoid the conversation, opened up the TikTok studio app, and began giggling.

"About five years ago, there was a guy I knew. I wasn't living in this hotel yet but in a trailer park on the outskirts of town. I met this grifter dropped off by a trucker. Normally, I don't deal with strangers, but this guy had hopped off the road from riding with a trucker with a half-pound of some really choice meth. Big chunks, uncut. I never asked, but I assumed he might have taken it from the trucker. A half-pound must have been a small sum for what stash the truck actually smuggled, because I don't think—let's call this guy Will—would have done such a thing unless he knew he could get away with it."

Aaron continued on, "I bought it from him for a fair price. It seemed like he was comfortable with the town of Mason, and the money he got from the meth had given him enough to last Will a year or more. This was before fentanyl, and heroin was rare around here. Pills were the thing, hillbilly heroin they called it. He bought two Roxy thirties a day from me for his daily habit and squatted in an old hunting shack in the woods. At night, he had a fire in the cabin when he could get away with the smoke.

"He liked his pain pills and occasional Xanax, like you, so of course I saw him regularly. I think he might have decided to stay longer in this town after skipping with the trucker's stash because he knew I could supply him with his daily dose and he had the money to make it last. Even though he was a homeless drifter, he somewhat had his act together. Will was going to let the money carry him for as long as he could in a town where he could always get high.

"Then one day Will came to me with a strange look on his face and had some sort of weird-looking piece of metal in his hands. He said an object crashed in the bank of the holler across from his shack, as he was standing outside. He was excited and thought that the government would give him a fortune for finding their crashed spaceship. He also said that there was a small leg from a dummy or doll that poked out of the wreck."

"Was this guy an idiot?" exclaimed Mukesh.

"Just let me continue," Aaron said. "Will wasn't that bright, and I didn't know him, so when I try to gauge someone and they talk crazy stuff like that and I'm not sure, I'll just listen to them and not say anything one way or the other until I figure them out. From what I was thinking, this guy either hallucinated or told stories, so until I knew for sure, I let him go on with his tale.

"One thing for certain was that it wasn't any ordinary wreckage. That metal piece was strange. It was a light grayish creamy color, not like any metal I'd ever seen, and when you bent it, the piece went back to the same position. But if you wanted to bend it, you had to bend it slowly. The harder you tried to bend it, the harder the piece got. It was like nothing I'd ever seen before. Will said he was going to town to talk to the authorities and then go collect his reward.

"Later that evening, he came to my trailer and banged on the door. I let him in. He was frantic. He paced around like he didn't know what to do. He told me he was going to abandon the things he had in the shack and light out as soon as he could with his cash. I asked him what was going on, but the more I pried, the more scared he got. He handed me four hundred dollars and asked me to get him thirteen roxy thirties and he was gonna leave as soon as he could. All he needed to do, he said, was get his secret drug and cash stash. I pressed him about why he wanted to leave so fast and why he was so scared. He brushed me off and asked me how long it would be before I could get his pills so he could skip town. I said an hour. He said he'd be back after he got his shit and we both went out the door. Before he left he looked at me red in the face, shaking, and said loudly 'I should have kept my stupid mouth shut!' I got him his pills and waited for him back at my trailer, but he never came.

"Around town, the word spread. Will had first told his story about the crash to the old men who hung out at Hardee's every morning, showing them the strange sample of the wreckage. It didn't take long for everyone in town to know about the spaceship. Later that first day, a group of people went down to the holler to check on his claims and came back scared. That's when the military started coming in, but that's later."

The Hacker and The Hillbilly

Aaron sighed heavily. "Will never came back. I knew something had to be up with that. He looked so scared..." Mukesh looked at Aaron, nervous at the strange tale unfolding before him, which according to what Mukesh knew about Aaron, had to be true.

"I waited the night out for him thinking he'd come, but I knew everything was fucked when the black helicopters and military vehicles started flying and driving around the area of the crash. What's even worse..." Aaron paled, swallowed hard, and began to shake. "The very next night..." Aaron paused again to collect himself. "Two men came over and knocked on my trailer door. I had heard about the men in black, and these men sure acted strange, just like that. They were stoic and different, with very pale skin and sunglasses, like their sole purpose was to intimidate. They never once took their glasses off even though they visited me at dusk." Aaron sighed heavily again.

"They knew everything." He stretched his hand out and stared at Mukesh. "Like they had talked to Will and he told them about me. They knew I was the first one to hear about the crash and warned me to never tell a soul. I remember at one point thinking to myself that I hadn't told anyone about it yet, so why should they worry about me saying shit? As soon as I finished thinking that, they both smirked like they could read my thoughts. I can't tell you how I knew, but it was like they could read my mind, and also, they even knew that I knew they could read my mind. Fucking crazy. That's why I warn you to be quiet about all your weird vision shit. Will was an outgoing person, and even though he was only in town for a few short months, a lot of people liked him. He wasn't very bright, but he was good-natured, and that added to his appeal. But after the 'plane crash' everyone seemed to forget about him totally."

"So what happened next?" asked Mukesh, simultaneously amused and concerned.

"No one saw or heard from Will ever again. It was like everyone in town knew the government must have gotten him, and the way everyone kept their mouths shut about his sudden disappearance made me think everyone in town must have also gotten house visits from the same two men in black, or in this case, men with matching blue suits. Mason had a lot of veterans and government officials move in after that, a lot of newly retired ones, which is even scarier. All kinds of people moved in here who never had any connection with this town. They all live quiet lives, never speaking to anyone, but they're still here. Listening, watching, ever since that so-called, 'plane crash.'"

"That's a wild story," said Mukesh, staring off to the side.

"It's all true. You just need to be careful who you talk to, especially if you actually have some sort of telepathic or clairvoyant abilities."

Mukesh stared silently ahead at the blank wall across from Aaron.

"Seriously, you'd better keep your mouth shut, Mukesh," Aaron admonished him. He spoke again, quickly with a start. "Oh! I almost forgot. A year after Will disappeared, I walked around the upper trail on Billy Gentry's land where you could see the crash site. There was no wreckage. Even the shed on the opposing bank where Will used to stay had been leveled and removed. Where the shed was bulldozed, there's a large spot that's still bare. A lot of trees had been removed, and makeshift vehicle paths were criss-crossed all over where the U.S. military hauled everything off. The final government narrative was that it was an experimental drone with small crash-test dummies, even though the initial town rumors talked of alien bodies. Even today, five years later, there is a large section at the crash site where no plants grow. That don't make any sense."

Aaron stopped and sat up in bed.

"Thank you for telling me this, but by doing so, you have broken your promise to the men in black. And you tell me to keep my mouth shut!"

"I didn't promise those two suits I wouldn't say anything, they just told me to be quiet. I don't like people trying to intimidate me or my friends. But they were very intimidating. The way the men in black questioned me, it felt like they could look into my soul. That's the only reason I never said anything to anyone until tonight. So with that, you know that I've seen some strange shit. When you talk about the 'problems' you have been having, I've seen enough to be able to believe you, but I'm still not convinced we should trust them."

Aaron slunk deeper into the two pillows that propped him up against the headboard. "My honest opinion on the government is, fuck them, being silent about UFOs and aliens. It is obvious they are up to something with all of the UFO sightings going on. It's on the news so much now, it's like they want us to talk about it. It's way too obvious that something is going on to keep silent about UFO and alien encounters anymore."

Mukesh didn't understand UFOs but was absorbed by Aaron's story. But it was also getting late. It was a good place to break the night off after such a conversation, and Mukesh wanted to think on his own about the vision he had earlier. He stood and stretched. Jen pecked at the keyboard on her new laptop with her headphones on, oblivious to their earlier conversation between the two men, and typed a description for her latest TikTok video.

Mukesh shuffled around for a while, thinking about the missing drifter in Mason from years before. "I really want a Xanax tonight, but I can see what you're saying about how I should slow down." Mukesh gritted his teeth. "But after a story like that paired with the strange things I have been experiencing, I sure could use one." Aaron couldn't help but grin as he opened the nightstand drawer and fumbled out another small blue pill.

"Take care of yourself, friend, and please listen to what I am saying about keeping your mouth shut in this strange town," Aaron said as Mukesh turned to leave.

"I will, and you take care as well." Mukesh walked out and shut the door. Aaron locked it behind him and hollered over at Jen loudly enough to get through her earphones.

"Jen!"

She took her headphones off and looked.

"Let's do a shot and screw." Jen closed her laptop quickly then walked over and sat beside her man and waited for him to work them up.

Chapter 17

The next day, while Mukesh was rolling sushi, he felt a vibration in his pocket, a rarity. He'd set his phone to notify him during work hours only when someone in his contacts texted or called. After finishing the rest of the sushi in front of him, he walked into the bathroom to pee and check his messages.

"I got some news about the good friend I see every day, the one with the hurt arm."

Mukesh laughed at the covert joke and texted back: "Let me know when your real good friend leaves and I will come over afterwards." Aaron's sly sense of humor was beginning to rub off on Mike.

Mukesh broke another record rolling sushi and was getting more efficient with the chores. He paced himself while washing the dishes so he wouldn't get too far ahead and be stuck pacing around, pretending with a rag.

At four-thirty, Mukesh finished his shift and left for home. He opened the curtains up all the way and propped the door to let out some of the stuffy air. Normally, Todd left Aaron's at around seven-thirty. Mukesh didn't feel like looking through the church footage for that long, so he took a drive and a short walk. As he hiked down the mountain trail, he realized it was the same one that overlooked the spot where Aaron spoke of the alien wreckage. Below him, off to one side, lay a barren spot with neatly hewn trees. Nothing grew in that small round section on the bank, not even outside its edges. Mukesh didn't know anything about the local foliage but even in his ignorance he could tell the bare spot was odd. The same could be said of the unnaturally flattened space across from the bulldozed wreckage. It had to be where the cabin once stood. Curious, Mukesh started toward the alleged crash site but decided against it before he'd taken two steps. It was a feeling, perhaps a premonition, as if he was about to slip and fall and never emerge again.

Closing the door to his Prius, he decided that was the last day he'd ever hike that particular mountain path.

When he got back to the motel, he opened the fridge and took out the marinated chicken and vegetables he had prepped the day before. He cooked the Indian stir-fry on his motel-prohibited hotplate and made himself a nice meal. He put the pot on a folded up t-shirt on the bathroom counter to cool and walked his plate to his computer setup and opened up the Bling cam app. It was six-thirty. Mukesh had an hour and a half to kill before he expected to go over to Aaron's to hear the big news.

Mukesh resumed the Wednesday church meeting where he had left off. The head pastor announced the name of the woman who had left the church the hefty sum, Eileen Baker.

"I'm surprised she didn't leave it all to her fifth husband," one member joked.

"I'm surprised she didn't leave any to her fifty cats," joked another. Most around the table chuckled at the two men's verbal digs.

One of the men, seeing the success of his friend's joke, tried a more hateful one. "Maybe she thinks giving money to the church will atone for all her sins." Two women began to laugh but stopped themselves at the head pastor's glare.

The Hacker and The Hillbilly

Wanda paraphrased Eileen's shady past. "I hear the Mountain Miner's Credit Union found out a year too late that she'd been embezzling money from them the whole time she worked there, and the statute of limitations had passed. Rumor has it she took the $250,000 she'd stolen from them and turned it into her large fortune by sleeping with an investor on a hunting excursion to get his insider trading tips. She had to think her large donation might keep her from going to Hell."

The head pastor intervened. "Alright now, let's remember the golden rule. We should only say nice things about people after they die."

"It is something nice, pastor. She died and left us four million dollars!" said Deacon George. He laughed at his own joke.

The co-pastor smiled. "Knowing that hateful woman, the money is dirty. I agree with Wanda. I think she gave it to our church thinking it would launder her soul."

The head pastor laid down the law. "Act like you got some sense, y'all. I know none of this is going to leave this room, but still..." Mukesh watched more of the banter and skimmed through the rest of the boring bits. He stumbled on a spot a few minutes in where the leaders discussed how they were going to spend the money. Mukesh paused the footage and walked over to his electric hotplate precariously straddling the bathroom counter sink. In the pot beside it, his food had cooled. He took out a few Ziploc freezer bags and divided the leftovers into three portions.

A text came in: "You can come over now, Mike."

Mukesh texted back, "Do you want any Indian food I made?"

"Hell no, I don't want to start to smell like curry all the time like you."

"I was asking Jen."

"Just this once, but I'll tell her if she eats any of that shit too often we're going to have to get a room with two beds."

Mukesh chuckled and took one of the packages of Indian chicken and vegetables he had portioned and put it into a plastic grocery bag and texted, "Leaving now."

He walked up to the door and knocked.

"It's open!" Aaron yelled from within. Mukesh entered, locking it behind him. He handed Jen the bag of Indian food, and she put it in their mini-fridge.

"Thank you, Mike. I'll let you know what I think of it."

Mukesh took to his usual chair and turned to Aaron, twisting in his seat. "So what's the news? Is it good or bad?"

"It's kind of both, but also neither. It's nothing that anyone can do anything about anyway. As a matter of fact, it's already been done." Mukesh thought that Aaron was leading him along to get some sort of reaction, so he kept stone-faced and silent as his friend spoke. After the short, uncomfortable silence, Aaron went on, "Todd signed a settlement with the insurance company."

"What!" Mukesh was confused, as it was early in the negotiation process. The plan was that Todd wouldn't take the first offer.

"He was supposed to wait until a later offer, I know," Aaron rolled his eyes, "but there are some other factors. Biggest one of them is Todd's mother needs an operation or she's going to die. I know Todd's family and that's actually the truth. She won't get the life-saving surgery unless she has the money, but

The Hacker and The Hillbilly

there's a bright side to it all. I talked to Todd's lawyer about his case and..."

"Wait, you talked to Todd's lawyer about his case?"

Aaron drew back and looked offended. "Sometimes drug dealers get special perks, especially me." Mukesh laughed. "No, seriously. Yes. I know I don't have to tell you, 'never say anything to anyone about what I say.' Yes, I have talked to Todd's lawyer. She even knows about our fraud. Most of the time, you want a crooked lawyer. Todd wouldn't know to emphasize important details to her, such as what it meant that the floor was mopped with the wrong detergent, but I do. When she stressed that point to the insurance agency, they changed their whole tune. When personal negligence is brought up in a court case, it makes it a lot more lucrative and winnable. Betty's a ruthless woman, and she loves the drama of the courtroom. The floor being too slippery from a worker's mistake would draw a lot of sympathy from a jury in the courtroom, and Betty's never afraid to go all the way."

"The lawyer is a woman?"

Aaron laughed at Mukesh. "You are a little sexist, but it's ok. You can blame it all on your traditional Indian upbringing, and I can blame mine on being Southern. Yes, she's as crooked as any personal injury lawyer, but that's also why she's so good."

"I don't really care about the lawyer. What I want to know is, how much money are we going to get?" Mukesh was getting annoyed at Aaron for drawing out the conversation.

"Well, because of the soap on the floor and the severity of the injuries, the offer that Todd took, from what the lawyer said, is close to the amount they would offer before the matter would be taken to trial. If the lawyer is fine with the settlement, then so am I." Aaron paused again. Mukesh rolled his eyes. Aaron laughed. He was playing with his friend, stringing him along.

"After the lawyer gets her money, we split three hundred and twenty thousand dollars. That's eighty thousand apiece for you and me."

"Yes!" Mukesh said, hopping up and down in his chair.

"I know, right? I never expected that much, and so soon. I am actually going to go back to that shed and swap the block of wood and sledge with two replacements. The originals I want to keep around. Matter of fact, I'll give you some money to give me a ride."

"I'll give you a ride to get them whenever you want. I'd like to look at them every now and then myself."

"Yeah, having that sledgehammer hanging on the wall would make a good story," Aaron added, "but one that I could never tell. That's kind of why I want it hanging on my wall."

Mukesh chuckled for a few seconds and then got serious. "So, when do we get our money?"

"In three weeks, Todd gets the deposit, so however long it takes for him to funnel money out without suspicion. I suspect we can have all the money in our hands in four or five months, and no one will ever know you and I got our cuts. We'll get the money by funneling it through one of my friends' construction companies. Don't worry about it. I have everything covered."

"What did I tell you about all this, Aaron? Doesn't it seem that the stars have aligned and everything is working out perfectly with our plans? It's like it is all by cosmic design."

The Hacker and The Hillbilly

"Let's try to keep God out of this. It's not good to talk about Him when you're speculating that He helped us benefit from breaking the law. I have to draw the line there. Getting too cocky is never good, and now you're trying to attribute our illegal acts to divine intervention."

Mukesh swiveled to talk to Jen. "And what do you think about all of this stuff?"

She turned around and looked at both men. "Everything seems to be working out, and I hope it continues to do so." She smiled at Mukesh, then went back to her computer and piddled with one of her new videos in TikTok Studio.

Mukesh asked Jen an open-ended question to find out more about her behavioral skills. "What have you seen of importance since I saw you last?"

"I have gone through two weeks of footage from the start of this month. Jerry looks like he's ready and willing to put his hands on people. I also found out the church is getting a four million-dollar donation from Eileen Baker's will. The church leaders were bad-mouthing the woman who gave it to them in the church meeting. Aaron and I had just finished listening to them talk about how they were going to use some of it, and then you came in." Mukesh noted the coincidence, how he'd stopped the footage at that exact point before he came over.

"They are going to use it for a no-bid church renovation that's going to benefit two of the church members' construction companies. Then they are giving a large amount to a charity, one that helps out an orphanage. I have seen the documentaries; in reality, the money will get funneled into the country where it gets laundered and lines the pockets of the church leaders. Crooked churches like the CCP rarely deal with anything charitable within the United States. They do everything overseas so they can steal most of the money. If we scam any money from this scumbag church, it will be just as good in our hands as in theirs. It will be Karma."

Mukesh leaned forward in his seat to signal that he was getting ready to stand. "I am glad that Todd's mother will be able to continue living after the operation now that Todd has all that money."

Aaron searched Mukesh closely to see if he had any genuine sympathy for Todd's mother. "That's a good way of thinking about it. This all could have happened because Todd's mother needed that operation." Aaron nodded and smiled. "That's called good Karma... and we helped."

Mukesh straightened his slacks and stood. "I hope it's like that. When it comes to Karma, I only want the good stuff," Mukesh said, chuckling. Mukesh paused before he left, telling Aaron, "Just try to find a sledgehammer that looks like the one we used and go switch it. It will be nice to have the original Toddhammer around."

Aaron laughed. "I'm going tomorrow. You can take me there if you want. I'll hide it by my side the next time Todd comes in and see how he reacts when I bring it out."

"Goodbye, friend." Mukesh grinned and walked out the door.

"See you later, Mike."

Chapter 18

The next day, Mukesh had a day off from rolling sushi at Food City. He opened up the shades in his motel room after he got dressed and took out his phone and texted Aaron. "Do you want me to drive you to get that sledgehammer today?"

"I've got someone who's going to take care of it. Come by and visit me later."

"Ok, let me know when I can come over." Mukesh assembled a backpack with a Sun Drop and two bottled waters and went out to his Prius. He went through the drive-thru at Bojangles and got a coffee and a chicken biscuit. He chewed on the biscuit and sipped his shit coffee as he rode around a mountain backroad, looking for a trail or dirt path to hike far from the UFO crash site. None of the ones he passed appealed to him, and the day was gloomy, so Mukesh went back to his room after his drive. He closed the shades and booted up his laptop to examine more church cam footage.

All the while watching, in the back of his head, Mukesh thought about how to celebrate the successful food pantry score. He decided to drive to the city later that evening to eat a traditional Indian dinner. Just forty-five minutes away, Indian Garden had an awesome buffet with authentic Tandoori chicken. Mukesh's mouth watered as he scrubbed through a sermon.

He got a good grasp of a week's worth of on-goings over four fast-forwarded hours. By then, his stomach was growling. He hopped in his Prius and headed to the restaurant. The buffet cost twenty dollars but was worth it. Their rice pudding was so perfect, Mukesh bought a quart of it to take home with him, despite the high per-pound price of nine dollars. He let his GPS lead him home along meandering country roads instead of taking the Interstate. Gloomy as the day was, the mountain scenery seemed magnificent. In any season, in any weather condition, the Appalachian skyline always proved majestic.

Mukesh got home at six-forty-five, expecting Aaron to hail him at around seven-thirty or eight. At seven forty-five, he got the text and went over.

Aaron updated Mukesh on all Bling cam news. "We're caught up on the church footage until the next live. We skimmed through the sermons and skipped over the cheesy worship songs but made sure to catch all of the church announcements. At last Wednesday's church meeting, we found out the church is going to sign two no bid contracts with their crooked construction friends, one for three hundred thousand dollars and one for two hundred fifty! I know I'm a crook, but I ain't crooked like that. I'm a drug dealer and a hustler and sometimes a thief, but I'd never take advantage of God to get my money. It's all about the lines you cross."

Mukesh stared silently.

Aaron continued on. "What I mean is, and I'll use myself as an example... I don't ever do anything that would hurt someone physically, unless it's indirectly by stealing items or cash from them. I'm trying to get the money just like any good American, and for the least amount of work possible, just like everyone else. I aim to take as much as I can from whoever, as easily as I can. But I'm not going to do something that could hurt someone physically. These church folks are scam artists just

The Hacker and The Hillbilly

like me, but worse crooks because they entice people to donate to them by pretending to do good with their money."

Mukesh nodded. "It is a cutthroat world like that everywhere. It is just like that in India. Americans are no different."

"I'm sure you're right. For example, and I'm not saying this to be bragging, if I get some fake or bad dope that's going to hurt someone, I'll take the loss. Not many people would do that, but I would. And I'm not going to tell someone that the dope they bought from me was safe unless I was certain. You'd be surprised at how many sociopaths and psychopaths are out there in the world now. Too many people are out there in the world today that would hurt or even kill someone if they could get away with it."

"I see," Mukesh said, nodding slightly. He had known a lot of crazy people from the dark corners of India, some who were near that level of evil depravity. The conversation was getting heavy. "Let me ask you," Mukesh smirked. "I'm only bringing this up because this is very important..." he paused and stared at Aaron.

"It's ok." Aaron braced himself for what Mukesh was going to say.

"The sledgehammer... where's it at? I want to see it," Mukesh said, grinning.

"Oh. I can't believe it! I almost forgot." Smiling, Aaron reached between the side of the bed and the wall and pulled it out. "Here it is." He held it halfway up the handle with one hand as he smacked the double-sledge end playfully on his other palm.

"Nice," said Mukesh.

"Yes," said Aaron, looking psychotic with the sledge. "As far as seriously hurting or killing someone, I haven't crossed that line yet, but not many cross me because they know I would if I had to. I just ain't been pushed that far."

Mukesh didn't say anything, as understandably every man has his limits. He knew Aaron well enough by now to believe he had no real malice towards people without good reason.

"Karma," Mukesh said again with emphasis. "You and I exact Karma on people who are suckers with their money. Sometimes, the old phone regulars I used to prey on seemed like they knew I was scamming them the whole time, and it was all a game to them. Some of the people who used to fall for my phone scams just wanted attention. With some of them, it was like they were punishing themselves for something they did, and they allowed themselves to be conned. I'd listen to their stories and fake-cry with them for an hour or more sometimes. The longer you listened to them, pretending to care, the easier it was to take their money."

"I saw something on the news about those Indian call centers. It doesn't look like they are that much fun or that it pays well."

"I don't really agree with that. If you are a good con man, you get good contacts and numbers and assignments. If you are not good on the phones, then yes, it's not much fun." Mukesh amused himself thinking of his past and his progression to more profitable cons. "And now we move on to bigger and better things. I pray this will be the one scam that will last us for many years."

"I'm going to leave praying and God out of it. I will count myself fortunate to benefit from someone else's Karmic

The Hacker and The Hillbilly

demise, but I am not going to ask God for anything dealing with my scams. The few times I've messed up and done that, it's always led to bad luck."

"I don't really believe in God," Mukesh confessed.

"Well, I do," Aaron said, unoffended. "Do you believe in Karma?"

"Of course I believe in Karma. That is in my culture."

"If you believe in Karma, then who or what controls the Karma and doles out Karmic justice? Who or what is watching who decides how to dole out the Karma?" Mukesh grew visibly uncomfortable at such a good question. Before he could answer, Aaron asked another question. "And what describes all of the unusual things that you say have been going on with you?"

Mukesh rolled his eyes facetiously.

Conscious that he broke his own rules by hinting at Mukesh's supernatural occurrences, Aaron tried to shut down any more mentions. "If all this works out with Jerry Dirk and the church and this turns out to be the big one, I'll believe everything you say about your unusual experiences."

Mukesh smiled and looked in the corner of the room at a makeshift clothes rack where a long coat splayed flat against the other clothes. He froze. The supernatural sensation swelled in his body once again. This time, he did not let it turn into anxiety. He closed his eyes, relaxed, and saw the same vision from the week before of him walking into the church. The coat on the rack was the same as what he wore in the vision when the church bouncer placed a hand on Mukesh's shoulder when he tried to walk in. The scene played out precisely as he saw it the week before. Aaron could tell Mukesh was having a psychic episode and looked concerned. Mukesh broke from his trance and beamed, excited.

"I had another one of them again, Aaron!"

Jen spun around at the outburst, glanced at the two, and went back to swiping on her phone.

"I could tell by the look on your face," Aaron said, half concerned and half annoyed that Mukesh was going to talk about his visions again. Aaron glared sternly at Mukesh. "I am going to have to lay down the law on this one, Mike. I am your friend, and I respect that you are going through some strange shit and it scares you. I understand you want a friend to help you process it. That's cool, and I want to listen to you and help you..." He paused and stared deeper into Mukesh. "But I insist, if you ever want to talk to me about this stuff, don't do it within earshot of any phone, or in any public place, or around a dishwasher or a toaster, even. Hell, don't even say anything around the wrong fencepost. Not to come down too hard on you, but I thought I was clear after last night's conversation. I've seen the wrong kinds of pressure come down on strange and unusual shit, and I don't want either of us to get on anybody's radar, especially government or military. I shouldn't have even told you what I did last night. I have told you over and over, and have become more and more direct. This is the laydown: after tonight, respectfully, don't talk any stuff like that around me, or I will make you leave our room. If you have to talk, we'll take a ride and walk in a field somewhere without our phones." Aaron hoped that would be enough to finally keep Mukesh from breaking the rules.

Mukesh's feelings were hurt, and he tried to defend himself. "Alright, Aaron, I won't. I have thought about it. I should keep my mouth shut, and I promise you, it's not like I'm bragging that I'm special or something."

"That too," added Aaron. He softened his facial features in case Mukesh thought he was being too hard.

"No one should really be saying anything incriminating around any phone, or anywhere in public," Mukesh added. He knew all about what could be done with phones and had the hacker tools to prove it. "I know all about the technology out there and the widespread surveillance that goes on now. You basically have to give multiple corporations full access to your computer or phone in order to use their services and apps. That's why I am not on social media."

"I don't do Facebook either," Aaron said. "So one last time and I'll drop it. If you need to talk to me, we can go ride somewhere and talk. I hope you understand, and don't mess up." Mukesh nodded. "I don't want to see you disappearing." Aaron's phone chimed, notifying him. He sat suddenly upright in his bed and joked, "See, I told you they were listening!" He looked down at his phone. "That's Todd wanting a morning shot tomorrow. That still counts, right?" Aaron grinned.

Mukesh smiled and shook his head. He thought about where their conversation had started that evening and where it ended. He looked up again at the overcoat that draped over the clothes rack, like it was waiting for him to wear it. He stared at it and closed his eyes and made up a plan. He finished his thoughts and faced Aaron, who braced himself skeptically, suspecting Mukesh had another one of his special visions.

"I think I should go into the church tomorrow and meet that man in the foyer in person," Mukesh stated. "I also want to wear that overcoat."

"That is not an overcoat. That is a trench coat." Aaron studied Mukesh some more and began to laugh. "So is this like a test run? You are going to go in and see how this guy treats a stranger, or is this where we collect on our scam?"

Mukesh smiled, "A Middle Eastern looking stranger in a long, tan trench coat is going to walk into Community Compassion Presbyterian tomorrow. I will even go into the church late so I stand out more. We'll see what Jerry Dirk does when I try to walk in."

"You're going tomorrow?"

"I assume he is going to be there as a volunteer tomorrow, right?" Mukesh asked.

"Second service," Jen spoke up from her phone. Even though she was always fiddling with something, nothing ever slipped by her. Mukesh was impressed with her skills and was thankful that everything was going well. Perhaps a hillbilly town in the USA was the right place for him all along.

"I am going there tomorrow, then. Second service," Mukesh said.

Jen let out a squeal. "This is going to be fun. Aaron and I get to watch it all here in real time. Hey, I forgot to ask, Mike. Since I'm caught up watching the church footage, do you think you could give me access to the other Bling cam hacks for fun? Maybe we can come up with something else for one of them."

Mukesh thought for a few seconds. "I don't see why not. As long as you don't do anything to let people know you have access to any of the feeds." Mukesh was willing to do anything to make Jen happy to hopefully keep her enjoying an otherwise unsatisfying chore. "I'll put them all on a thumb drive and bring them over tomorrow. As far as the value of the other accounts,

The Hacker and The Hillbilly

I don't see much in them. A couple of them are doorbell cams and yard surveillance. Actually, you might have some fun watching one of them. An Indian convenience store is among one of the hacks."

"That should be fun! A local one?"

"Yes, the one in the town thirty minutes down the interstate. But you cannot use the Bling cam footage to interfere with any of their affairs."

"Of course not, Mike."

"Alright, I will bring them to you tomorrow." Mukesh looked at Aaron. "Will you let me use that coat?"

Aaron was impressed with the rapid expansion of Mukesh's balls. Not long ago, he'd have whined about not wanting to go to the church in person. "Sure you can use the coat." He looked up and laughed. "Just come over here before you go, and we'll see how you look and get you set up nice and dapper for your first visit to the CCP."

Jen smiled at Mukesh, no longer underestimating the Indian immigrant who had become her boyfriend's best friend. "Don't forget the thumb drive with those hacks!"

Aaron grinned at Mukesh. "Get you some rest. You have a big day tomorrow. I can't wait to watch it live myself. Come get the coat tomorrow morning. Just don't get any blood on it when Jerry beats you up in church." Mukesh thought of the dangers of going in himself while appearing to be a threat and the possibility he could get hurt and be the one with the lawsuit, but he decided to follow the vision anyhow.

Aaron expressed similar fears to his friend. "If you get hurt too much tomorrow, I'll feel sorry for you. When we get the money, I'll stop feeling sorry for you as I count mine."

"I am following my—what do I say?—gut on this one," said Mukesh. After some goodbyes to Aaron and smiles to Jen, he left Aaron's motel room to rest for tomorrow's church mission.

Chapter 19

After a restful night's sleep, Mukesh woke up at eight forty-five. A text notification sounded while he was in the shower. It was from Aaron: "Come and get some coffee. Text me when you wake up."

"I was in the shower. Want to ride and get biscuits?"

"No. Church is at 11." Aaron texted back.

Mukesh didn't want to watch the first service and wasn't concerned about the time. He made coffee and crushed up a granola bar into the rest of the rice pudding he'd gotten from Indian Garden. He ate the light breakfast and took his Keurig coffee in a to-go cup over to Aaron's.

Mukesh knocked.

"Who is it?"

"It's me." Mukesh said while rolling his eyes. This time, after Aaron opened the door for Mukesh, he looked around outside before closing it. He walked over to the bathroom where Jen sat in front of her laptop. Mukesh followed.

Jen turned around and looked at Mukesh and smiled. "Good morning Mike! Are you excited for church today?" Mukesh grinned at Jen. The mood was pleasant among the three as they watched the laptop split into four screens: two cameras in the sanctuary, one in the foyer, and one in the parking lot.

"Let's just do a large split screen of the foyer and one of the sanctuary cams," Mukesh suggested. Jen clicked a couple of times and the screen was split into two distorted pans. Jen resized and zoomed in on the sanctuary panel to get a good frame of the preacher on stage and the projector screen behind him. The foyer cam she sized smaller and placed in the left corner of the monitor. A couple more clicks and they heard the sermon audio. The preacher's vocals, mixed with sentimental piano, tinkled out of two external speakers Jen had connected to her laptop setup. Aaron started laughing.

"What do you find funny about that?" Mukesh asked.

"The piano music." Aaron laughed more. Mukesh stared, confused, until Aaron collected himself and explained. "I don't know why it's so funny to me. It's like the piano player plays some sort of theme music according to the topics that are being discussed in the sermon. Sort of like bad background music in a motion picture soundtrack." Mukesh politely chuckled . "Wait until you hear the music they play when they pass around the collection plates."

"No thank you," Mukesh said as he walked over to the chair by Aaron's bed and faced it towards the laptop and Jen. Aaron went over to his bed and lay down.

Jen turned down the audio on her laptop. "Aaron and I know a lot about Jerry and the Dirk family. Jerry is the brother of one of the most powerful judges in this region."

"Yeah, a very corrupt judge, though of course no one can prove it. Rumors are he owns a lot of stock in the local regional jail, one of the for-profit ones. It doesn't take much to see a pattern when the same judge who owns a cut of the jail is known for laying down the heaviest sentences. Then there are his crooked civil case verdicts. One time, Judge Dirk oversaw a case and favored his rich friend instead of recusing himself for knowing the defendant. Even though the judge ruled in my friend's favor, the judge's ruling was one-third of the insurance quote. Judge Dirk helped his millionaire friend save six hundred dollars by screwing a poor common man."

Mukesh wasn't surprised. It was the same in India. He looked at his phone. It was ten-thirty. His eyes panned from the coffee cupped in his hands to the trench coat still draped on the clothes rack in the corner.

Aaron noticed him looking, and said: "Just your size. It's also more threatening than the average coat because of what you could potentially hide underneath. It's definitely going to make you look more threatening. Since Jen and I will be watching the live feed, we really need to know about your plans."

Mukesh leaned back in his chair and folded his arms behind his head. He looked at the coat again. "What is more suspicious is that the weather is not right for a coat like that today." He stood up and took it off its hanger and put it on, buttoning one top button and spinning once like a runway model for Aaron and Jen.

Aaron grinned and pointed over at Jen and the laptop monitor. "Check this out. The pastor is always trying to make the congregation feel guilty. This church is sitting on four million, and look how he is talking to the people."

Mukesh walked to Jen's side to watch. "... and we have to fund this great mission to build and renovate our orphanage in Honduras, so we really need more donations from the congregation..."

Mukesh shook his head. "All they're really doing is going on vacation. It is the same with all of the Christian missionaries I have seen in India. Not all of them, but most of them. I met a lot as a teen. I was fascinated with Americans and their culture.

I'm fascinated by people in general. Everyone in India was fascinated with American culture back then.

"We all saw the meeting they had last Wednesday," said Mukesh. "Even the people who can afford the trip to Honduras are getting their travel and accommodations from church donations instead of dipping into the four million in funds. They're also bringing ten thousand from Eileen's will money to hire local help so they can do less work. Just like the ones in India I used to hang out with, they'll make it a point to help out on the roof one day to get some pictures of them doing a grueling job." Aaron rolled his eyes, knowing Mukesh had probably never worked on a roof, either. Mukesh rolled his eyes back at his friend and continued on. "The men take pictures of themselves on the roof with tool belts and the women and kids will get some pictures smiling and eating with the natives and holding their babies. The real motive is to go overseas to see an exciting new place, launder money, and virtue signal." Mukesh turned and looked back at the computer screen. "Best thing about the missionaries in India is they had a lot of spending money and were gullible. That was the main reason I hung around and one of the biggest reasons I got into cons."

"But of course." Aaron looked over to the side at Mukesh. "Those coat sleeves are too long."

Mukesh hopped his shoulders up and stretched both his arms out in front of him then dropped them back by his side. "They are not too bad."

Aaron looked Mukesh up and down a few times then turned back to the monitor. He got excited and waved his hand at Mukesh. "I want you to hear this music that they play when

The Hacker and The Hillbilly

they pass around the collection plate at the end." The ushers walked up front and grabbed several braided reed baskets lined with red cloth and began to coordinate among the congregation. The piano lady played some watered-down money-giving music.

Mukesh grinned at his friend. "You are a strange one, Aaron. You find a lot of things funny that I just don't understand." It was ten-thirty. The congregants from the first service were leaving, and the second service started at eleven.

Jen turned around and spoke to the two men behind her. "Jerry's coming up to take his place in the foyer right now." The men turned towards Jen and looked at the computer screen. Mukesh leaned in to get a better look. Jen zoomed in on a close-up of Jerry Dirk's face. Mukesh felt the relaxed confirmation that accompanied most of his visions.

Aaron wanted to have everything square before Mukesh left. "Mike, what are your plans? We got distracted by your runway performance and fabulous coat."

Mukesh began to laugh. "My plans are to look like I might be some Middle Eastern terrorist and walk into the church sanctuary to worship like anyone else and walk in fifteen minutes late. I hope he tries to stop me or put his hands on me. I think that is what he will do."

Aaron nodded at Mukesh and said, "I don't know about him putting his hands on you. Jerry might look aggressive, but I think he's more of a privileged prick. He's not going to do anything that he can't get away with, and he'll have to have a good reason to put his hands on you, but I agree with you. It does look like he's hoping for a confrontation, maybe to become a hero or to have some kind of story to tell."

"I hope," Mukesh said as he raised his eyes at Aaron. Mukesh stressed again, "I hope he puts his hands on me. I'm not sure what else to think about after that. I hope I am tough if I get hurt," he said as he took off the trench coat. He folded it twice lengthwise and draped it over the side of his chair. He sat down and looked at Aaron. "What I am thinking is," he paused and cleared his throat, "if we can send someone in to him who could sustain some sort of assault injury, we might create a nice lawsuit." Mukesh closed his eyes as another thought occurred. "If the church isn't considered responsible for the injury, from what you say, Jerry comes from a rich family that can pay if the church won't. I guess if it happens to be me who gets hurt then so be it."

"If you say so," said Aaron. "I have been holding my tongue about some of my ideas until I had a better feeling about our plan. Perhaps..." Aaron paused and looked into the air, "I might know of someone I trust who can pull something like this off, someone who looks threatening because he is different. We'll see what happens after you go to church today. I have a personal connection to this person, and I don't want him to get hurt too badly. I have some real good ideas of my own that fit in nicely with this idea, but I want to see how Jerry responds to you today, first."

Mukesh wondered what type of person Aaron would want to bring on for this, because it obviously couldn't be someone like Todd. "Have I told you," asked Mukesh with a smirk, "that I have a good feeling about all this?" Aaron smiled and looked away. Mukesh got up and tucked the trench coat under his arm. It was five after eleven, time for Mukesh to make his way

The Hacker and The Hillbilly

over to the church. He planned to get there at fifteen after, when the choir and congregation would be singing.

As Mukesh walked to his car, he stopped midway and closed his eyes. A vision of his Prius pulling into the perfect parking place, as well as some other thoughts on how to look more threatening, entered his mind. He smiled, opened his trunk, and put the trench coat inside, knowing it would look more ominous if Jerry saw him fiddling in his trunk for something before he walked into the CCP.

Just like in his vision minutes earlier, the exact spot was available for Mukesh to park, right in front of and facing Community Compassion Presbyterian. He pulled into the spot, on the right side of the road and facing the entrance of the church. Jerry Dirk stared at the Prius through the glass from a distance of what seemed to be about thirty yards. Mukesh fought back duper's delight as he put on his darkened prescription glasses. He sat in the car for a full minute to make sure Jerry took special notice of him. He braced himself for whatever was about to happen as he thought about his plan. He counted another thirty seconds to himself silently while staring at Jerry through the glass entrance of the church foyer. Jerry glared.

Erratically, Mukesh opened and staggered out of the driver's side and glanced back at the church as he stumbled to the trunk of his Prius. Jerry continued to watch. Mukesh paused dramatically and breathed heavily before he popped the trunk. He smiled as he slowly donned Aaron's trench coat, half-hidden behind the trunk hood. He imagined he was a secret agent or an actor in a Bollywood action movie, and tried to contort his face ominously like he was about to rob a bank.

He took his time behind the trunk hood. After an uncomfortable amount of time, he closed it and stared towards the church. He buttoned one button on his trench coat and began to strut towards the foyer entrance. Mukesh power-walked the distance between his parked Prius and the glass Community Compassion Presbyterian doors. He replayed the vision over again in his head to keep a mental track of what to do, replicating even the rhythm and speed of his gait in his vision as he walked.

As Mukesh neared the church steps, he could see Jerry was triggered. The man's hands dropped as Mukesh climbed the steps. He kept a brisk pace, bouncing rhythmically as he went. When he reached the top, he jammed both his hands into his pockets. He paused at the glass door, tore his left hand out, and pulled hard on the door handle. Mukesh glared at Jerry Dirk's face, stern and frowning.

Jerry's wide eyes narrowed. His face fixed in a scowl, and he spread both of his arms out as rigid as a rock face. Apprehension overcame Mukesh as the church door closed behind him. He slowed down but was still closing quickly on Jerry.

Three strides before Mukesh reached the sanctuary threshold, Jerry Dirk sidestepped into the middle of both doors. A nervous energy overcame Mukesh as he continued forward around the burly man's side. Without a word, Jerry caught hold of Mukesh's shoulder.

Mukesh abruptly stopped. Jerry eyed him with evil intensity. Mukesh stepped back. Jerry's fingers peeled off with visible reluctance. Fear struck. Mukesh realized he had not planned for anything after Jerry's outstretched arm. But

The Hacker and The Hillbilly

instead of panicking, an uncomfortable drive overcame him, and he spoke as if under a spell. "I am trying to go to church!"

Jerry postured with his arms out as if ready to fight, spreading his legs and planting his feet firmly in front of the double sanctuary doors. "Are you sure this is the right church for you?" Jerry glared at Mukesh.

Mukesh was nervous, but again, as if under possession, he spoke. "I come here to worship the one true god, Allah." Mukesh shuddered for a second as he realized he'd made the statement with a middle eastern inflection.

"Get out of here! This is not your church," said Jerry Dirk. Jerry stepped toward Mukesh and said louder, "This is a Christian church, it ain't that Muslim crap. You best go on and carry your Islamic ass down the road somewhere!"

As Mukesh walked away from Jerry, he turned before he opened the double glass doors, looked back, and said "Allahu Akbar!" loudly. Mukesh broke out of whatever had overcome him and walked back to his Prius. He stripped off his trench coat and threw it on the passenger seat beside him. By the time he glanced back into the foyer, Jerry was gone. Mukesh thought he probably went into the sanctuary to tell people about what had happened. He didn't want to wait around for anyone to come out and see him or get his plate number. He inserted his car key and started the ignition.

As he sat in the idling Prius, Mukesh texted Aaron, "Be over in a while."

Before he could set the phone down on the seat beside him, Aaron shot back, "OMG! Just watched a Sunday Church Special. Lol. Come on by!"

Mukesh drove to Bojangles and got everyone gravy biscuits and coffee. He skipped going to his own motel room, and parked directly in front of Aaron's instead.

Chapter 20

Mukesh put on the coat and knocked on the door.

"Who is it?" Aaron could hardly ask through his laughter.

Mukesh tried to think of something funny to say but, without divine inspiration, could only stick with his usual, "It's me." Aaron and Jen jumped out of their seats to greet him as he walked in. Aaron doubled over, laughing. He grabbed Mukesh's shoulder and shook it playfully. Mukesh handed Aaron the trench coat.

"You can keep that," said Aaron with a smile.

"It's not really my style," replied Mukesh. He folded it over two times and handed it to Jen. She unfolded it and put it on a wooden coat hanger. She shoved a handful of clothes on the rack to one side, burying the trench coat in their other long clothes. "I appreciate the gesture, but you know I can't be seen wearing that coat around town."

"You're right. Don't draw attention to yourself."

"Never," affirmed Mukesh.

"It was exciting watching you in the church," Jen said as she returned to her laptop. She scrubbed the footage forward to live from where she had paused it to greet Mukesh. She swiveled her chair to face him. "After you left, the man pulled aside some other church members, and they were talking in the foyer. Then the co-pastor came out and... here," Jen turned to her laptop. She dragged the line with her mouse and released it right when she saw one of the double wooden doors open to the sanctuary and Jerry Dirk walk out with another gentleman.

"I think that guy's name is Tom," said Aaron.

The men let the sanctuary doors close, and Jerry spoke. "I just had a Middle Eastern guy in a long trench coat try to walk into our church a few minutes ago. He was up to no good, so I stopped him."

"What do you mean? Who tried to walk into the church? And you stopped him? What about a trench coat?" Tom asked, incredulous.

"He looked like a terrorist. He wore a long coat like an active shooter. He was even wearing dark glasses. I got in between the two doors to block him, but he tried to step around me and walk in anyway. I grabbed him by his shoulder."

"You put your hands on him?"

Jerry Dirk got red and agitated. "You want me to keep this place safe! There have been a bunch of attacks against churches lately, and this man was a threat!"

Tom shook his head. "Let me go get the co-pastor." Jerry Dirk paced in the foyer, mumbling. A couple of minutes later the co-pastor, George, arrived at the foyer, followed by Tom.

"Tom tells me there was an altercation in the foyer this morning. What happened, Jerry?" George asked with his chest puffed out and his hands in his pockets.

"It is not a big deal, George. I handled things. I stopped an Islamic guy in a trench coat from rushing into our church. Look at the footage! I am not dealing with this mess today. I try to do the right thing and volunteer to protect our church, and this is how I get treated?"

George gestured with his arms out to his sides as he tried to comfort Jerry. "Relax, Jerry. We, of course, have to look at the tapes. I just want you to tell me what I'm going to see so I can understand your actions."

"I ain't ashamed of nothing I did," huffed Jerry, loudly. "He rushed me. He was wearing a trench coat. He even said he was a Muslim coming in to worship and said 'Allah Akbar' or something and left. I can't believe this."

Tom knew Jerry well enough to know he was abrasive. This was the first serious altercation addressed to leadership involving the new church security, and Tom had been concerned about how some of the volunteers would approach delicate situations. Out of all of the volunteers, Dirk was the most worrying. Jerry took his coat off the foyer's corner rack and glared back and forth at Tom and the co-pastor. The two knew there was no use in saying anything else and didn't want to agitate Jerry any further. They would watch the Bling cam tapes to know exactly what happened.

"Go home, Jerry. We'll look at the footage later today and talk about it sometime after that," said Co-pastor George.

"Sorry I got a little upset with you, pastor. I'm just trying to protect the church. This man was a threat."

"Ok," Jen said, pausing the footage and chuckling. "Get a load of this part coming up."

"I know, right?" said Aaron.

The glass door slammed, and Tom and the co-pastor watched Jerry walk down the church steps.

"Maybe he actually did something so we can take him off the volunteer list. He isn't a very warm and welcoming person," said Tom. "He's exactly what you guys asked for, is what he is, volunteer church security. I think Jerry might like to cause drama instead of avoiding it. These big guys in the foyer 'protecting' our church are really just for show, anyhow."

"Our congregation expects it. If it's too obvious the men are serving as church security, it's because our church needs to see them there. Do you want to come look at the footage with me?" asked the co-pastor. "It'll be good to have a second set of eyes to process everything."

"Sure. When?"

"Right after the congregation and all the other staff leave, I'll meet you in the office, and we can watch it then. We can do it right after counting the offerings together."

"Ok," said Tom. They made their way back into the sanctuary.

Jen switched the feed to a single-cam view of the church office in real time to wait for the men to view the footage and put that window in the top right hand of the screen. Then she switched back to the live feed of the sermon.

"Let's take a ride," said Mukesh to Aaron.

"Why?" Aaron asked.

"Let's take a ride and talk," said Mukesh, hinting at wanting to speak about some of his recent visions.

Aaron looked over at Jen and said, "I don't need to see it live, I guess. Mukesh and I can watch their reaction video when we get back."

Aaron put his hand out for Mukesh to walk out ahead of him, but Mukesh turned to Jen first and said, "Log out of the Bling cam app for a while. We can't risk them noticing you're logging in, remember?"

The Hacker and The Hillbilly

"Kay. We can watch it later together, I guess." She closed the app, got up from her chair, and locked the door behind the two as they made their way to the Prius.

Mukesh looked over at Aaron inside the car. "Thanks for coming out with me. I am a little excited from the drama with Jerry and wanted to get out of the room and talk. You and Jen both need to get out of the motel more often. It would be nice to be able to talk sometimes without your girlfriend around."

Aaron shrugged the suggestion off and asked, "What do you have planned? Please let's not be out for longer than an hour and a half. A friend comes by every Sunday afternoon, and I can't miss that."

"Let's ride around the country for a while, then stretch our legs and walk in the fall air."

"It's nice outside," added Aaron. "I've got an idea. Let's go over to that new Sheetz by the interstate. I want to show you an old con. A friend and I used to pull it off all of the time in places that had self-serve registers when we were on the road for long stretches. It works every time." Mukesh drove ten minutes down the road and pulled into the Sheetz parking lot. He looked over at Aaron.

"Alright, here's how it goes. You go get a drink and a couple of snacks. Scan the drink and set the snacks down, then pay for it and leave with exactly what you paid for, the drink. You leave the items at the side of the self-serve register. Then we wait like five minutes. A few more people go through the line. Most of the time, they don't ever mess with any items lying beside the self-checkouts. Then I come in behind you and buy something and then place the items by the ones you set there earlier. I'll bag everything up when I go through the line, including the items you set there that weren't scanned. If I get caught, I wasn't paying attention and just bagged everything up by accident. I didn't bring the items to the self-checkout in the first place, so no one can prove I was stealing. It's worked every time, and it's like the slushie lottery scam I told you about, plausible deniability."

Mukesh smiled at that clever turn of phrase and basked in the complexity of Aaron's simplest street scams. "Ok, but please let me be the guy who accidentally leaves the items at the self-checkout." He stepped outside of his Prius to go into the busy store.

"That was my plan." Aaron stepped out of the car and yelled dramatically, "Get me a Monster Slim Jim Original and some Rolaids!"

Mukesh got Aaron his Slim Jim and a bag of Hawaiian BarBQ potato chips and, since they had no Rolaids, a tube of Tums instead. He grabbed a Sun Drop from the fridge and went to the register. He scanned the Sun Drop, left the other items lying there, and paid for his drink. Mukesh made it back to his car undisturbed.

Aaron opened his door as Mukesh got in.

"I thought you had to wait five minutes or so?"

"I'm going to use the bathroom," said Aaron. "It's also real busy, and I want to get a feel for the employees and how they act. I want to know if they pay extra attention to people like they want a raise or if they don't give a fuck. Jen used to know some clerks in her shoplifting heyday who always looked the other way for me and her. You'd be surprised at how many clerks will watch people steal and never say anything to their bosses. Normally with clerks, it only takes one time for them to learn not to worry about thieves, especially if there is no video surveillance. Most owners don't pay for their workers to be witnesses if they have to go to court." Aaron closed the passenger door and walked inside the Sheetz. Mukesh kept the Prius running like it was a getaway car. Seven to eight minutes later, Aaron came back and set a bag in between him and Mukesh. Aaron took the Slim Jim out of the plastic bag. "I said monster sized, dumbass!"

"I don't know anything about nasty Slim Jims. And you better not open that fart-smelling thing up in my car!" Aaron grinned at Mukesh and slapped the Slim Jim on his lap while he sipped the Barq's root beer he bought.

"Let me know where there's a good place to pull over to stretch our legs," Mukesh told Aaron. A couple more miles down the country road, Aaron signaled a spot with his Slim Jim. Mukesh pulled over into a gravel stretch that was the entrance to a longer, private road. A small hayfield lay to the left, and a section of trees and brush to the right. The two men left their phones in the car and walked out into the field.

Mukesh followed Aaron fifty yards into the field. "Thank you for coming out here and talking with me. That was the strangest experience I have ever had today." Aaron could see the concern on his friend's face and kept silent, letting him continue. "Everything worked out like in the vision I had a few days ago, with this guy Jerry putting his hands on me, everything. I never told you about it because you asked me not to say anything more about my strange visions. Aaron, I promise you, every detail, from Jerry's hand on which shoulder to the exact color of the trench coat you had for me to wear, I swear I saw it beforehand."

Aaron stared at his friend, puzzled. "I hate to say it, but I am beginning to believe you."

"But there was something else today that happened. At the end of the scene where Jerry put his hand on me, it felt like an outside force was guiding and controlling me. All of the words just spilled out, the same with my body movements. Not only that, but it felt uncomfortable, more than any of the other visions." He shook his head but remained strong and didn't sob. "I don't know what's going on."

"Something is definitely going on, Mike, but you have to remain clear-headed. You can't talk to anyone about this, because people will think you are crazy. Even worse is if the wrong people believe you. You don't want either of those."

"I understand that, and I thank you again for coming out to talk to me. I am kind of glad some of this psychic stuff feels uncomfortable. I can't assume any of these visions are positive, even though everything is working out."

"Listen, Mike. I can't be any more than a friend who listens. I don't understand what you are going through. I hope maybe one day you can get a handle on what's going on... without showing up on any radar."

"Alright," said Mukesh. "I won't bother you too often, but I wish I could have told you about the vision of Jerry putting his hands on me before it happened so you know I am not lying."

Aaron stepped towards Mukesh and put a hand on his shoulder. "I believe you. I know you well enough to tell when you are bullshitting me. I'll go on a ride with you anytime you want. Now, let's go back to the motel. I really want to see George and Tom review the tapes. Talk about a reaction video!"

The Hacker and The Hillbilly

"Jen is pretty crafty. She's doing great," Mukesh said.

"I told you she was perfect for this. I'm glad that you figured that out. Let's go back. I'm enjoying watching this all unfold as much as you are, and I'm beginning to have faith, just like you, that everything is going to work out."

Mukesh and Aaron drove back to the motel. Jen was grinning from ear to ear. Aaron and Mukesh stood on either side of her, eager to see the footage. "Don't spoil anything for us," Aaron said to Jen.

"I've watched it twice already." Jen chuckled. "This is too much fun!"

She queued up the footage of George and Tom watching the video of Jerry and Mike. They sat down in front of a monitor in the church office and watched the church foyer footage from beginning to end.

The co-pastor turned to Tom after watching it, "What the heck was that?"

"I don't know," said Tom, "I think we need to watch it again." They rewound the footage and watched it two more times and turned the monitor off.

Tom was the first to speak about the incident, "I don't really know what to think about this. That guy did wear a menacing-looking trench coat, but it still looked like he was only trying to walk into the sanctuary. Jerry put his hands on the guy for trying to walk past him is all. It doesn't matter that he's a Muslim. Other than his appearance, and the fact that he was walking a little fast, I can't see why Jerry put his hands on this man."

"When he stepped back and said he was there to worship the one true God, it makes what Jerry did seem more appropriate," said George.

"It doesn't make what he did appropriate," said Tom. "So what if the guy was Muslim. I told Jerry I would call him and talk to him after the elders review the tapes. We'll bring them up at the elder's meeting tomorrow and see what they think. Everyone is going to give Jerry a pass because of who he is and because the guy was a crazy and menacing looking Muslim. I know how they will vote. Just in case we have something like this happen again, we need to come up with some church policies to keep us out of trouble. Let's talk to the elders, and we'll address all the staff in the next Wednesday meeting on how to handle another situation like this one. We can call a special church security meeting afterwards to inform the volunteers after we figure out what to do." George took out his phone and tapped it. Tom got up from his chair and messed around with some of the settings on the Bling cam system.

"There," the co-pastor said and put away his phone. "I just told the elders about the importance of this meeting."

"What do you want me to say to Jerry in the text?" Tom asked.

"Make sure to let him know he isn't in trouble so he'll show up at the meeting, and we can go over the new policy. I don't want to hear any whining from him until then." The co-pastor stood up and waited for Tom to walk outside the office. He shut the door behind him and locked it.

Jen froze the footage and turned around toward her boyfriend and Mukesh and said, "So..." She grinned. Both men smiled.

The Hacker and The Hillbilly

Aaron looked over at Mukesh, "So now, after Wednesday, we'll know everything about what they plan to do the next time they think someone is a threat. I have some ideas that I've talked about with Jen, about who we could send in there to confront Jerry, but I want to see what they say in this meeting before I decide if it's right."

Mukesh was curious about who Aaron was thinking of, but he quit wondering, because he didn't know anyone Aaron knew besides Todd.

Aaron checked and put away his phone. "Wrap it up, Jen. Being Sunday, Todd just texted me, and he's coming over early." Jen closed the Bling folders and logged into the TikTok Studio app. She leaned over and cradled her phone in her lap. "That means you have to leave, too," Aaron told Mukesh. He stood up to let him out and locked the door after he left.

When Mukesh got home, he watched YouTube for the rest of the afternoon and evening. He lay on his bed with his phone until he grew tired, set his alarm, and fell asleep, anticipating another relaxing day of sushi rolling.

Chapter 21

The next morning, Mukesh awoke ten minutes before his alarm and got out of bed. He made sure to cut the alarm off so it wouldn't sound while he was in the shower. Afterwards, he dressed in his Food City sushi-rolling uniform: black slacks, a blue shirt, and a black mesh trucker hat with a fish and knife emblem. He reviewed Tom and co-pastor George watching the security cameras a couple of times, and three times he viewed the footage of his altercation with Jerry Dirk.

He observed himself closely in the feed when he confronted Jerry. Mukesh's back was turned to the camera, so he couldn't see his face. He contemplated the supernatural sensation that seemed to take control of him at the point where he backed away from Jerry. Though all his previous visions had jarred him, none had such a punctuated, negative body tension or feeling of lack of control as the vision that overcame him with Jerry the church bouncer. It felt like his body was under some foreign entity's grip or control. Mukesh looked at the time. Nine-thirty. He folded down his laptop and drove to work.

Rolling sushi had become second nature to Mukesh, which allowed him to devote most of his attention to his thoughts and plans. He imagined the details of their potential church plot and fantasized about what type of person they might want to send. Whoever Aaron had in mind, he had to look like a credible threat in Jerry Dirk's eyes.

Mukesh finished the morning prep duties and settled into his next task, counting shelf inventory. On Mondays, he

The Hacker and The Hillbilly

adjusted the amount of sushi rolls he replenished for the week based on what was leftover from weekend sales.

The old Japanese man complimented Mukesh on his work. He was halfway finished wiping off the stainless steel and sliding glass doors when Kim came to him with another task: two party platters. She brought a special book out of her office and placed it before Mukesh to the side of the rolling station.

"We need two of these." She pointed at a picture of a round sushi tray. The size of the sushi platters was sixteen inches in diameter, with a large inner portion of the decorative wheel reserved for the finer pieces, which Sugami would make. "Easiest way to do this is for you to prepare the rolls while my father is plating his sliced sushi. My father will place his gourmet sushi in the center, and you will have your sushi rolls ready and cut up to place on the platter after he is finished. I think you can do it by looking at picture. If you have problems, ask father."

"I think I got it," said Mukesh. He smiled at Kim and her confidence in his work. Out of everything Mukesh had done in his life, he was most proud of his new job rolling sushi. Mukesh glanced at the pleasant old man slicing fish at his station and smiled. The old man smiled back. Mukesh had all of the rolls prepared before the old man had his sushi ready. While Mukesh waited for the man to finish his art, he wiped the fronts of his workstation.

"What are you doing? You have to cut up the sushi rolls," Kim said to Mukesh as she walked by.

"I will cut them and place them when your father is done with his duties so I don't have to handle them twice."

"Oh," said Kim.

196

"Here, I am ready," the old man said. Mukesh put down his dishrag. He washed his hands and put on some new gloves and took the two trays from the old Japanese man. He cut up the rolls and placed all the pieces directly in the concentric circle patterns that corresponded with the chart. He garnished the trays with some Oriental lettuce and wasabi dabs. Instead of placing all the soy sauce packets in a pile, Mukesh decorated them in lines to separate the different types of sushi. Lastly, Mukesh assembled four neat piles of folded ginger slices on the four corners of the sushi wheel. Mukesh looked at the glossy training photo to see how he did. He had smeared a small dab of wasabi paste on the laminated training picture and fetched his rag and wiped it off. Sugami saw Mukesh going into the walk-in with the finished tray and went over to see his work. Mukesh lowered the tray in front of the Japanese man. The old man smiled at Mukesh and nodded quickly. "Very good!" he exclaimed.

"Thank you." Mukesh smiled at the old man, put the finished tray in the walk-in cooler, and went back to plate the second tray. He finished it exactly as the first and walked to the back office after washing his hands to tell Kim he was done."

"I figured you would be fast." Kim smiled at Mukesh. He looked down and bowed humbly. "Let's go see. I'm sure you did fine." She followed Mukesh to his workstation where the second tray lay. "Oh, you only did one?"

"No. The other one is in the walk-in refrigerator."

"If it looks like this one, everything fine. You can take that to the walk-in with the other one," said Kim with a smile. "You do great job. I do not need to see other tray." Mukesh hoped

The Hacker and The Hillbilly

Kim was a good enough boss to give him a raise after ninety days and he wouldn't have to ask.

Mukesh wiped down the workstation and tackled the monthly chore of taking everything out of the fridges to clean the insides. His big chore that day was to run all the metal grate fridge shelving through the dishwasher. Mukesh wrapped up his day with the dishes and departed Food City for the motel.

Instead of going straight home, Mukesh decided to go on a drive in the mountains that evening. It had been a long time since he'd hiked the first trail where he stumbled upon the spot of the Mason UFO crash and missing shack. Mukesh gathered up his nerves and decided to walk that path again. He parked his car at the top of the mountaintop and made a beeline along the ridge. All of the old crisscrossing vehicle trails were blocked by chains, and he was still too nervous to go down to check them out on foot.

Mukesh approached the section with the bare spot and its ring of sparse growth surrounding the center of the suspected crash site. He surveyed the spot and the other side of the holler where the shack once stood. He saw several small impressions of sections that looked like footers. Other than that, the former shack space was nothing but a flattened section of saplings and weeds. Mukesh recalled Aaron's tale and noticed how unusual it was that even the foundation of the old shack had been removed.

Before he got back into his Prius to ride back to the motel, Mukesh texted Aaron, "Call me after your friend leaves."

"Someone else is taking Todd to the gas station tonight. I need to watch the evening news, and tonight Jen has her TikTok live-stream," Aaron texted back.

Mukesh put his phone in his pocket and laughed. He looked over the holler again. From the tallest viewpoint, Mukesh could see an eerie grid pattern carved along the ground from all of the vehicle paths. He shook off his anxious energy and cleared his head of worries about his future and the psychic visions he'd been having and headed back to the motel.

It was dusk when Mukesh pulled in. He walked to his room and flicked on the lights. He turned on his computer and opened the Bling church footage. Mukesh configured it so the foyer, parking lot, hall entrance, and church conference room were in view in four equal sections. He toggled on the option to notify him of any movements in the cameras to let him know once the church meeting was underway. He minimized the app and watched YouTube videos until the app chirped at him a motion detection. Halfway through the latest episode of Darknet Diaries, the Bling system notified him of movement. Mukesh zoomed in on the two parking vehicles that triggered it. Just then, Mukesh received a text from Aaron, who of course was watching the same thing.

"Want to come over and watch the evening news with me?" he asked.

Thinking it wiser to watch the footage without his neighbor's commentary, Mukesh politely declined. "I don't want to watch any news. I will come over after I am done with this YouTube documentary."

A man walked to the church with two other people holding pizza boxes. Mukesh recognized one of the three as co-pastor George, who unlocked and held the door for the other two. They walked down the hallway and into the kitchen adjacent to the conference room, all the while chatting about NASCAR. The

The Hacker and The Hillbilly

two men spread five pizza boxes out on the counter of the serving area joining the kitchen and conference room. The head pastor placed some disposable plates and napkins at the front of the line. He opened up the first box full of garlic knots and took two for himself. He dipped one into one of two containers of marinara sauce, bit off half of the knot, then dropped the half-eaten part on his plate and dribbled marinara sauce on top from one of the plastic ramekins. The three engaged in small talk about fishing while they ate.

"I'll go get the TV and bring it in here for when everyone arrives," one of the men said. He came into the room five minutes later, rolling in a monitor and a computer on a portable cart. He plugged in the power strip for the cart and toyed with the remote control. He cued the footage to the beginning of the foyer altercation and paused it to turn off the monitor so there was no paused screen thumbnail. Tom and the head pastor and two other men trickled into the room and seated themselves.

"You men get some pizza," said George as the men entered the meeting room, waving toward the serving station. "It's Sal's. Only the best for us elders now after Eileen's death." Mukesh rolled his eyes, glad he wasn't watching with Aaron and Jen. They would be commenting and laughing at everything. After more small talk and a lot more munching on pizza, George stood up. He was the only one besides Tom who had seen the complete footage of Jerry and Mukesh.

The co-pastor outstretched his hands. Everyone chewed with closed mouths as the head pastor said, "We should pray." They swallowed and closed their eyes. Most bowed their heads.

"As we are gathered here today in your name O Lord in fellowship and understanding we beseech you to have mercy on us and guide us all in wisdom and love and compassion as we humbly assemble to discuss your will in this great house. We pray that you guide this blessed and highly favored church and congregation and lead us to continue to love and forgive and guide the community with compassion, understanding and wisdom as we preach to them of your great works. Thank you dear Lord for the unexpected donation bequeathed to our church by a wayward local woman and God forgive her for her transgressions. Please guide the CCP to spend her donation wisely among the leaders of the Mason, Tennessee community. Amen."

As the head pastor finished his blessing, the crowd echoed, "Amen."

"Amen," Deacon Bill added, "and thank you, Lord, for our dearly departed friend Eileen Baker and all of her dirty money. Thank you for choosing us, oh Lord, to help clean it up." He raised and toasted a sagging slice of pepperoni and sausage.

"We celebrate her donation with some of the best pizza in town, Sal's!" bellowed Elder Ennis with a dramatic church vibrato. Enough people chuckled at the pair's insensitive jokes that the head pastor decided not to openly admonish them but instead rolled his eyes.

George took Tom's silence as a sign to begin his speech. "As you all are aware, after Sunday's email, we had an altercation during the second service where security volunteer Jerry Dirk put his hands on someone that tried to enter the CCP. The duties of our church security are not something that can be taken lightly. Tom and I have already viewed the footage and have mixed thoughts, but just in case something like this ever happens again, we are gathered here today to discuss how to approach the next situation if one arises." Without saying anything else, he turned on the monitor and started the foyer footage. The men watched intently.

When it was over, the head pastor said, "Let's watch it again."

"Pastor, d-did you s-s-see how—" Elder Larry stuttered.

The head pastor interrupted. "Let's watch it together one more time and take everything in again before we comment."

"Yes s-s-sir," Larry said. They all watched one more time, and George paused it on Jerry standing, arms folded in front of the double doors as Mukesh turned to retreat."

"I think I've seen that Indian guy in the trench coat somewhere," said Elder Paul, the oldest elder. Everyone ignored him.

"I have my thoughts, but I'd like to talk to all of you to see what you think before I make up my mind about this," said the head pastor.

"I don't think he should have laid a hand on that feller," said Elder Jimmy.

"Neither do I," said Elder Cliff.

"Our security volunteers are a crucial part of modern-day church greeters. Just about all churches have some form of them now," George said. "What do you think about it, Mark? Any thoughts, Tom?"

Mark was the youth minister and one of the more respected men of the church. "I don't want to say anything about it one way or the other. It's true that some churches have been attacked recently, so we have to be on guard. It is only by God's grace that some of these massacres have been stopped. I hope we don't get to the point where all church bouncers need guns."

"Let's not get into that mess, Mark. There will never be guns in our church," the head pastor told everyone.

"I don't want that either, but it's a fact that a couple of tragedies have been stopped by armed men in houses of worship," Elder Cliff said confidently.

Tom decided it was time to give his thoughts, which he'd stressed to the co-pastor the first time he reviewed the altercation. "I'm in the air about it. The way the Muslim man talked about Allah like he didn't know he was in a Christian church was suspicious, or at least that gives us good evidence he was crazy. But Jerry did grab him too fast, just as soon as the man got within his reach."

"I don't think that guy's Middle Eastern. I think I've seen him somewhere working in a convenience store," said Elder Paul again.

The head pastor looked around the room and thought it was a good time to close up. "The guy had dark glasses on and looked kind of menacing. That, with the trench coat, made me suspicious. Sure, Jerry grabbed the man too quickly, but he did look like he was going to step around Jerry to get into the church when Jerry blocked the sanctuary doors. I think it's fifty-fifty on whether Jerry was right to handle things the way he did."

The co-pastor tried to hurry the meeting along. "What are we going to do if this ever happens again?"

Tom stood up, got another large piece of pizza, and halved it with Elder Cliff.

The Hacker and The Hillbilly

"Well, we could fault Jerry or we could praise him for what he did, based on the footage. But by that, we won't have any judgment either way. We all know Jerry has the heart of a good Christian and is a leader in the community. Here are my proposed rules of engagement for any people who we don't know that enter the building in an unusual manner." The head pastor paused and looked around the room to make sure everyone was listening. "Rule number one is spoken engagement. The greeter must always speak to any person they don't recognize to assess their mental state or intentions. Rule number two is no physical engagement unless you think the person is a threat and the perceived attacker enters your personal space. For cases where the intruder puts up a struggle or acts aggressively, all of our church security will be taught nonviolent submission techniques at Deacon Mitch's MMA classes. That way, if there's ever another misunderstanding, no one will get hurt."

"Maybe this is a good time to review our policy about guns in the church," Mark added.

"There will be no guns in this church," said the head pastor forcefully.

"Well, that don't include off-duty policemen, does it?" Elder Cliff asked.

"Of course not. Off-duty law enforcement can wear a sidearm wherever they are, even a concealed one, wherever they want." He looked around the room to get a feel for who agreed about the no gun policy. "This doesn't leave this room, and I don't care what people think," the pastor glanced over at the Elders to discern their reactions. "Unless something changes and church attacks become more than just one sensational story a year, maybe then I might allow volunteers with guns. For now, our church security greeters are not to carry guns. Does anyone disagree with that or have anything more to add?" The head pastor looked around the room.

All seemed to nod, then Elder Jimmy asked, "We ain't going to say nothing to Jerry? I think he was a little hasty with that feller."

"I swear, I think that Indian guy in the trench coat works at Checkers," added the geriatric Elder Paul. The head pastor glanced at him, nodded and smiled, and continued on.

"No," said the pastor. "We won't congratulate him, but we also won't condemn him. We aren't going to say anything to him at all. Since we elders all agree on the rules of engagement, if any of the volunteers don't like them, they can walk around with collection plates in the sanctuary instead." The pastor stood sharply to signal the meeting was over. Everyone shuffled slowly out of their seats.

"I'd like to take a piece of sausage and pepperoni home, and also a slice of deluxe for the missus," said Elder Charles.

The pastor nodded his assent and walked over to the kitchen section to do the same. He got another garlic knot, dipped it into some sauce, bit down, and swallowed. "As for these garlic knots, they are really only great when they are fresh. He put a piece of pepperoni pizza in one of the empty pizza boxes and walked out the door. The other men followed, all with leftover pizza in hand.

Co-pastor George stayed behind to straighten the chairs and wipe off the table and kitchen counter. He watched the elders leave happily now that the new security orders were in place. Mukesh was happy, too, to finally know enough details for him and Aaron to put their plan into action.

Chapter 22

Mukesh closed the Bling application and powered off his laptop. He paced around the room a few times and pulled out his phone and texted Aaron. "Are you free?"

"Come on over, friend :-)" was his reply. Mukesh walked over and knocked. Aaron opened the door and peeked out before shutting and locking it behind Mukesh.

"Todd might be over here in a while, but I couldn't wait to talk to you. Before I tell you about my idea, let's talk about that meeting."

"Good thing you weren't here," Jen said with a laugh. "Aaron talked the whole time." Mukesh suspected as much and held back his grin.

"Shut up, woman," said Aaron playfully.

Jen was going to rewind and watch it again, but Mukesh said, "No need to replay it. It wasn't that complicated, and I'd rather talk about it before Todd comes. What do you all think about it?"

Jen swiveled her chair around and faced the two men.

"Well," Aaron began, "first of all, this is entirely too much fun. This is like fishing with dynamite." Aaron chuckled harder. "We know exactly how they are going to treat the next security situation. I already have so many ideas."

"I am glad you are having ideas. I have done most of my part. Picking the right person to send into the CCP is on you. I am sure you will come up with the right person," said Mukesh.

"Of course, we need someone who is less threatening than a foreign guy in a trench coat if we can. He has a scuffle with

The Hacker and The Hillbilly

the church bouncer, and we make a big civil case out of it. If we can prove excessive force was used by Jerry, depending on the type of injury, we could make many more times what we did at the food pantry. I know a person who would be perfect for this, but I need to think about it some more. He is my older brother, and I don't want him to be severely injured."

Mukesh was taken aback. To get a good sum for all of their trouble, the person going in the church would have to get at least a sprained wrist and maybe thrown around some. "Your brother?" Mukesh asked him.

"Yes. I know I don't talk about my family often. I'm like that with anyone. Since my father died, I have power of attorney over my older brother, who gets a disability check. If the preacher said he'd allow the church bouncers to carry guns, I wouldn't want to send Nate in there. My brother's real tough. His dream is to own a house in the country by a pond or stream, and to get a truck with a trailer and a nice fishing boat. Both of us have been roughed up pretty bad before, so Nate can take a good beating. All I have to do is tell him if he lets someone beat him up some, he'll get his house, truck, and boat in the mountains. I know he'll be excited about doing it for us if we help him achieve his dream."

"Are you sure he can pull it off, being disabled like he is?" Mukesh asked Aaron, noting the power of attorney Aaron had over his older brother.

Aaron rolled his eyes and smirked, "He's not disabled. He has autism. He might not be the brightest of guys, but he's just different is all. He has a hard time doing day-to-day things like paying bills, and he doesn't like large crowds or loud noises. He gets anxious a lot, and his emotions can sometimes be all over the place. He's a nice guy for the most part, but he's difficult to deal with. He talks in monotone and inflects his voice like he's not smart, but I blame that more on him being in the special needs classes with the Down Syndrome kids when he was in grade school."

"I don't know much about autism. Go on."

"He's quirky, a loner who's a little aloof, but he's a gentle, kind man. He's no threat, but to our bouncer boy Jerry Dirk, he will certainly seem odd and menacing by how he looks, moves, and talks."

"What is his name?"

"Nathan. We call him Nate."

"As long as your brother doesn't mind getting injured, that sounds like a great idea. He's your brother, so I know we won't have to worry about trust issues," conceded Mukesh. Jen sat on her chair, listening intently.

"Nate won't say anything. My brother would sell both his kidneys to get his little house and boat. We'll get him his dream home and supplement his disability money, and he'll be in heaven. All he'll need to do is hurt an arm or leg or take a good ass-whooping. We take care of all of Nate's needs, and we get the rest."

Mukesh was confused because they had never talked about how they were going to split the money. "What are you talking about?" Mukesh asked politely about a split.

Aaron could sense what Mukesh was getting at, so he clarified: "this time, unlike with Todd, my brother will get, I guess, roughly a quarter stake in some kind of trust after we buy his house, and you and I split the rest. Of course, Jen's cut will come out of my share. I respect the fact that you purchased

The Hacker and The Hillbilly

the Bling cam footage on your blind hunch. Plus, I'm Nate's power of attorney. Any sum he gets will go through me, and no one will know what I do with it if I don't want them to. Nate gets taken care of for the rest of his life, and we split the rest."

"Ok, that's a deal," said Mukesh. They shook hands.

"I've never treated my brother badly or done him wrong with his money. I pay his bills, and he gets the rest, which right now ain't much. I'm glad he's working now with a couple of guys as a laborer. If not, he wouldn't be able to make it on his disability check. At least Nate's smart enough to work as a construction helper, and he's very strong for his size. He'll be able to follow all of our directions, and he's sure to keep his mouth shut about our true plans."

"We should plan for this to happen a month from now if this is what we are going with. We have to make sure the footage of my scuffle with Jerry is out of the CCP's minds and also out of the thirty-day Bling cam rotation."

Jen had been quiet for too long. She lifted her head from her phone and spoke up. "Can you imagine the loads of money we can get from a lawsuit like this? If we can get Jerry to hurt Nate, he would be harming a disabled person. Depending on how badly your brother gets injured and if Jerry clearly had no reason to lay his hands on him, this could mean half a million, maybe more." Jen glanced at Aaron, who was sensitive about his brother. Aaron gave her a look. "I mean, not disabled but autistic, Aaron. But get real, now. What's the meaning of the word disabled? Your brother wouldn't be able to make it without you or someone else's help. That's the definition of disabled." Aaron smirked at Jen's smart-ass comment and kept silent.

"Alright!" exclaimed Mukesh. "So far so good. I'm sure we will hear more about the CCP's plans after their Wednesday church meeting."

"One more thing," Aaron said before Mukesh was about to leave, "it's also great that Jerry's brother Robert Dirk is a powerful and corrupt local judge. He and the town will want to keep everything quiet, especially something that embarrasses the Dirk family. We might not even have to go to trial to get exactly what we want, and I hope we get the whole four million. Well, split fairly between us, I mean. Let's try to get it all. We hold all the trumps and can see what cards the Compassion Community Presbyterian is holding and how they will be playing them. Nate goes into the church and Jerry injures him. We play the autism victim card and maybe net a fortune."

"Well, I need to leave before Todd gets here. Is he still coming here every night for a shot?"

"Yes," Aaron said. "He's probably healed up enough by now to do it on his own. He's just milking it for all it's worth. I'll get reimbursed in full for all I've done for him once Todd gets his share." Aaron grinned.

Mukesh stood up and drew a deep breath. "Well, I will see you later. I have to roll sushi tomorrow, and I think I'll go watch some more church footage."

"See you later, neighbor."

Mukesh walked out, and Aaron locked the door behind him.

Mukesh went home and watched part of the second service sermon, where Jerry walked inside after the altercation to get Tom. He rewound and watched his scuffle again with Jerry. His skin pricked as he got to the part where he had felt guided by an outside force. He closed his laptop and switched to his

The Hacker and The Hillbilly

phone to listen to a Let's Read live-stream on YouTube. He laid the phone beside his head and listened to Joel's soothing voice and stories until he fell asleep.

The next morning, after driving back from work, Mukesh nosed around a few computer networks to search for weaknesses and exploits. He skipped his normal drive and short walk in the mountains and fixed a quick sandwich and noodles. While slurping desktop ramen, he got a number of names and phone numbers he could call to figure out how he could breach their networks. After three hours of hacking, he got bored and switched back to watching YouTube. In the middle of the latest Why Files video, he got a text from Aaron.

"You can come over now if you want, Mike." Since Mukesh hadn't asked Aaron if he could come over, he was sure Aaron had some news.

He texted back: "In a few minutes I will." He finished the latest Why Files video about the Anunnaki and walked over to his friend's place.

Mukesh let himself in and locked the door behind him.

"Hi, Mukesh," Jen smiled at him before he sat down.

"I think she likes you," said Aaron, grinning.

"Shut up, Aaron," Jen barked back playfully.

"Yeah, you should have seen earlier how much fun she was having watching a guy mow his lawn while his wife pruned from one of those hacks you gave her."

Jen shot Aaron another look.

"You know, you probably could get better Bling cam hacks than that if you wanted on the dark web. I know how much you like to watch," Mukesh joked to Jen.

She beamed at him. "I'd love that, Mike!"

Aaron looked at Mukesh sternly as Jen turned her back and shook his head from side to side—a silent, "No." Mukesh chuckled and asked, "Anything new at the church?"

"We've been through everything we can, some things twice. Jen is keeping an eye out for movement, but other than George going in to get a couple of books from the office, we've seen nothing interesting this week." Mukesh wondered if Aaron had something important to tell him or wanted him over just for company.

Aaron saw Mukesh's puzzlement. "Todd just left. Tomorrow, I'll have the first of what you'll get from the food pantry payment, twenty thousand dollars. I hope you understand that in order for you to get all the money in cash and to make sure it's laundered, we have to sift it through my buddy's construction company. For that, it's going to cost us a few thousand dollars."

"That's fine, I guess. How much exactly?"

"Six thousand apiece. That's about seven percent. There is really no other way we can get this money from Todd without looking suspicious unless we do it like this through my friend's company."

"I understand. If anyone ever knew Todd gave money to the witness of his fall, we could all get in trouble. Six thousand apiece is an acceptable amount."

"Yeah," said Aaron. "Todd is going to be building a very costly shed, as well as some expensive trailer remodeling. Every month or so for the next six to eight months, we'll get ten to twenty thousand dollars until we get our eighty thou apiece, or with the laundering fee, seventy-four. I will text you tomorrow when I have your money. Just remember one thing.

The Hacker and The Hillbilly

Bring a bookbag or something. No one here ever brings in and leaves a bag or walks out with one they didn't come in here with."

"I understand," said Mukesh. Aaron looked at him then back over at Jen, who swiped through TikTok.

"You know you can watch that on the computer and it's better for your eyes," Mukesh said to her.

Jen smiled, held her index finger up and flexed it a couple of times. "It's not the same." She looked back down at her phone and continued to swipe.

"Not to mention your posture," Mukesh added to the woman in the bathroom foyer, hunched over with her phone in her lap. Jen stayed bent over and grinned.

Mukesh was ready to go back home. He said to Aaron, "Do you have another Xanax? I could use another good night's sleep tonight."

Aaron dug in his drawer and took out a bottle, "No Xanax today, but I have a Klonopin. Four dollars."

"I know. I got one from you before. They are not the same, but it will do."

"Here you go. That will be four dollars." Mukesh leaned to the side in his chair, took out his wallet, and handed Aaron four ones. Mukesh swallowed the pill and stood up.

Jen looked up from her phone and said, "See you later, Mukesh. Thanks again for including me in this Bling cam fun. Don't forget you promised me some spicy hacked accounts."

"You're welcome, my dear," Mukesh said to Jen. Jen was having so much fun, she had no clue how happy he was that she was doing all the work of slogging through surveillance footage. It was the perfect chore for a device-addicted woman on meth.

214

Mukesh went back to his room and fell asleep while listening to serial killer stories on YouTube.

Chapter 23

Mukesh poked around some networks to try to find a few easy admin passwords after he got home from Aaron's. He found a username with a common password, but the account was not an admin. Mukesh took that as a sign and went to bed.

Wednesday morning, he woke up and went to work at Food City. Like always, he saved the dishes for last. He glanced behind him at the digital clock on one of the ovens in the deli and paced himself perfectly for a second day in a row.

He drove straight home after work. The same as the day before, Aaron texted Mukesh first thing as he pulled into the motel. "Want to come over and watch the game?" Mukesh considered watching the church meeting with Jen and Aaron that night but decided against it.

"I will be over afterwards if that is ok. I have a few things I need to do around here," was his reply. It was five-thirty, and the CCP meetings on Wednesdays started at seven. Mukesh browsed the internet for a while until six-thirty, when he opened up the Bling cam app for some early spying. Five minutes after he opened up the program, cars began to pull into the church parking lot. Two women got out of their vehicles, met on the sidewalk, and walked together into the church. One of them took out a key and opened the church door. Mukesh activated the audio for the foyer. They were gossiping about someone in the church who had cancer and was going for an operation that week. Their conversation moved into the conference room, where it continued well after the pair took their seats in the cubicles.

More cars and church leaders trickled in, but there was no sign of Jerry Dirk or any of the other volunteer church security. Mukesh switched to snooping in on the meeting hall while everyone filed into the room. Mukesh turned up the audio and listened intently. First, the members talked about what projects they had in mind for Eileen Baker's four million. They discussed CCP church renovations and the construction projects planned for the orphanage in Honduras, for which they had apparently increased their donation amount to one million dollars.

At seven-thirty, more vehicles pulled in. Jerry Dirk arrived in his Chevy Avalanche along with the other church bouncers. They made their way into the building and sat patiently outside the fellowship hall while the main Wednesday church meeting took place. Tom looked at his watch and wrapped the meeting up, dismissing most of them. The volunteer bouncers, mostly tall guys with big biceps and chests and fat bellies to match, waddled into the room and crushed into their adjustable rolly chairs.

"Gentlemen, it is good you are all here for this meeting," the co-pastor said to the six volunteer bouncers before him. "We had an issue in the church foyer, and we have to address some new policies with you. Last week, as you may have heard, a suspicious-looking foreign man came into our church." George paused to discern the volunteers' reactions. He summarized the altercation as carefully as possible, trying his best to neither chide nor validate Jerry's actions and to only stress the new security policies.

The Hacker and The Hillbilly

George gave the meeting over to Tom, who was tasked to explain the new procedures to the men. He stood up and eyed the six of them intently before speaking. "If someone approaches in a suspicious manner, or walks up to you aggressively, you are to always speak to them first to get a reaction and gauge their intentions. You will not lay your hands on anyone unless they are a clear threat. If you are approached by someone that you deem to be a threat, you may not put hands on them until they clearly invade your personal space, that is, unless they have a weapon, in which case you can engage them from any distance."

Jerry was the first to speak up. "What do you mean, 'if they have a weapon?' Am I supposed to disarm a guy with a gun or a knife with just my bare hands? What about the Charleston church shooting or the West Freeway Church incident in Texas, where the shooter was stopped by a member of their volunteer security?"

"Yeah!" another bouncer said.

The head pastor interrupted, "As far as the official policy goes for our volunteer security greeters here at Community Compassion Presbyterian, no one in this church is to be armed unless they are off-duty policemen. You are allowed to carry a folding pocket knife if you want, but that's it."

A few of the men looked like they were ready to open their mouths to protest, so the head pastor loudly added, "No exceptions!"

"But with the increased threats to churches today, we could use a couple of armed men in here," whined one bouncer by the name of Stan. His point was valid, but the head pastor knew of two skilled men in the church who conceal-carry at all times.

They were the real security. The fat men up front were just for show, though the elders kept that knowledge to themselves. "There will be no armed men in church!" he stressed. "Everyone will get a voucher for Mitch's Gym and MMA where each of you will be taught non-lethal submission techniques to apply if there is an emergency. All church volunteers will be expected to get their certifications within two months."

A couple of bouncers grumbled and rolled their eyes.

Tom glared at them and added amidst their groans, "You won't have to pay for the courses. Deacon Mitch will be providing them as part of his tithe."

The head pastor noticed most of the men looking down into their laps like they were not happy with the new policy. "We will be praying that nothing too serious ever happens here at the CCP, but absolutely no one here better bring a gun into church. No exceptions. Do you hear me?"

Everyone except Jerry Dirk answered, "Yes, pastor."

The pastor noticed Jerry's pensiveness and glared at him. "Is that clear, Jerry?"

"Yes, pastor," he answered, keeping his eyes on the table, confused as to why he wasn't praised for his actions a few days prior.

"Well, men... I'm sure you are ready to go home back to your wives," George joked. A couple of men chuckled politely, and all of them stood up and huddled off to the side to decide among themselves their schedule for bouncer duties next month. Everyone agreed on the usual schedule and began to exit the building. After tidying up a couple of pieces of paper left on the table, George got a Pepsi from the CCP fridge. He locked up, the last to leave.

The Hacker and The Hillbilly

Mukesh smiled, reveling in the Bling cam hack. He smiled wider when a warm, comforting feeling fell over him, which he attributed to his visions. But before he could experience anything truly supernatural, a notification pinged from his phone.

"Come over," Aaron texted.

"K," Mukesh messaged back. He walked out, locking his motel room door.

Aaron had already unlocked his. Mukesh entered and found Aaron reclined on two large pillows at the head of the bed, like always, and Jen was rewatching part of a foyer conversation. She paused the security footage and turned to greet him.

"Hello, Mike," she said.

"Hi, Jen." He turned to Aaron, who stared at Jen. "Hi, Aaron."

"What do you know?" was all his friend asked.

Mukesh was familiar with that colloquialism, but answered literally regardless. "I know Community Compassion Presbyterian is going to lose a lot of money in a few weeks." Jen and Aaron chuckled. "Soon we are all going to be very rich."

"Potentially," corrected Aaron, who glanced sideways over at Mukesh to make sure he knew not to jinx things by being cocky. "You need to take me more seriously when I say not to be over-optimistic about our plans. When you are cocky, you're not on the lookout for problems that arise, and you are less prepared for them when they pop up. Do you understand what I'm talking about?"

Mukesh conceded to Aaron, though he felt that his supernatural confidence was more of a broad optimism and had little to do with being cocky.

Aaron continued to stare at Jen, deep in thought. He turned to Mukesh. "I've made up my mind. Let's do it. Since none of the volunteers will be armed, I feel comfortable going forward with the plan to bring in Nate. No amount of money is worth my brother getting shot. I brought the idea up with him yesterday. I warned him he might get beat up or maybe break a bone, but he's fine with that. I told him about the house and boat he will get if he helps, and he's excited. He's a good guy and deserves to be happy. We both had a rough time growing up. Our father never paid Nate much attention because he was different and not very smart." Aaron chuckled once to himself and looked at Mukesh. "I think everything will work out. Just don't get cocky, is all I am asking. It always ruins my plans, and you and I are partners in this."

"I will try not to be cocky, Aaron. I like your idea. So the plan is to send your brother into Community Compassion Presbyterian to get roughed up by Jerry Dirk? We need to think of a good excuse why your brother will be in such a hurry to go in. Maybe… like he thought it was another church and he left something in there?" Mukesh trailed off in thought.

"Yeah, something like that," said Aaron.

Jen faced away from the men and toward her computer with her legs spread and hands clasped in front, elbows on her knees.

"We'll think of something," Aaron continued. "My brother is perfect for this. Let me rephrase that. My brother is the right man for this scam. I'll tell him, when he walks in, I want him to

The Hacker and The Hillbilly

look extra googly-eyed, and we'll also get him to wear a trench coat."

Mukesh perked up in his chair with an idea, "Let's use the same one that I wore, Aaron!"

"Why would we do that? That ties the coat to you. We don't want them looking back at the footage to see you and my brother wore the same jacket."

"They don't know who I am in this town, and why would they think it's the same jacket? I say your brother got the jacket from Goodwill after I donated it."

"Fuck Goodwill," interrupted Jen. "Ten dollars for a pair of used jeans, which half have broken zippers! Twenty dollars for a dirty pair of stained tennis shoes? Then they ask you to round up every time for one of their charities! They have fooled everyone into thinking that they are a charity organization because of their name, but in reality they are a for-profit corporation. The last pair of shoes I bought there, the soles began to peel off after only two weeks. Goodwill takes advantage of the poor and hides behind their deceitful name. The Salvation Army or the YMCA Thrift Store are the only places to shop. Fuck Goodwill!"

Aaron looked at his girlfriend, shocked by her tirade, but since she was one hundred percent accurate about how awful Goodwill was, he let her have her two cents.

"Salvation Army then," Mukesh grinned, corrected. "I think Jerry, being the unintelligent brute that he is, will be triggered subconsciously by the same jacket I wore."

"That's a good point. Anything that will add to Jerry's triggering," said Aaron, staring pensively, this time more at the ceiling than at Jen. Abruptly, he shifted his legs over the side of the bed. "So that's the plan. When did you say the Bling cam footage gets archived?"

"Monthly."

"Alright. We'll discuss it further and should have a solid and detailed plan by then. You can give me a ride one day, and we'll both talk to my brother. You'll like him. He is a decent guy, just awkward."

"Sure," said Mukesh. "This Sunday I have off. We can do it then if you want."

"Might as well. Then you can get a feel for how he is, and that might help you come up with some ideas."

"Alright. Sounds like a plan."

"You are sounding more American every day. You definitely have some good language skills."

"Thank you, Aaron. You are pretty smart yourself, for a redneck."

"Hey now," Aaron replied playfully, "see these mountains around you? I am more of a hillbilly than a redneck, but I'm a redneck as well, so oh well."

Mukesh smiled at Aaron.

Aaron smiled back.

Chapter 24

Sunday came. No work, so Mukesh slept in. He woke up at ten o'clock, matching Aaron's morning schedule, so he texted him before breakfast, "Still want me to take you to your brother's later?"

Within ten minutes, Aaron texted him back, "Sure. Let me call him, and we'll go sometime after twelve."

"K."

"K? lol."

"You know I really mean Ok. Lol."

Mukesh showered and put on comfortable slacks and a light sweater. He flipped his laptop open and peeked into the real-time church cams. It was between services at ten forty-five. Mukesh activated the foyer audio and watched one stream of church members file in while another shook the head pastor's hand as they exited. Plastic smiles showed on every face going in and out. Their shallow banter was too much for Mukesh. He thought of how much he appreciated Jen's help as he logged out of the Bling cam app and crawled around on YouTube for a while instead.

At eleven-forty-five, Aaron texted Mukesh, "You can come over now. I told my brother we'd be over around twelve thirty." Mukesh locked his motel room and went to Aaron's.

Jen was devouring a bowl of cereal while watching the second service file out. She leaned into her laptop screen, as if that could help her pick out individual conversations better through the CCP foyer's banter and bustle.

Mukesh couldn't help but laugh watching her watch the footage. She was deep in her task. He sat down in the chair pointing at Aaron's bed instead and stared. Aaron reclined on his bed, quietly.

Finally, Mukesh asked, "What are you thinking of?"

"Oh, nothing. Just going over the plan in my head and trying to come up with more ideas."

"That's how I do it, too." Mukesh wondered why he hadn't had a full-blown vision in a while. Being under pressure or in a sense of urgency seemed to bring them on.

Aaron stared at the ceiling. He reclined on his bed with his hands fanned behind his head. Without warning, his arms jerked to his sides; his whole body braced, and he leaned upright. He squared off with Mukesh sitting in the upholstered chair in front of him. "Come on," Aaron said. "Let's go meet my brother. Jen!" Aaron called out loudly.

Jen pulled a headphone off one ear and asked, "What?"

"Mike and I are going over to Nate's."

"Ok, babes. Tell him I said hello." She smiled at him and slipped the headphone back on and delved back into the live feed. Aaron waited for Mukesh to leave the room first and closed the door behind them. They walked to the opposite side of the parking lot and got in the Prius.

"Take a left out of the parking lot." Aaron guided Mukesh on the ten-minute drive to Nate's apartment above an old, abandoned office building in a dead business area downtown. "Park behind the building in one of the spots on the left. I know it says no parking, but the sign is there for those in the know to park here as long as they don't abuse it." Mukesh parked in the furthest spot in front of a large section of painted brick.

The Hacker and The Hillbilly

They both got out. Mukesh followed Aaron into a side alley that led to Main Street. "Nate doesn't let strangers go in the back entrance of his apartment, so we'll have to go in front today. Nate's strange about a lot of things. I don't understand why he thinks or does half the things he does most of the time, but he's a solid dude with a good heart. It's not like he can't socialize with people. He's just different and doesn't like to be around crowds. I think you'll like him."

"If it's all about being a social hermit, you and I both check the autism box, Aaron."

"No," Aaron said, staring at Mukesh. "There's lots of other things with him. You'll see."

They walked upstairs to a glossy door at the end of an off-white hallway. Aaron knocked. Nate opened up and poked his face out of the crack at Aaron and Mukesh. He flashed a radiant smile at his younger brother and quickly opened the door, pulled Aaron into his chest, and hugged him.

Nate sported a goofy-looking bowl cut, and his hair was blonde where Aaron's was brown. He was shorter than his younger brother—Mukesh guessed maybe five foot nine—and had a heartier than average build, slightly overweight. His clothes were unkempt and stained.

Nate looked at Mukesh and grinned. "Hi!"

"How are you?" Mukesh held out his hand. "My name is Mukesh."

"Mine is Nate-Nate," Nate stuttered nervously at the stranger. He stood stiff as a freezer in the doorway, his arms to his sides, staring nervously into a corner of the door frame.

"May we come in, Nate?" asked Aaron.

"Yeah…" Nate looked Mukesh over once again and swung his apartment door open and backed in. His place was messy, not filthy as in food trash, but papers and other household items were scattered around haphazardly. Clothes were strewn along the tops of the furniture as well.

Aaron pulled a joint out of his front shirt pocket and offered it to Nate. "Want to smoke? I got the sticky-icky!"

"Yeah…" Nate droned, hanging his head and nodding. Aaron looked back at his brother with a loving grin. Mukesh smiled at the two brothers' banter, which seemed to ease Nate.

They walked into Nate's apartment and through his kitchen to the laundry area at the rear. Aaron lit a nice cherry at the tip of the joint. He puffed on it gently, inhaling a few times in quick succession. It was the first time Mukesh had ever seen Aaron smoke a joint, and he rarely smelled marijuana in Aaron's motel room. Nate smiled and hit the joint a couple of times before passing it to Mukesh, who waved it off.

Aaron didn't know Mukesh's habits with the herb and asked him, "You don't smoke?"

"No. I can't say that I'm not curious, though."

"Best medicine ever, with the best side effects. Fuck that Big Pharma antidepressant shit. No true pothead ever took up an AR and shot a bunch of people." Aaron turned away from Mukesh and looked at his brother Nate. "By the way, you stopped taking that Seroquel the doctors prescribed you, right Nate?"

"Yeah…" Nate said, droning out the word longer than normal.

"Good," Aaron rolled his eyes and looked over at Mukesh. "Can you believe they had my brother on a fucking antipsychotic? He almost lost his job from being tired at work. I think some of these doctors over-medicate people so they don't annoy them as much when they see them every month." The brothers passed the joint between them a few more times before Aaron rolled the cherry against the sides of a glass ashtray until it spluttered out.

"I wanted to let you meet my good friend, Mike. Mike and I had the idea that's going to make all that money for your house, and we're happy you want to help." Nate stared at his brother, angling his head slightly down. Mukesh watched the pair and how it seemed Nate's whole countenance changed as his brother talked to him about his house and boat.

"I don't want to get in trouble, Aaron."

"It's nothing that you can get in trouble with this time, Nate. Don't worry about that part. We only need you to walk into a church and do as we say. You won't get hurt too bad, and there is no way you can get in trouble. You do that, you get your house." Nate smiled again when Aaron mentioned his home.

"I don't want to go to jail, Aaron." Nate knew Aaron made his money by breaking the law, and Nate didn't like doing anything illegal.

"I promise, it's nothing you can get in trouble with," Aaron reassured his brother again. Mukesh began to look around the room, bored, and stopped paying attention to the two brothers. Aaron noticed Mike's boredom and began to wrap up the conversation so they could leave. "I'll tell you more about what we need you to do later. Just remember, if you do this for us, it's all you need to do to get that house near the lake and the truck with the boat. You'd love that, right?"

"Yeah…"

"This is a sure thing, brother." Aaron put his hand on Nate's shoulder. Nate shrugged Aaron's hand off, but Aaron pressed on. "You won't be doing anything wrong, I promise. None of us will. We plan to..." Aaron looked up at Mukesh and smiled, "inspire someone less intelligent than us to make all the mistakes." Mukesh nodded at Aaron's description, happy to finish up the meeting with Nate and have his brother fill him in on details later. "Do you think you might want to help?"

Nate looked up sheepishly and said, "Yeah..." again.

Aaron smiled back. "Good. I'll tell you more about it later when Mike and I come up with a solid plan." Aaron reached out and grabbed his brother's hand. "It'll be easy. Of course you might get hurt, but you're my tough older brother, right?"

"I'm your tough older brother," Nate repeated in monotone, grinning. Aaron grinned back.

"That's right," Aaron said, and stepped away from Nate. "I'm gonna leave you this half a joint, and also this..." Aaron pulled out of his pocket a small bag of pot and set it on the table. Nate beamed. "I wanted you to meet my friend Mike today and let you know we're proud of you for wanting to help. Jen is especially proud of you, Nate, and she told me to make sure to tell you hello." Nate smiled harder at the mention of Aaron's girlfriend. "I'll come back in a week or so and we can go over the plan. I promise you, it's nothing that can get you in any trouble." Aaron glanced over at Mukesh. "Can we leave out the back?"

"Yeah..."

"Nice to meet you Nate," Mukesh added before they left.

"Yeah..." Nate repeated.

The Hacker and The Hillbilly

"Goodbye!" the visitors said together as they walked down the rickety rear steps of the downtown apartment building. Nate stood on the back perch of his apartment as the two men made their way down, waving at them the whole time. As the two opened the door to Mukesh's Prius, Aaron looked up and waved at Nate, who was still watching and waving at his brother Aaron. Mukesh looked up and waved as well. Nate waved back extra hard, excited at his new friend's added goodbye.

Aaron and Mukesh sat inside the Prius. Aaron leaned his chair back and stared forward as they drove. Mukesh glanced over at his friend a few times, but unsure of Aaron's mood, stayed silent. After a while, he tried to break the uncomfortable quiet by asking, "Do you need to go anywhere or want to ride around for a bit? The fall leaves are starting to turn and the mountain view is beautiful."

Aaron shifted in his seat. "Yeah, let's go riding around for a bit. It will be nice to look at the fall scenery."

Mukesh stopped at a convenience store to get gas. It was the same Sheetz where Aaron had shown Mukesh the clever self-checkout scam. Aaron stayed in the car while Mukesh pumped gas and went in. When Mukesh got back to the car, he handed Aaron a monster Slim Jim and a Sun Drop.

Aaron burst into laughter. "You're never supposed to pay for a monster Slim Jim, Mike, especially for how much they cost now. And why did you get me a Sun Drop? You know I prefer Mountain Dew!"

Mukesh opened up his own Sun Drop and took a sip. "Yes, but Sun Drop is better than Mountain Dew."

Aaron scowled playfully at Mukesh and smirked. "How would you feel if you told me to go into the store and I bought you a Pepsi instead of a Coca-Cola?"

Mukesh chuckled and said, "I would be furious. But you didn't tell me you wanted anything, and this is a gift."

"Fair enough. I can forgive the Sun Drop, but never buy a Monster Slim Jim ever again. Slip the next one in one of your pant legs, instead."

"Eat your fart-smelling meat stick and shut up," joked Mukesh. The mood in the car lightened noticeably as Mukesh drove, and he hoped Aaron would open up to him about whatever was on his mind. Mukesh guessed it was something about Nate, and tried to get Aaron to open up by saying, "I am glad I met your brother. He seems like a nice guy."

"He is," said Aaron. "He's really going to love his new life if we can pull this off." Aaron shifted in his seat, uneasy.

"Do you think he'll go along with this once you tell him the full details of our plan?"

"Yes, I do. That's kind of my whole issue," Aaron confessed. Mukesh was happy Aaron was finally going to open up about what had been bothering him. "Nate loves me, and he'd do whatever I want him to. I'm really fortunate to have a brother that has such a big heart like him." Mukesh glanced over at Aaron and smiled at him a little too long while driving. He drifted into the grass along the side of the road, dangerously close to the ditch. Rocks kicked up from the passenger-side tires and plinked on the underside of Mukesh's Prius.

"Mike! You gotta be careful on these mountain roads," Aaron shouted. "If you run off the road in the wrong place around here, we're both going over a cliff!"

The Hacker and The Hillbilly

"Sorry, Aaron," Mukesh said with his eyes back on the road.

Aaron looked over at Mukesh and back at the dash. "My brother and I had it rough in a lot of ways. That's why we're both so tough. I'm glad he's the type of person who can defend himself, and I never had to fight too many people for him. He is so good-hearted, too good-hearted. People used to take advantage of him. That's something no one does around here anymore, because several people were..." He paused to come up with the right words. "...adversely affected by that awful decision. Maybe I'm having a time with my conscience right now. Bringing my brother in on something like this isn't like bringing Todd in and breaking one of his bones."

"With a sledgehammer," Mukesh added, this time keeping his eyes firmly in front of him.

Aaron chuckled and echoed, "Yes, with a sledgehammer."

"That was amusing. I have seen some crazy things in India, but that definitely made me cringe." Focused on the road, Mukesh realized he'd drifted somewhere insensitive in the conversation, so he switched topics and offered Aaron some friendly assurance. "Hey, it's not like Nate is going to get hurt too badly."

"I hope not," said Aaron.

Mukesh glanced over at the passenger side and quickly returned his eyes to the road. "I think I would let someone beat me up for a few hundred thousand dollars."

"Oh, I would, too. This is too good of a plan, and my brother has the perfect qualities to not be a threat but look like one to an idiot like Jerry. Then there's the other part, Nate's autism will get him sympathy in court, if we have to go that route."

"I have a good feeling about this. Don't worry about your brother. He'll be fine." Mukesh said with a grin.

Aaron smirked. "Speaking of, did you need to go walking around in the field today?"

"No. Nothing has really changed, and I haven't had another... thing."

Aaron laughed at Mukesh's choice of words. "I'm glad you have a good feeling about this. I hope it all works out. You're damn right, I want some easy money, and I've never really taken advantage of Nate. I take some of his money, 30-50 dollars each month out of his assistance check for having to pay his bills, but nothing more than that. I don't know what it is about autism. He's not good with money. He can't seem to handle any kind of responsibility. I give him one hundred fifty dollars a week from his check after his bills, and he works to make another two. No matter how much I give him or how much he makes, he's always broke at the end of the week. We'll build him a house and get him a truck and a boat by the lake. Those are the top priorities. We have to get my brother what he needs first if we still want to go through with this."

"I agree with you, Aaron. Of course we'll take care of Nate first. Community Compassion Presbyterian has four million dollars to spare, and it would be nice to get one or two from them. I looked up autism the other night on YouTube, and the world is definitely very sensitive about them now."

"I know. When neuro-divergency started trending, I had to tell Nate too many times to quit going around telling everyone he was autistic. He started to think he was special. I had to remind him that some of his autistic ways were annoying, a couple of them infuriating."

The Hacker and The Hillbilly

"Infuriating?"

"Yes. One of them really pisses me off. Nate has a big heart and would do anything for you, but he won't let me ask him for money. It makes me so mad. I've given him hundreds of dollars before when he was in need, but ask to borrow twenty dollars from him and he'll flat-out refuse. But if a stranger asks, he will give it to them. A month or two ago, he really pissed me off. A guy had traded me a nice leather jacket that looked like it might fit Nate. I gave the guy a twenty bag for it and wore the coat to go see him. We hadn't gone out to eat in a while, and I always paid for all the meals when my brother didn't have his job. Nate complimented me on the coat I was wearing. It had to be a three hundred-dollar coat when it was new. After we were done eating I took the jacket off and gave it to Nate. All I asked him to do was to pay for the next meal when he started working again. When the time came and I wanted to go out to eat with him, I reminded him about his promise. He fucking ghosted me. Two days later he still wouldn't answer my calls. I had to get someone to take me by his house to set him straight. Even still, it was, 'I'm sorry, I'm sorry,' but he still never offered to pay for the next meal, and I didn't bring it up because I knew it would be the same old thing. It pisses me off so much how he can be so unselfish in areas, and completely selfish in others. He'll attach no value to money with certain things, and too much value to it in others. If I wasn't around and hadn't set some major examples with a couple of locals, Nate would have two or three townsfolk mooching off of him at all times. I do so much for my brother and he never seems to take notice. But someone else could ask him for some money and he will give it right up."

234

"Your brother really loves you, Aaron. I can see it in how he looks at you."

"I know, Mike. The money issue is only one example of some of his bad behaviors. How he thinks and feels about certain things defies all logic sometimes. But that's autism. I love him, and I'd do anything for him. We had a rough childhood together, I imagine rougher than most, probably a lot rougher than yours."

"It was plenty rough in my family too, maybe in different ways. My father was very traditional and overbearing. I was happy when he moved to America and left me to handle the glassblowing business in India. He never let me pursue any of the types of things I liked to do or was good at. Everyone in the family expected me to fit into the hole my father wanted me to be in. He caused a lot of division in our family, and we have never been close. My father even tried to control all of our personalities. I still think my youngest brother, Mufa, is gay. One thing I'm sure of: he has absolutely no interest in women. He's so anti-gay now from my father's misguidance; when I tried to have a conversation about it after our father died, we got into an argument and he still holds a grudge. Mufa was very effeminate from a young age. My father was always screaming at him, 'Quit acting like a girl! Lower your voice! Stop being such a sissy!' All I did was try to open up a dialogue with Mufa about his tastes to try to help him, and he hates me for it."

Mukesh shook his head. "Even from the grave, my father still controls our family. That's how he was, good at getting his way at all costs. When he knew he couldn't get his way with you, he made it clear he would have no more use for you unless

The Hacker and The Hillbilly

you bowed down to his demands. There was not much genuine love in my family, just a lot of going through the motions."

"I understand that, Mike. I'd never tell you any details," Aaron added, "but my father was somewhat of a psychopath. He died of a drug overdose eight years ago. Best thing that ever happened to my brother, because at the time Nate was living with him, and my father only provided for his basic needs. Every bit of Nate's check, after the bills, my father used on drugs. My mother left him when I turned fourteen, and I have no idea where she is. At least, that's what we all were told. A lot of people still think my father killed her and told everyone that she had left him. He was the type of a man capable of doing something like that."

"That's horrible!" Mukesh said. They were almost back at the motel.

"Of course, that's speculation. I probably shouldn't have told you that, but you're my best friend. It isn't like it's much of a secret in the town of Mason, anyhow. My father was questioned many times and even investigated by the state police."

Mukesh pulled up at Aaron's door. "I'd come in, but I have already had my fill of you today."

Aaron grinned at Mukesh as he got out of the Prius. He turned back around and poked his head inside the car. "Fuck you." They smiled at each other, and Aaron walked inside his room. Mukesh pulled around and parked in front of his unit and went inside himself.

Chapter 25

For three more weeks, Mukesh bided his time before the big scam by rolling sushi, riding around town after work, and hanging out with Aaron and Jen. In two days, the Bling footage with Mukesh would be archived and no longer accessible on the church Bling system. It was time to finalize the plans. Jen continued to monitor the church footage but not as feverishly as before. Mukesh had told her about some darknet sites that could provide content to satisfy her voyeuristic tendencies. She had hooked up with some online friends that had given her a dozen "hacked" Bling accounts, and now she had lots of content.

It was Sunday, and Mukesh wanted to meet up with Aaron to discuss the plan for the upcoming scam. "You want to go on a ride? Maybe get a biscuit?" Mukesh texted.

"You and your biscuits. Sure. When?"

"I am hungry now."

"You are going to have to wait a few minutes. I'm expecting company."

"Ok," thumbed Mukesh.

"K. Lol," Aaron thumbed back. Thirty minutes later Mukesh got the ok to come over. He put on his shoes, got in his Prius, and drove over to Aaron's motel room door.

"I'm outside," Mukesh texted. A couple of minutes later, Aaron walked out and got in Mukesh's car.

"Haven't seen you in a few days," Aaron said. "You still like your job?"

The Hacker and The Hillbilly

"It's peaceful rolling sushi. It's one of those jobs that does not require your whole attention, so I can think, and it's always good when your boss isn't looming over you at all times." He pulled out of the hotel parking and onto the road. It was twelve o'clock, but Bojangles had breakfast all day. They bought a two-for-four sausage and egg and two gravy biscuits and got everything for under ten dollars. To help with the gas, Aaron paid for the food. Mukesh insisted on paying for both of their coffees, which they got later at McDonald's.

"Anything good on church TV today?" Mukesh asked Aaron.

"I don't watch anymore unless Jen has found some drama. Jen still watches everything, and then shares things with me. I don't really care now that we have a plan."

"I don't watch it much anymore either," Mukesh said. "By the way, that's the main reason why I wanted to ride out today. We should do this soon. We need to figure out step by step exactly what we're going to do that day."

"Alright. What are your thoughts?" Aaron asked.

"I will drive him over there—" Mukesh started.

"That's not a good idea. You don't want anyone to see you drop him off at the church," Aaron interrupted.

"I won't be dropping him off right at the front door," Mukesh told Aaron. "I will drop him off a few blocks away. Nate will wear the trench coat that I wore the first time and walk up the same street up to the church entrance that I parked on. We can even have him walk up the same side of the street I did. I'm sure that will trigger Jerry and set him up to be thinking of a conflict."

Aaron looked down at the floor of the Prius and back at Mukesh. "I like the idea of Nate walking to the church along your same path, but it's not necessary for you to give him a ride. I can get him a ride. Or better that he can get his own ride. That way I am in no way connected to him whatsoever and especially not you."

"I was wearing my prescription darkened glasses that day. No one is going to know who I am. Hey, Nate can wear sunglasses too! That will make him look more threatening."

"That's over the top. Nate is going to appear plenty strange to Jerry. Plus, Nate has a funny-looking lazy eye. I'll tell him to walk up to Jerry extra googly-eyed. We don't want the church to remember the confrontation you had with Jerry. They can't know we are all friends."

"I think they will always cover that up, since there was no good reason for Jerry to put his hands on me that day," said Mukesh. "If Nate walking into the church causes another confrontation, they're not going to want to show any evidence of Jerry acting aggressively any time before. I think we're safe."

"That's a good point. So Nate walks into the church. What's he going to say when Jerry addresses Nate as he enters? It won't look suspicious if Nate doesn't answer Jerry or says hi and just tries to walk past him into church."

"I don't know," answered Mukesh. "I'll have to think some more about that. He can't just say, 'I'm going into church.' Then Jerry might just let him in."

"That's one I'll think some more about," said Aaron as he looked out the car window at the mountain view. Mukesh pulled in at the end of the road near the trail where the alleged UFO crash had occurred. "You know, I don't normally like

The Hacker and The Hillbilly

coming over to this holler, but it's been so long," Aaron said. He held his phone up at Mukesh and set it on the dash as they pulled over to park. Mukesh followed and put his own phone on the dash in front of him. They both got out of the Prius and started along the trail. Aaron kept his hands in his pockets as he walked. After about a hundred yards, Aaron took them out and pointed over to the right side of the holler. "That bare spot there is where the UFO crashed, and that spot on the other side of the holler is where the cabin used to be. I don't really know why they let people trespass up here. Maybe it's because everything has been cleaned up and they are trying to dismiss the incident by letting people walk openly on the old crash site."

Mukesh felt a surge of horror and stopped in the middle of the mountain trail. His body froze. Aaron turned around to see what was going on. Mukesh lost control of himself, heaved forward, and fell. His lips parted, beaded with spit, and a scene flashed before his eyes of Nate walking into the church. Jerry spoke, and Nate paused for a second and said, "I have to go in, I am going to explode!" He held his belly with his right hand and reached to unbutton the top of his coat with his left. In a panic, Mukesh lifted his head, free from the trance. He shook in terror and cold sweat, glad his body was again under his control—mostly. He couldn't stop the heaving breaths.

"Mike! What happened?"

"I had another vision! This one gripped me so hard... I could hardly move. I did something... to break from its grasp... and I finally was released."

"I thought these visions gave you a pleasant, confident feeling?"

"I had a couple of uncomfortable ones like this before, remember?" Mukesh asked in answer.

"What did you see?"

"I saw what Nate's going to say in the foyer on that day with Jerry." Aaron nodded for Mukesh to continue. "Nate goes into the church and acts like he needs to go to the bathroom. He clutches his stomach as he unbuttons his trench coat and says, 'I need to go! I am going to explode!' And then he holds his belly like he has to go to the bathroom real bad. Maybe Jerry will get caught up in all the drama and our triggers, and think Nate is some kind of suicide bomber."

Aaron doubled over, laughing. He regained control over himself and stood up. "That's fucking brilliant! So that's how you come up with all of these great ideas, just go into some sort of trance?"

Mukesh stared at Aaron, looking pissed. He was doubled over on the ground in the middle of a mountain trail having a panic attack while Aaron stood over him, laughing. Mukesh got up on one knee and caught his breath. He glanced up and shook his head at Aaron. "Jerk!" he muttered sharply.

"I'm sorry," said Aaron as he backed away and waved his hands. "I had a knee-jerk reaction and laughed. That's such a great idea! Genius! You've convinced me of your strange visions, but please don't tell anyone else, and make sure you don't mutter anything around a television or phone. I'll listen to you and help you out in any way when you have these episodes, but you can never tell anyone about them." Aaron glanced over again at the two sites on opposing sides of the holler and back at his friend on the ground. Mukesh was still kneeling. He braced his hands on either side of himself as if to stand. He looked up at Aaron and then back in front of him down the trailhead.

Aaron extended an arm down and out at Mukesh to help him up. "Come on, Mike. This is good news. These visions are good things. That's the best idea! I'm more confident than ever this is going to work and everything is going to be ok. I can't wait to go back and tell Jen! She's going to bust out laughing as well." Mukesh took Aaron's hand and rose. They turned in the direction of the Prius. Aaron hung back watching Mike walk away.

"I really am sorry, Mike," he said as he began to walk after him. "I can tell that one scared you, but if those visions help you come up with ideas as good as that, think of it as taking one for the team!"

Mukesh smirked and continued to his car. Aaron shut his mouth and quit trying to cheer up his friend. They got inside the Prius.

Mukesh hung his head and looked at Aaron sidelong. "It's ok. I just wish I could understand what's going on. Something about that vision made me feel uneasy. You are right. I probably could have seen some more of what is going to happen if I didn't panic and try to fight it off. The good news is, so far, no matter how any of my episodes have made me feel, things still seem to work out."

Aaron jerked his head up and remembered that both of their phones were still on the dash. He reached over and tapped in front of Mukesh's phone above the steering wheel to remind him to quit talking about stuff.

"Oh," said Mukesh.

"I know it's hard," said Aaron. Both men grabbed their phones off of the dash. Aaron checked his messages. Mukesh put his phone beside his lap. He had calmed down. He glanced again at his phone. "Thank you for helping me up after I fainted, my friend."

"You're welcome," said Aaron. "That's what friends are for." He stared ahead as Mukesh drove back to the motel, grinning, excited to talk to Jen. Mukesh dropped off his friend at his room and drove to the other end of the lot and parked in front of his own.

Chapter 26

For the sake of additional hysteria, Mukesh and Aaron planned the church fraud for Halloween Sunday, October thirty-first, two thousand twenty-one. Mukesh took out his phone on the Friday two nights before the church scam and texted Aaron, "What are you doing?"

"A friend is coming over this evening and will be hanging out here for a while. If you want to come over, the next time will be tomorrow when you get off work."

"I took tomorrow off."

"Ok. Tomorrow around noon, I'm going to visit my brother. You can come if you like," Aaron texted.

Mukesh trusted Aaron's judgment to take care of everything with his brother. "I have some errands to take care of and things to do. When you are back, text me."

"K," texted Aaron.

"Lol. Shut up, Aaron," Mukesh texted back. Mukesh nosed around some networks for vulnerabilities and watched some YouTube videos and went to sleep.

The next day, he did his weekly hotel room cleaning and bought necessities. In the evening, he took a drive and a stroll in the mountains. Just as he was getting a breakfast biscuit at Bojangles after his hike, he got a text from Aaron.

"Come over when you want."

"I'll be over in thirty minutes or so." He drove back to the motel and parked in front of his door. He went inside and ate his gravy biscuit, then dipped his sausage and egg biscuit in the excess gravy. After watching a couple ten-minute videos on YouTube, he closed his laptop and went over to Aaron's.

Jen rolled backwards and turned around in her little computer chair in the bathroom foyer and smiled at Mukesh when he entered the room.

"Hi, Mike," she said. She swiveled in her chair and glanced back and forth at her computer and phone. Mukesh strained his eyes and peered at her monitor from a distance. He jerked his head away from it with a smile when he noticed she had a live Bling cam image of a couple on the couch together watching TV. It was not from the batch of Bling cam hacks Mukesh had purchased. He thought to pry and see what kind of people Jen was hanging out with to get a hack like that but decided to focus on the important task of buttoning up the church plans. As long as she didn't get in any trouble until after the Community Compassion Presbyterian fraud was over, everything should be ok.

Mukesh pulled his usual chair closer to Aaron's bed and pointed it squarely at the man himself before sitting down and folding his arms. They looked at each other. Aaron nodded.

"What's up?" asked Mukesh to break the silence.

"Hard dicks and airplanes," said Aaron. Mukesh had never heard that before and smiled. "I squared everything up with my brother today. He's ready for tomorrow. We are ready tomorrow."

"The main thing is your brother. I don't know him all that well, but are you sure he is going to follow every detail?"

"Yes, Mukesh. What? Do you want me to go over the plan again to let you know I understand it through and through?"

Mukesh grinned. "I guess so."

The Hacker and The Hillbilly

Aaron grinned back. His confidence made Mukesh feel even better about their plans. "The details," Aaron began, "Nate gets a ride a few blocks from the church at eleven. A friend is going to drop him off at your old convenience store. That will give him a nice fifteen minute walk on the way to Community Compassion Presbyterian. I gave Nate twenty dollars to give to said friend for the ride. I told him I'd help him out with some high-speed chicken feed for doing the favor as well, so Nate's ride is set. I gave Nate the trench coat and told him I wanted him to take the approach to the church on the right side of West Street and walk in fifteen or so minutes after eleven during the second service. He's going to walk up to the church on the sidewalk on the right just like you did.

"I told him what to say when he walks into the church, to hold his belly and start to unbutton his coat and to say he was in a hurry because he was going to explode. Nate is even going to hold in a bowel movement and need to pee real bad when he goes in so it will be less of an act. I told him specifically to sidestep the man at the door after saying that and try to go around him in a hurry like anyone would if they really had to go to the bathroom that bad."

Aaron looked in the air for a couple of seconds to make sure he had covered everything. He cocked his head up and spoke after he remembered, "And I told him not to take Jerry out the second he puts his hands on him, but if Jerry puts his hands on him or hits him first it is ok for him to push him away one time. Then I told him to sound really pitiful like, 'Stop! No! I got to go real bad,' or something. I told Nate after he pushes Jerry off of him, he will have to let Jerry rough him up some so he can get his house. I told him he's not gonna get hurt any worse than what our father used to do, so he's fine with it. I'm sure he understands. I said, 'big brother, all you have to do is go take an ass whooping like the real man I know you are, and you will get your house, truck, and boat.' He was like, 'Yeah...'

"Every time I talk about his new house, he gleams. I have a hard time understanding all of his strange ways, and he's going to be a pain in the ass to me sometimes, but he'll live the rest of his life in peace and happiness. And so will we. If he has to get hurt a little bit to live out his dream, so be it. He'll be able to live the rest of his life comfortably in mountain solitude without having to deal with any drama other than his own. That's all he needs to be truly happy, and we don't really need that large of a settlement to give him all that. Of course, he gets what he needs first, and we take the rest. His assistance check should pay for all his bills with more left over once he owns a home and doesn't have to rent. If we have to give him some money here and there, we'll be able to afford it."

"Sounds like a plan," said Mukesh. He stared straight ahead to take in Aaron's thoughts. It occurred to him that there were no solid plans for after Nate's encounter with the church bouncer. "And after that, then what?"

"Then Nate comes and complains to me, and we file a lawsuit." Aaron answered. "I'll file a preservation request to get the church footage a day or two later. That should be all we need to get the suit rolling, unless the encounter is serious and authorities are called in. I'm not going to call the law, but it's possible someone at the church might. I'm not trying to press charges on Jerry and the CCP if I don't have to. He'll get off with the least penalty anyway." Mukesh and Aaron looked

The Hacker and The Hillbilly

sheepishly at each other, scared to show their nervousness and excitement.

Mukesh looked over at Jen facing the computer, watching on her laptop the same couple on the couch leaning into each other, nuzzling. Mukesh placed his forearms on the sides of the chair to get up when he shuddered abruptly and fell back into it. His mind was flooded with the supernatural knowledge that he had to be in Aaron's room the next day to watch the surveillance footage with them, a detail not part of his original plans.

Aaron scrunched his face at Mukesh. "Was that some of that heartburn you've been having lately?" Aaron asked with his head twisted to the side so Mukesh would know it was code.

Mukesh, confused by his vision, said, "No." Exhausted, he positioned his body at the front of his chair intent on trying again to stand. He looked at Aaron with a sudden desperation. "Do you have a Xanax? I want to get right to sleep tonight and wake up tomorrow morning and get this over with."

Aaron grinned and reached into the drawer and fumbled for a bottle in the back. "You're in luck. I have one left." Mukesh stood up and reached into his pocket for his wallet when Aaron stopped him.

"Don't bother," Aaron said. "The night's sleep is on me. Let's hope we pull this off tomorrow."

Mukesh smiled at Aaron, swallowed the Xanax, and made his way out of the door.

Chapter 27

The morning of the caper, Mukesh showered, dressed, and opened up his laptop. It was nine-fifteen, and the first service had already started at Community Compassion Presbyterian. Mukesh texted Aaron: "I was thinking of going to get a biscuit and join you and Jen in your worship service this morning. Do you want anything?"

"I'll take a gravy biscuit and a sausage biscuit, sausage and egg if you want one as well and we can split the two-for-four deal."

"Want any coffee?" Mukesh texted back politely.

"Bojangles coffee is nasty."

"I know it is. I'll get the coffee at McDonald's. Be there in a few minutes." Mukesh drove to the fast food chain and pulled into his parking spot back at the motel with two coffees and breakfast. He walked over to Aaron's room and knocked.

"Who is it?" asked Aaron.

"It's me," said Mukesh.

Aaron unlocked the door. Mukesh walked in. Aaron sat back down on his bed, and Mukesh positioned his chair in front of Aaron.

"Good morning, Jen," Mukesh said.

"Morning, Mike," Jen replied. She had the church Bling cam footage up on a split screen, on one side of the monitor was the church service, and on the other side was the church foyer, where a corpulent church bouncer stood in front of the double doors to the inner sanctuary. His arms were folded in front of his puffed-out chest, and he wore a look of sly determination on his face.

"So you are sure that for the second service today, Jerry will be the church security volunteer?"

"I listened to them talking about their schedules in the last meeting. They said they were keeping them the same," said Jen.

"This isn't like the food pantry episode," Aaron interjected, staring blankly at Mukesh. "It's not all or nothing like it was with Todd's collar bone injury." He smiled. "I can always text Nate and call it off if Jerry doesn't show. It reminds me of when you had to piss on the floor when it didn't get mopped. You said you saw that in one of your, uh, dreams? Another brilliancy."

"That was the first uncomfortable one, actually," Mukesh pointed out. Aaron and Mukesh broke off their conversation and stared at Jen's monitor.

"I wanted to stress something to you," Aaron said, nodding and gesturing his hand at the computer screen. He told Jen, "Put that church guy standing there in the Foyer up on full screen." She obeyed and minimized the service camera and maximized the foyer one with the stern-faced brute. The church service audio droned on in the background.

"Look at that guy. He thinks he can do something. Big guy like he is, he would be easy pickings for a lot of people in a fight. If his big ass stood still, I would dance around him and beat on him all day. And if he decided to move around, then he would go wherever I wanted him to. I would throw his big ass around like a blowup doll."

Mukesh laughed at Aaron and looked back at the computer screen. It was ten-fifteen. According to the normal Sunday pattern, Jerry would come in just before ten-thirty every Sunday he was scheduled to volunteer.

Aaron looked at the bag of food Mukesh had set on the floor. "Let me get that sausage and egg and gravy biscuit. Do you want any, Jen?"

"You can fix me a small plate if you want."

Mukesh picked up the bag of food at his side. He was embarrassed when he realized he forgot to ask if Jen wanted anything, but from what Mukesh had seen, she rarely ate. He handed Aaron his food. Aaron ripped off the top of the biscuit and gravy container for a makeshift plate for Jen. He squished her off a quarter of the sausage and egg biscuit and portioned off half of his gravy biscuit and laid it on top of the torn container. He handed it to Jen and returned to his bed and end table. They ate silently, watching the foyer cam. Just as Jen was finished with her food, Jerry entered the frame and shook the morning service church bouncer's hand. The first service volunteer moved aside, and each took a side of the double sanctuary doors. Jen switched over from the church service audio to the foyer audio. The pair talked quietly about football and joked about their wives until they heard a bustle in the sanctuary. The two men opened up both sanctuary doors, and the first service filed out. Second service started trickling in at fifteen till eleven. At five after eleven, the two men closed the sanctuary doors.

"You have a good day, Jerry," the morning service church bouncer said.

The Hacker and The Hillbilly

"You too, Bill," Jerry said. Bill ambled out the front of the CCP. Jerry took his place before the church double doors. He folded his arms and spread his legs apart.

Mukesh chuckled and gestured at the monitor towards the stoic church brute. "So welcoming looking. Your brother will be coming up any minute now, I expect."

"I told him to make it anytime after eleven fifteen. It's ten after now," Aaron shifted over to the side of the bed closer to Jen to get a better look at the monitor. Aaron tapped his right foot nervously.

"It's going to be alright. We all are going to be alright after today." Mukesh patted Aaron's knee with his hand. "Your brother will have his house, and we can finally get out of this cheap motel."

"I like this motel," Aaron said. "My traffic isn't as noticeable compared to some of the other dealers here. Though I would like to get a trailer somewhere near the house we'll build for my brother."

"That's a good idea. I don't mind this motel either, but it would be nice to be comfortable enough to afford a private place in the mountains, one with an actual view. I think I would enjoy that life and maybe even learn some things about gardening and hunting. Waking up every morning and staring at a beautiful view does wonders for your life."

Mukesh looked at the clock. It was eleven-fifteen. Aaron sat at the edge of the bed with his elbows on his knees and his hands cupping his mouth while he watched the footage. He stood up quickly and paced over to the door and back to the foot of the bed. He walked behind Jen and leaned over her left shoulder to look closer at the computer screen. A look overcame Jerry Dirk's face, who unfolded his hands slowly at his sides. Jerry squatted slightly and parted his lips, leaning to his left to peer out the glass entrance. Aaron glanced back at Mukesh, who stood up from his chair. Aaron folded his arms.

"I see it," Mukesh said as he folded his own arms nervously into his chest. "It looks like Jerry sees your brother. I like how he looks startled." They stared at the monitor. Jen turned the volume up to the point where they could hear an ambient hiss. Terror and confusion were pouring out of Jerry. Everyone in the room knew Nate had to be close.

Nate popped into frame at the bottom center-right, approaching quickly in his trench coat. Jerry Dirk put his palm out to the man and asked, "What are you doing, buddy?"

Nate paused and shifted to the side a couple of times, his back turned to the camera. Jerry glared at Nate with his arm still outstretched. Nate brought his left hand up and fiddled with a button on his coat and gripped his belly with his right as he tried to sidestep the church bouncer, all while shouting, "I gotta go! I am going to explode!"

Nate had almost slipped behind Jerry to open the sanctuary doors when Jerry Dirk grabbed Nate's shoulder and spun him around to square him up. Jerry reached out and grabbed Nate's other shoulder. In return, Nate took hold of the lapels of Jerry's blazer as the bouncer struggled to get Nate on the ground.

"Stop, you're hurting me! Don't! I gotta go!" screamed Nate as he summoned up enough strength to shove the fat man away from him. Jerry fell backwards and knocked over the coat rack on his way to the floor. Per Aaron's instructions, Nate braced himself to take whatever punches or submission techniques the bouncer would throw at him next. "I got to go!"

The Hacker and The Hillbilly

Nate shouted and held his belly again. Jerry, still on the floor, reached toward his ankle and pulled out a small pistol and shot twice. Nate went down, screaming.

Aaron jumped up and yelled, hands thrashing in the air. He whipped around and bolted for the door. He almost had it open when Mukesh intervened. He tackled Aaron out of the half-opened threshold, closed it, and both men fell to the floor.

Aaron flushed red, screaming, "That fucker shot my brother! I'm going to kill him!" He tried to scramble up, pushing and shoving at Mukesh.

"You can't do this, Aaron!" Mukesh said loudly as he wrestled Aaron on the motel room floor. "It is fucked up, I know, but if you go out there, everything is ruined. You have to think about this!"

Aaron darted his eyes around, breathing heavily. "No!" He screamed. His eyes began to line with tears. He scrunched his legs up into his chest and wept. Mukesh shimmied over on his butt and blocked the motel room door with his back.

On the monitor, four more church members were now in the lobby, two attending to Nate on the floor and two blocking Jerry from going near Nate and questioning him on the side.

"Why did you shoot him, Jerry? What the hell were you thinking bringing a gun in here anyway? We were clear about that in the meeting!" said one of the off duty bouncers.

"B, but," Jerry stammered.

"I don't want to hear it," said Tom sharply. "Wanda, are they on their way?"

Wanda was bending over attempting to console Nate, who sobbed pitifully on the floor. "Yes, pastor. I think he's going to be alright. It's a gut-shot. The other shot missed him. What the hell were you thinking, Jerry?" Wanda screamed.

Jerry Dirk swallowed his stammer. "He was looking cross-eyed and deranged when he came in. Then he pushed me with freakish strength, saying he was going to explode. He's possessed, I tell you!" Jerry doubled over with his hands on his knees, panting. "He said he had a bomb and was going to explode!"

"Jerry, you're a fucking idiot. Look down here," Wanda told him. A large pool of what was obviously urine began to spread out from Nate's waist, and the smell of a fresh bowel movement wafted in the air. Nate cupped his stomach with both of his hands, and Wanda's palms were pressed on top of them to stop the bleeding.

"Don't say another word and go to the office," Co-pastor George screamed. Jerry leaned down further to pick up his gun. "You leave that there!" George yelled again. Jerry stood up and turned, pouting, and walked into the sanctuary.

"Active Shooter code 2!" Tom screamed into the open sanctuary door.

"What the hell does that mean?" George asked him.

"That's a code from our church shooter drill that lets everyone know to leave out of the back of the church calmly," Tom said.

The co-pastor walked over and latched the lock on the sanctuary doors. "Son of a bitch," he said. George looked over at Wanda. "Isn't this the mentally-challenged boy who lives downtown?"

"He's not mentally challenged; he's just autistic. He's a nice guy."

The Hacker and The Hillbilly

"I know," said the pastor. "I've even invited him to our church service before. And look what happened here!" He faced Nate and asked, "What did you do to Jerry?"

"I had to go poop and pee. I told him, and he tried to block me from going inside!" Nate said, lying on the floor. The puddle of urine began to spread wider in the foyer area. Everyone scrunched up their noses from the stink of shit.

The motel room was dead silent as everyone stared at Jen's computer screen. Five minutes later, Officer Morton came into frame at the bottom left hand of the screen, followed by a female officer to his left, both with guns drawn.

"You don't need those, guys," said George.

"What the hell happened here, George?" Officer Morton asked the pastor.

"Jerry shot him."

"Jerry Dirk! What?" The police officer exclaimed.

"I don't know what happened, guys. It's all on video. Jerry is in the back waiting in the office. I'm going to go back there and talk to him now."

"Make sure he doesn't go anywhere. I'm going to wait for another officer to come and process the scene. We'll make sure this man is taken care of, and then I'll be back there to talk with you both. We'll also need copies of the footage."

"I'll go back there and pull up the church foyer footage now," said the co-pastor as he readied himself to confront Jerry again.

"No, the crime scene processors will want access to everything. One of the investigators is on his way and will take care of that. I'm sure this was just some horrible misunderstanding." Officer Morton bent down and looked at the gun. It was shucked partly back with a spent round stuck in the chamber. "Getting off two shots is actually a rare accomplishment for a Raven 25."

Jen looked back at Aaron. He sat on the floor in terror with his back up against the bed. Mukesh sat on the floor as well, still blocking the door. "Nate is Ok, Aaron," said Jen. Aaron looked pale.

"I guess we really should have thought things further," said Mukesh, staring at Aaron, who was wide-eyed as well. "What do we do now?"

Aaron looked down at the motel carpet. He brought his head up, breathing from his mouth. "I think you need to go back to your room, Mike." Aaron hung his head in thought. "I want to be with my girlfriend now. Nate should be calling me anytime now as well. Since this involves Jerry Dirk, and his brother Robert is a big time judge, all of the town and police are going to be interested in this. Until we can figure things out, it's best you stay away from me for a while, because from here on they are going to be watching me very closely."

Mukesh, relieved Aaron was in his right mind again, stood up from blocking the door. "That reminds me," he said, and walked over to Jen's computer to remove the hacks but stopped himself. "I was going to wipe your computer, but it might be better to wait. We might see something else later that helps us get what we want from the CCP."

Aaron had finally collected himself. "In the meantime, all we have to do is what we have been doing all along, staying one or two moves ahead of Community Compassion. I'll go see my brother in the hospital after he calls. I'll know more about how best to move forward from here after I talk to the authorities

The Hacker and The Hillbilly

and the people from the CCP. They're probably going to try to gaslight me and make this out like it was a big accident or tell me Nate was being aggressive. I don't plan to bring a lawyer into this unless I have to. Well, I'll threaten to, of course, but what I'd really like to happen is they settle directly with us out of court so we get all the money. I hate that my brother got shot, but now that I know he's all right, I feel more confident about getting an extremely large sum." Aaron smiled and Mukesh smiled back. "I think we can get it all. I'll know more by how much the police and the CCP try to fleece us on how well this will go. I'm not a lawyer, but what Jerry did was a crime any way you cut it. They will have to pay dearly to keep one of the Dirk family jerks from going to jail. Just go home, Mike. I will text you once I find out more. Don't be surprised if it takes me a couple of days to contact you."

Aaron's phone rang. He picked it up. "Yes... What?... What!... Hold on, look, I'll be right there!" He hung up and looked over at Mukesh. "Just go home. I don't want anyone asking questions about you. The Dirk family is capable of anything. They'll have someone watching me at all times to try to get something on me for leverage. We can't make any mistakes until this all blows over and we get what we want." Aaron thumbed some more on his phone and put it up to his head. "Hi, Larry. Look, this is an emergency. My brother is hurt and I need a ride to the hospital. I will give you twenty dollars and a treat if you drop me off there... See you in a few." Jen continued to watch the church feed.

"If I don't hear from you, I'll text you in a couple of days, Aaron," Mukesh said as he got up to head out the door.

"Alright. We have to be extra smart and careful until this thing is over with."

Mukesh poked his head back into Aaron's open door. "Everything will be ok," he said. "I can feel it."

Chapter 28

Mukesh waited for two whole days with no word from Aaron. If he didn't hear anything after the third day, he decided he would text him. That third evening, Mukesh pulled out his phone.

"How is it going?"

Unexpectedly, Aaron texted right back. "Oh. Sorry Mike, so much has happened. Can you text me tomorrow evening and we can talk then?"

"Yes," Mukesh texted.

The next evening when Mukesh got home, he texted Aaron, "Good evening."

"Come over after eight," was the reply. At ten after eight, Mukesh walked over to Aaron and Jen's. Nervously, he entered their motel room. Jen sat at the computer. Aaron, who had just unlocked the door in preparation for Mukesh, stood behind his girlfriend.

Aaron turned with a smile and said, "The gift that keeps on giving." Aaron smiled wider at Mike's confusion and spoke again, "I am talking about the Bling cam footage. It is good that we didn't immediately hop off the church's system. They have cut off some of the camera footage around the church—more on that later—but Jen heard on Facebook that Jerry's brother, Robert Dirk, and the sheriff, the head pastor, and a couple of other church bigwigs are going to be meeting over dinner in a few days."

Mukesh scrunched his face up in thought.

"They are planning something," Aaron said. "I talked to the lawyer. I haven't retained her yet, hoping we can settle for what we want without her. She says that if she brought it to court, she thinks she could easily get ten million or more, even with a crooked judge to sway the amount in the CCP's and the Dirk family's favor. The autism thing is key. Protected status."

"What the hell is protected status?" asked Mukesh. Jen started laughing.

"Nevermind, Mike. I think they are going to make me an offer," said Aaron.

"I hope you are right," said Mukesh. "And I hope it's a big one." Aaron walked over and sat on his bed. Mukesh situated the chair in the room to face him and sat down as well.

"I want all of it. All four million." Aaron held his head in his hands to try to straighten it out. "That reminds me, I have to tell you what I've been going through the past few days. I would rather have four million now than wait a few years for ten. If they spit out a number in this meeting, I am going to think for a while for drama, then spit one back, and that number will be four million."

"All of it?" said Mukesh. "Don't you think we should leave them some room to bargain so they settle quicker? And don't forget I have a say in this."

"You have a say in this, but of course I know you want it all too. We don't know what other money the CCP has or if anyone from the Dirk family will help them with the settlement. I am sure they have a lot, though. Judge Dirk and the sheriff will convince them to settle if they are hesitant. Remember that church meeting where they were mocking Eileen? If I ask for the whole four million, Community Compassion Presbyterian

The Hacker and The Hillbilly

might take that as a sign. I'll remind them politely that I'll be nice and won't press charges or make too big of a deal about Nate getting shot. They can call my bluff if they want to, and then we'll go to court. I hope they want to settle with us, because then we can expect the money within a few months. I think they'll go for it. I know these people. Well, I don't know the pastor, but I'm very familiar with the sheriff and the judge." Aaron chuckled, and Jen angled back at him and laughed. Mukesh stared at the block wall behind Aaron, politely grinning.

"That sounds good to me," Mukesh leaned back in his chair. "So, you meet with them this weekend. That is good. How is your brother?"

"He's better. He shouldn't have any permanent damage, other than losing his spleen, whatever that is. All I know about a spleen is that sometimes gunshots and car accidents can make you lose them. Ask Jen." Jen turned around at Mukesh and raised her hand and smiled. "Now we can get out of this motel and hopefully be set for life."

Mukesh sighed. "I would love to rent a place off of the country roads in these beautiful mountains."

"I don't know much about investing money, but when you have four million dollars, you don't rent a house, you buy one. Nate is excited about his house, and even though I didn't talk too much in the hospital for fear of recordings, I let him know with a thumbs up and a wink that he's going to be good. You should see him, lying back and grinning, talking with me about his new house, truck, and boat, loopy on fentanyl, repeatedly pressing the pain meds button and calling for the nurses. He is so happy."

Mukesh smiled. "Good. Tell your brother I said hello."

"I will," said Aaron. Mukesh stood up. "You don't have to leave so soon."

"I am glad to hear all the good news, but I am feeling restless tonight. Should I continue to lay low for a while?" Mukesh asked as he straightened out his shirt and pants.

"I'm optimistic everything is going to be ok after this weekend meeting from the way the sheriff sounded when I saw him at the hospital." Aaron leaned back in his bed and lay down. "Jen, would you lock the door when Mike leaves?" Jen nodded, "yes" as she stared into her computer. "The Dirks have more money and power around here than God. I'm sure Robert Dirk and his family will take care of some of the settlement. The church will be alright, and Judge Dirk will have another town institution tucked tighter in his robe."

Mukesh was at the door and held it open. As he was leaving, he turned and said to Aaron, "Do you still want me to lay low?"

"I would," said Aaron. "I am sure I'm still being watched. At least I know I have no warrants, or they would have picked me up already."

"Good night, Aaron," said Mukesh, who closed the motel room door. Jen got up and locked the door behind him and went back to her TikTok.

Back at his room, Mukesh looked at his laptop folded up on the table. He made sure to always close it to protect it from the dust he could see floating in the sun when the shades were open.

Mukesh reviewed the past few months in his mind. He had changed so much since he first came to the States. Months ago, he stayed wrapped up in his computer all day, either scamming

The Hacker and The Hillbilly

someone or amusing himself with content. Now, he was happy his life had developed in this new, exciting direction. He had formed a genuine friendship with a Tennessee hillbilly that was stronger than any friendship he ever had before.

Mukesh glanced around, eyeing the room in a different light. He suddenly became aware of the ugly stains on the motel's block walls that, for cleaning purposes, were painted with gloss. He felt the lack of feng shui and vowed to move out of the stuffy place to a real home in the mountains, hopefully with his close friends around him if things went well with their perpetrated fraud.

Finally, he thought. Mukesh was bored with the CCP Bling cam footage and couldn't wait to remove the hacks and hacker tools from his and Jen's computers. He brushed his teeth and went to bed.

The next day after work, Mukesh took a drive and pondered his future. He loved his part-time job rolling sushi. It was a peaceful, low-stress environment. His mind was free to wander and clear itself with the repetitive patterns it took to create the Japanese culinary treats. As he gently rounded a mountain bend, he wondered what sort of new hobbies or projects he should get into next. He decided he would attempt to find software security exploits. Mukesh's gift for pattern recognition should serve him well in trying to find chinks in code.

He returned home at dusk and sat at his computer. He opened up a Tor browser to surf the dark web and look at the message boards. The Bling trend was still strong and likely always would be due to the ease of hackability. He opened up several sets of browser code and began to poke for holes.

Finding and selling exploits would be one of the safest avenues of all the hacking endeavors. As long as he wasn't the one to use them to cause damage or steal money or information, he should be alright. If he found a good one, he could always sell it on the dark web. Some zero-day exploits brought millions to those who found them, and that was in legitimate money from companies trying to patch their own bugs. If he found a good enough exploit, paired with the right dark web buyer, he could be looking at the potential for much more. He looked over sections of code in several browsers until he grew tired. He went to bed with his mind in a flurry of possibilities.

That evening, he had a vivid dream. His brain flooded with a series of codes in bright red and blue letters on a background of swirling electric white. Inside the vision, Mukesh felt the same peace as before in a few of his more pleasant waking premonitions. This was the first one he experienced in a dream. When he woke up, he had in his mind an exploit that combined Internet Explorer with a remote computer controller app and the Java plugin. It would allow him to breach any firewall on computers that had both Internet Explorer and Java. Mukesh could not figure out how the exploit could work, but based on the supernatural confidence and the success of all his other visions, Mukesh trusted it would.

He took a shower and put on his work clothes. Mukesh thought it best to shelve the new zero-day exploit for later, or at least until everything was over at the church. He left for Food City.

After finishing rolling up the last tray of spicy tuna rolls, he looked at the time and paced himself washing dishes and tidying up counters. Aaron was supposed to have a meeting

The Hacker and The Hillbilly

with the CCP and town authorities that day, and Mukesh couldn't wait to hear the news. He finished cleaning the silverware last and gathered his things and headed home. He rode around for a while like always, but not as long as usual. He was anxious to speak to Aaron about the meeting, but waited patiently for his text.

At eight-thirty, a text came through. "Come on over, Mike." Mukesh went over. When Aaron unlocked the door and Mukesh walked in, he could see his friend was very happy. Jen was not on her laptop but seated sideways in her computer chair, looking at her phone. Mukesh stared silently as Aaron paced back and forth between the bed and bathroom foyer glancing back and forth at Mukesh and the floor.

Finally, Aaron spoke: "I think I have good news," he said as he abruptly sat down on his bed. "They came to me and kind of insulted me with the first offer."

Mukesh smirked, "What was that?"

"Two hundred fifty thousand dollars," Aaron said, grinning. Mukesh laughed.

Jen looked off to the side at Mukesh and said, "Right?"

"And what did you say to that, Aaron?" Mukesh asked.

"Well," he paused, himself chuckling, "I had to keep a straight face, thinking that I was prepared for whatever they were going to throw at me, and I had slight changes for every possible scenario. They think I'm not smart, and I pretend as much to them so that I always have an edge. If I'm being underestimated, I always have the upper hand. You should have seen them all look ill when they got all the way up to two million and I still refused. After asking what I thought was appropriate, I said plainly to them that I know how much the lawsuit was worth, but I was trying to be nice. You should have seen the look on the preacher man's face when I said, 'Four million dollars.'"

"You should have said five million and then they might have come back to four. They might need to bargain, and now you have left them no room!" Mukesh protested.

"No, Mike. I gave them the white boy price. I don't do that Indian haggling mess. One fair price, take it or leave it. I know how much the Dirks are worth, and we know how much the CCP has. They'll go for the four million. I told them to get back with me in a week and that my brother kept asking me when we were going to build his house. Just to add to their discomfort, I added that if they weren't fine with four million we could go to court and they could give me ten." Aaron chuckled. "I told them that in a few weeks, if we can't come to an agreement, we will settle the matter in court. Jerry shot my brother Nate, for God's sake! I was blunt with the sheriff and Judge Dirk about how pissed I was, but stressed I wasn't seeking any jail time. My brother Nate has already forgiven Jerry." Aaron grit his teeth and banged his fist on the bed. "Get this! That motherfucker actually visited my brother at the hospital and no one told me anything about it or asked! I guess it's good, because they can feel better about staying out of too much trouble if they make things right. If they don't agree with the four million, we'll get a lawyer and they'll pay a lot more for every million they have to give us. I am one hundred percent certain they are going to give us the four."

Mukesh smiled and turned and spoke to Jen. "Anything new on the church Bling cam?"

The Hacker and The Hillbilly

"Actually," Jen said, setting her phone off to the side on the bathroom counter, "They have disabled the footage in the conference rooms and office. The only ones still up are the parking lot, foyer, both sanctuary cameras and the hallway cam."

"Let me see," said Mukesh as he got up from his chair and went over to Jen's laptop. He got on the Bling cam system and checked. "No, they haven't physically disabled them, just turned off the feeds. Until they disconnect the wiring to the cameras, we can always tap in. As a matter of fact, I'll start working tonight on a program so we can tap into the feed undetected while the cameras are still wired up. I'll have one written in a couple of days."

"It would be nice to hear what they say about the settlement and the money Eileen Baker gave them. I heard about some of Eileen's ways. She was an old-school con-woman. She is probably staring up at us right now grinning, having watched our brilliant con from beyond. After that, I don't really care what goes on at Community Compassion Presbyterian, or the CCP, or whatever you want to call it," Aaron said, smiling.

Mukesh got up from Jen's computer. Aaron was lying on his back again on his two large pillows, his hands fanned behind his head. Mukesh looked back at Jen, "We are going to have to delete the Bling cam footage after this next meeting. The CCP must be spooked now that they don't want their more sensitive church areas surveilled. The police must have found something embarrassing when they looked through the footage. I'll start working on that Bling cam hack tonight. It's been a while since

I coded, but I am pretty good at it," he said as he eyed the door to leave.

"Take care, Mukesh," said Aaron.

"Do you think I should worry too much about being noticed anymore?" asked Mukesh with the door halfway open.

"No," said Aaron. "Just don't go walking all over town in a trench coat until we settle up. And quit holding the door open and talking to me when you leave!" Mukesh smiled and shut the door.

Chapter 29

Mukesh went back to his place and sat at his laptop. Memories of his vivid dream returned to him. He had forgotten all about the exploit as well as the dream while listening to his friends' good news. Now that he was alone, he could think of nothing other than checking the computer code. He opened up Internet Explorer and the remote computer app and ran Java. It should be fine, he told himself. Whether it works or not, no one would ever know he tried it out, especially if he tested it on Jen's computer. He knew exactly how her computer was configured and would be able to detect any changes the next time he saw Jen. He typed her IP address with those same two ^^ symbols at the beginning and the four symbols #$>* at the end that he'd seen in his dream. Their computer synced. Mukesh could see her through her camera in a small window in the top right. The rest of the screen on Mukesh's computer was exactly like Jen's, her cursor movements flashing. Aaron reclined on the bed in the background like always. Mukesh snatched his hand from the mouse, sure Jen would freak out at a sudden movement in the cursor.

Mukesh waited for three minutes before Jen finally looked off to her right side and leaned down. Mukesh moved his mouse. The cursor split in two, one from his movement and one from the original location of Jen's. His cursor flashed where Jen's stayed a solid white. It was like his computer and Jen's computer had cloned and split into two, and Mukesh had full control of Jen's computer on a separate dial which she wouldn't be aware of. He went through her system. He had total access as an admin. On every website or app he visited that asked for a password, it would already be typed in. All he had to do was press "enter." He checked even the most mundane apps and saw this was consistent. Mukesh shut his computer off in horror as he realized what he had stumbled upon: a multi-corporate combination exploit, near undetectable, which one hundred percent had to have been intentionally designed.

Mukesh freaked out. He stood up from his computer and started pulling on his shirt frantically, trembling. He knelt down for a few seconds and caught his breath. There was no way for such a perfect hack to have occurred by accident. This was on purpose, an exploit conceived from several different corporate entities, designed and written for some explicit future event or rarely used so it stayed a secret. The horror tortured him. He needed a Xanax.

Mukesh frantically picked up his phone and texted Aaron, "May I come over?" Mukesh stared down at his phone, awaiting his friend's answer.

Much to his relief, Aaron texted right back, "Sure, Mike." He walked briskly, breathing heavily, and braced himself in front of the door to compose himself as best as he could.

Mukesh was visibly agitated when he entered the room. Aaron noticed and said right away, "Are you alright, Mike?"

"Aaron, I need a Xanax."

"I got you bro. I just want to know if you are alright. I have never seen you like this before." He corrected himself. "I mean, the last time I saw you like that, we were on that walk." Mukesh frowned, knowing he could never discuss this particular computer breach, ever. Aaron sighed and opened up

The Hacker and The Hillbilly

the drawer and brought out the same labelless pill bottle he always kept tucked in the back. He shook a few pills out into his palm, blue and green. He scooped up all but two different colored ones with the bottle lip and let the two pills fall into the tips of his fingers and held them out to Mukesh. Mukesh stretched out his palm under Aaron's hand. Aaron dropped the two pills in his friend's hand, a green and a blue one. "You look real keyed up, Mike. We can talk about it later if you like. I would try taking half a Klonopin and half a Xanax right now. The Xanax kicks in fast and the Klonopin lasts longer."

Mukesh placed the Klonopin on the armrest of the chair behind him and tried to break apart the Xanax. He was shaking.

"Let me get that, Mike," Aaron said. He took the Xanax out of Mukesh's hand and snapped it in half. He handed it back with one hand and snatched the Klonopin off the chair with the other. He broke the Klonopin in half and gave them to Mukesh as well. Mukesh swallowed the two different colored halves and cupped the others in his hand. Aaron could guess by the way Mukesh continued standing that he wanted to leave, so he helped him on the way. "I am sorry that you are 'going through it' again. Go get you some rest, and think about the good news. The big three have a meeting with me again tomorrow. I think they are ready to sign off. And those two pills are on me." Aaron smiled hard, trying to get his friend to smile, too.

Mukesh mustered up a fake grin and said shakily, "Thanks Aaron. Let me know tomorrow. I'll be alright." Mukesh walked out of Aaron's motel room with the pills cupped in his hands, but Aaron didn't stop to chide him. As Mukesh walked back to his room, the truth sunk in. He must have discovered and used a high-level shadow government or NSA hacker tool. As the

Xanax and Klonopin kicked in, he realized that if anyone had noticed he used the exploit, he would soon find out. Or maybe he wouldn't. He drifted off to sleep hoping to wake up the next morning in his motel room without getting snatched up or unalived in his sleep.

Mukesh did wake up the next morning, though he didn't feel refreshed so much as at ease. He powered his way through his anxiety while rolling sushi with the other half of the Klonopin. When he got off work, he chose a long mountain back road to clear his head. Halfway back to the motel, he took a side path and drove by the old mountain trail with the strange UFO tales and even stranger spot where nothing seemed to grow. As he passed where he'd had the uncomfortable vision a couple of weeks before, he felt another swell of anxiety. He fished the other half a Xanax out of his watch fob pocket and swallowed it.

Mukesh considered his predicament. He removed Internet Explorer from his laptop, scared to open it after using the exploit. It was the most perfect hack, undetectable and brilliant. Mukesh sighed, reasoning if any authorities had known about what he had done, he would have been picked up already.

Unexpectedly, he chuckled to himself, thinking of his strange life. There was no good without the bad. That's a part of Karma, and as long as things were working out, Mukesh decided not to be too concerned and just roll with it all. As he pulled into the motel parking lot, Aaron texted him, "Come over whenever tonight, just let me know beforehand."

"I'm coming over now," Mukesh answered.

The Hacker and The Hillbilly

"Are you feeling better, Mike?" Aaron asked Mukesh as he entered the room.

"I am. I walked on the path earlier where I felt the last one, and everything was ok."

"Let's talk about it. I want to know the details. We can ride out now if you like."

"No," said Mukesh. "As I said, I just came back from a walk."

Aaron stared at Mukesh in disbelief. Normally, Mukesh always wanted to talk about his episodes, and Aaron wondered what his friend could be hiding. "Ok then. Just wanted to check in with you and make sure you are all right." Mukesh stood there silently, looking nervous. Aaron shifted his head and eyes at Mukesh and the chair beside him like he should sit down. Mukesh sat.

Aaron's eyes lit up and he stood and swung his arms and clapped his hands together dramatically. "Today I signed a settlement for four million dollars."

Jen looked back at Mukesh with a sneaky smile. Mukesh closed his eyes and lifted his head like he was praying, then he looked back down at Aaron and smiled.

"I know, right?" said Aaron. "They are going to transfer all the funds over to my bank account in a couple of months. I went over to see Nate today. He's at home now. I told him we'd go to an architect and talk about some plans for the house we're going to build for him next week. He is so happy. It's also been a week since he had any blood in his urine or stool."

Mukesh looked back and forth at Jen and Aaron a few times with his mouth open. "In one month you are going to have four million dollars?"

"Well, it will be a joint account, you and I. We will have four million dollars. Of course, that also includes Nate and Jen." Mukesh stared at Aaron's shoes in disbelief. "I was thinking, let's go out and look over some of the land they have around here. Somewhere with access to a lake or stream. I was thinking we could buy a place with a small cabin on it for you, build my brother something better on the property, and Jen and I will live in a trailer at the base of the drive. It doesn't have to be a new trailer, just a nice trailer. Then we improve the value of the land we buy and protect our money with a nice real estate investment."

"I like that idea," Mukesh said. His mind flashed briefly to Jen's computer and the exploit he had used on it. Mukesh stood up too fast, so he walked slowly over to where Jen sat with her laptop. "Remember, we have to remove this software. We don't want anything to tie us to this church." Mukesh sat down at the bathroom sink in front of Jen's laptop. He began checking around.

"I would hate for them to find out after they'd given us all that money we'd been spying on them the whole time," Aaron said. "I don't put it past these people to exact some kind of revenge if they ever found out we got 'em this good."

Jen walked behind Mukesh and looked over his shoulder as he sat at her computer. "But tomorrow they have a meeting in the conference room, remember? Let's listen in on that last one, the day after they had to sign the settlement, and see what they have to say about it. I'll understand though if we can't. As Aaron says, these people may be big public figures and government officials, but they are very dangerous, and we need to know what they are thinking after our con."

The Hacker and The Hillbilly

"That's a great idea." Mukesh smiled. "What time is it tomorrow?"

"Seven o'clock," said Jen.

"That's enough time for me to get off work and clean up. Want me to bring the popcorn?" joked Mukesh.

Aaron started laughing.

"No," said Jen. "Why don't you get some pizza. That's what they were eating that time at the meeting where they announced the four million dollar donation and celebrated Eileen Baker's death."

"That's a great idea!" said Aaron. "Get some Sal's pizza. That's the gourmet shit."

"I will. What kind?"

"Sal's deluxe!" Jen and Aaron said at the same time.

"Good. I like deluxe pizza as well," said Mukesh. "It will be funny. We will celebrate our four million the same way they did with the same gourmet pizza." He walked away from Jen's computer, having briefly looked over it for evidence of his breach but finding nothing. Mukesh turned to Aaron. "Do you have another Xanax?"

Aaron narrowed his eyes. "You took both of those already? You looked like you were freaking out last night, but you know you can't take those things like you want whenever you want." He reached into the bottle in the back of the drawer and fished out one Xanax with his right index finger. Aaron handed the small blue pill to Mukesh.

Mukesh took it from Aaron. "I took the rest to get me through today."

"At least you don't look that wound up anymore."

"I feel better. I will be here tomorrow to watch the meeting with you, and I will be bringing a Sal's pizza."

"Come early," Jen said as Mukesh was leaving. "We can watch them file in. Some of the conversations they have in the foyer are better than the ones in the meetings."

"Wait. Give me five dollars for that Xanax," Aaron said to Mukesh as he was about to open the door. Mukesh reached in his wallet and handed Aaron five dollars. "The pills were on me last night. Tomorrow night, pizza can be on you." Mukesh smiled and walked back to his room.

After work at Food City the next day, Mukesh went straight home. He got in the shower and washed off the smell of fish. He put on some comfortable evening clothes and called up Sal's and ordered a pizza. If his friends could stand a deluxe pizza, they could stand a gourmet upgrade. He ordered a large pepperoni, sausage, onions, green peppers, black olives, fresh tomatoes, fresh garlic, and fresh sweet basil. Then he got in the car and bought the stinkiest parmesan and a small cheese grater from Food City and General Dollar.

When Mukesh got to Sal's, they were pulling the pizza out of the oven just as he walked in. Mukesh salivated the whole walk back with it to his Prius, holding their prized pizza along the box edges because of the fresh heat. Inside, the cramped hybrid quarters reeked of the deliciousness. When he pulled in front of Aaron's, it was six-thirty.

Mukesh sat patiently in his Prius, grinning. The weighty deluxe pizza sagged in the back seat. Keeping with the norm, Mukesh texted Aaron. "I wanted to watch that one movie with you. I brought some pizza!"

The Hacker and The Hillbilly

Mukesh waited in the Prius a few feet from Aaron and Jen's door. The windows were cracked slightly the way Mukesh liked them in the fall weather. The pizza fogged and smelled the car up so good, he stayed in the car for another minute before opening up the Prius and getting the fresh pie out of the back. He heard a text notification and assumed it was Aaron responding with some sort of "Come in."

He walked over to Aaron's door and propped the pizza up on his right knee and knocked.

"Come in!" said Aaron.

Mukesh hollered, "I got my hands full!" Aaron opened the door. Mukesh walked in with the pizza and put it on the small table behind him that went with his chair and opened the box lid. Jen and Aaron shifted from their posts towards the taunting smell. Aaron snatched up a slice and turned away from the table, propping the piece on his outstretched fingers until Jen came back from the corner of the room with a plate and paper towels. Aaron sat down on the edge of the bed closest to the bathroom foyer. Jen set a plate on her boyfriend's lap and Aaron laid his twice bitten slice down.

"Oh, look! They are filing in for the meeting," Jen said. The three stared at the screen intently as they ate. Jen had the parking lot camera set up as a small square and the foyer video maximized with sound. One of the church deacons walked in with five Little Caesars' pizzas.

Aaron bounced up and down on his bed, laughing. "Oh man. That's too funny. From Sal's to Little Caesars in less than three months. And now that we got their money, we are the ones celebrating with the Sal's."

Mukesh licked pizza grease from his lips and grinned.

Jen spoke up. "All of them have been quiet while filing through the foyer. I am going to switch to the conference room." She clicked over but couldn't find the feed.

"Oh, I forgot." Mukesh laid his slice on top of the pizza box lid. He walked over to Jen's computer and reached in his pocket. Jen rolled her chair backwards to let him work. He pulled out two thumb drives, a blue one and a red one. He stuck the blue thumb drive in a USB slot on the left and laid the red one down on the right side of her computer. He pulled up a command screen and typed something in and hit enter. He pulled up the Bling software and the screen filled with the scene of the church leaders either seated around the conference table or helping themselves to some Little Caesars' Pizza-Pizza! Mukesh activated the camera's audio and stepped away from the computer screen.

"Where's Jerry?" one of the church leaders asked.

"I told him he better be here!" yelled another.

George bowed his head and was one of three not eating any. "He'll be here. He's probably ashamed."

"He should be ashamed. Even after the deputy told Jerry the accident was his fault, he still called the boy a retard a few times in front of the sheriff. We all should be fortunate they settled with us and Nate's brother didn't get a lawyer. Good thing we shut off the camera footage in the church just after the incident. Think of how much we would have had to pay if a jury saw and heard Jerry talk about the man he just shot like that."

The pastor weighed in, "At least the Dirk family helped us out. If we would have been deemed accountable by a judge

The Hacker and The Hillbilly

and would have had to cover a large court settlement, our church would have folded."

"When is that one and a half million dollar donation coming in from the Dirks, Patrick?"

"On January first, twenty-twenty-two," answered the church treasurer.

"Haha, just like we thought!" laughed Aaron. "I wonder what kind of sissy charge Jerry will be getting for what he did. Probably something like the discharge of a firearm indoors."

"How is your brother?" asked Mukesh.

"He's really great." Aaron said. "I told him we are going to break ground at his new home in a couple of months. He's seeing a doctor about all the medicine he'll need to take for the rest of his life tomorrow."

"Shut up you two! For God's sake! This is getting good!" Jen yelled. She'd reduced the church foyer cam to a small square in the top right corner of the screen. "See!" she said, pointing. "Jerry is coming in now." The foyer cam showed Jerry's back as he walked into the glass double doors to the CCP. All three took bites from their pizza and continued to watch the meeting.

"Why did we let the Dirks get away with not replacing all the money Jerry cost us!" Wendy said loudly. "Robert and Jerry Dirk should have replaced the whole four million. This is another case of one of the Dirk family causing problems and other people paying for them!"

"That's just the way it works, Wendy," the pastor shot back. "You have to think of it like this; if they had a lawyer, everything could have been so much worse. The CCP would be dissolved, people would have gone to jail..."

Jerry walked in. "I hear you talking about me!" he came through the door yelling.

"Damn it Jerry! This whole meeting is about you and what you did!"

"Listen to me, all of you!" the head pastor said, standing up. "The main point of this meeting, which we all have to accept regardless of what has happened or any future outcome, is to deal with what we got. It is not about the money. It is about the kingdom of God and the growth and success of this church. And most of all, it's about love, especially loving your fellow church members in spite of their flaws."

"What about the money to the orphanage in Honduras?" Bill asked. "I was really hoping that we could donate to that wonderful charity to help those poor starving kids out."

"We will still be donating to our fine charities," the head pastor said as he lowered his head in sadness, "though now, unfortunately for those poor kids, not so much."

"Eileen Baker was an evil bitch and that money was cursed! We all knew how evil she was, and this is our confirmation. That money flowing through our church almost ruined us. It was affirmed when Nate's brother wouldn't settle for less than four million. That wasn't a coincidence, asking for the exact amount in Eileen Baker's will. That money had to be cursed!"

"We have to move on," said an elderly lady hunched in her chair. A half-eaten piece of pepperoni was on a plate pushed away in front of her.

"If that boy wasn't retarded, we wouldn't have had to pay so much," said Jerry.

The Hacker and The Hillbilly

"You can't say that word, Jerry. Dammit!" Tom said.

Jerry looked up the wall and straight into the camera. "I thought you said that we were getting rid of the cameras in all the rooms where we held private conversations."

"They're not on. We haven't called the technician here yet to remove them," the co-pastor said. "We'll do that next week."

"Fuck that!" Jerry said in a fury. He grabbed a metal folding chair and dragged it underneath the camera. Jerry climbed up on the chair. His fat-reddened face filled up Jen's entire monitor. He puffed out his mouth and bit his lower lip. Straining, Jerry took both hands and ripped the camera off of the wall. The church feed became static fuzz, and the three friends in the motel room looked around at each other in wonder.

"There's your sign," said Aaron.

Mukesh stood up. "What a fitting end. That's that," Mukesh said. He walked back over to Jen's computer. She slid to the side in her rolling chair, and Mukesh leaned down. He grabbed the red thumb drive he set on the counter and transferred it to his left hand. He removed the blue thumb drive in one of the left slots and stuck the red one in its place. Mukesh typed a couple grand gestures on Jen's laptop.

The screen flashed purple, then black with a fading white line, then all black. Mukesh pulled the red thumb drive out of the computer and stuck it in his shirt pocket. "And that's that," he said again dramatically. Mukesh smiled, thinking that if there was any evidence on Jen's computer that might document his breach a few nights prior, it was now gone. "Jen,

I will come back here tomorrow with another computer. This one had to be completely destroyed. So does my own. I know it is not fun to lose some of your videos and data, but it had to be done."

"I understand," said Jen.

"Now I need to go over to my place and wipe my own computer. Then it's all done. I'll see you both later, my friends."

"Later, Mike," said Aaron.

"Later," said Jen.

Mukesh walked out of Aaron's motel room and into his own. He looked around the room, glad to soon be leaving the dingy block walls and poor lighting behind for a future mountain home. He walked over to the table and opened up his laptop and powered it on. He took the red USB stick and put it in the slot on the top right corner by the number pad across from the minus key. The screen flashed a bright white and then went completely black.

Mukesh got into bed. He lay on his back, grinning as he drifted off to sleep, relishing in the present.

Chapter 30

Mukesh washed dishes at the end of his workday. Sugami brought him two pans.

"I got more for you," the old Japanese man said.

"I'll come over and get them when I finish this one."

It was twelve o'clock on a Friday in the middle of twenty-twenty-two. Mukesh had to pick Jen up and bring her over to her new trailer, which had just been set on a foundation at the border of their shared property. He finished all of his duties at twelve-twenty, ten minutes before he was supposed to leave. Just as Mukesh expected, the old man waved him off early for home. Mukesh got in his Prius and headed to the motel.

Mukesh parked in front of Aaron and Jen's old room and got out and pecked on the door. Jen opened up with a box and a smile. "There's another couple of boxes on the bed if you don't mind carrying them for me to your car, Mike."

"I don't mind," Mukesh said and smiled back. He walked into the room and stacked the boxes on top of one another and put them in the back seat of his Prius.

"I am going to miss this little motel. Sometimes it feels good to be holed up in a cave," Jen said as she walked past Mukesh to go into her room for the last time to get her purse. She pulled the door closed. It self-locked. She walked over with her box and climbed inside Mukesh's Prius. She texted someone and laid the phone on her lap, smiling radiantly.

Mukesh stared at Jen and took in her profile. He had never seen her out in the sun before. She was the type of girl whose skin still looked lively even though it was pale.

284

"I went out and saw the foundation when they first set it for our trailer. That day, I walked up the hill to check out the work on Nate's little house, and I saw your cute place. It's a nice cabin, Mike."

"Yes, I like it very much, indeed. I like what you said about the motel feeling like a cave. It's kind of funny. Caves are sometimes safe, sometimes not so safe. You always need an exit if you live in a cave."

Jen laughed. Aaron's clever sense of humor was rubbing off on Mukesh. "You are exactly right. I have been hemmed up in a hotel a couple of times by the cops. I guess it's the same way with a cave."

"False sense of security," said Mukesh.

"Exactly. It feels cozy, but it really ain't." Jen's head bobbed along with the bumpy mountain road. She smiled harder, amused at the thought. Mukesh passed the logging trail of the UFO folklore, which was one property away from the one the three friends had purchased. As Mukesh came around the corner and approached his new driveway, Aaron and Jen's new mobile home came into view. He drove his Prius up the drive beside the freshly set trailer and stopped it in front of Jen's new home. Jen stepped out and opened the trailer door. Mukesh walked around and set the two boxes on their small deck.

"Aaron is coming over in an hour and a half with the truckload of furniture we just bought," said Jen.

"Yeah, I know that," said Mukesh. "I am going to take a shower, and then I am going to get us some beer and some moving day pizza."

The Hacker and The Hillbilly

Jen reached in her purse and pulled a twenty out of her wallet. She handed it to Mukesh. "You know what we like," she said to him, winking.

"How about some Sal's? Did you say Aaron is having some friends over to help you move?" Mukesh asked.

"Two of his friends are coming over. If you could help, that would be four men moving furniture."

"Sure thing," said Mukesh. "I will get two pizzas then."

"Only one deluxe, the other, pepperoni. I don't know what his other friends like."

"Got it," said Mukesh. "Let's get some gourmet pizza. Let's celebrate!"

"Let's celebrate again," said Jen.

He hopped back in his Prius, dialing Sal's but getting no reception so deep in the mountains. That was okay. Aaron and his friends needed some time to get there, anyway. He could order in the store.

He turned his focus to the country roads, remembering his friend's warning about being careful on them when he drove. That seemed like such a long time ago, when he and Aaron almost ran off the road. Mukesh passed by the UFO crash site. He wondered if the land would ever go up for sale. They had the money. Why not try to buy it if they could? Mukesh tried to remember the name of the town resident who owned the crash site land. Billy Gentry. Mukesh decided he would talk with his friends about contacting him to see if he wanted to sell the spread. It was right by their place and that's what you do when you own land, try to buy up everything else around you. In America and in India.

Mukesh's stomach rumbled. All he could think about was how good his car was going to smell on the drive back—back home, to the best friends and family he'd ever known.

Ending Author's Note:

Regardless of whether you liked this novel or not, please consider leaving a review. It really helps us struggling authors, especially in Indie publishing. I hope you enjoyed this novel, and there is more, and perhaps better to come from the fearless free speech-minded author, Tilson Klaus.